How Long, O Lord?
Reflections on suffering and evil
Second edition

D. A. CARSON

HOW LONG, O LORD?
REFLECTIONS ON SUFFERING AND EVIL
SECOND EDITION

INTER-VARSITY PRESS
Norton Street, Nottingham NG7 3HR, England
Email: ivp@ivpbooks.com
Website: www.ivpbooks.com

First published in Great Britain in 1991
Reprinted 1992, 1993
Second edition 2006
Reprinted 2007, 2009, 2010

British Library Cataloguing in Publication Data
A catalogue record for this book is available from the British Library.

ISBN: 978-1-84474-132-8

Typeset in the USA
Printed in Great Britain by Ashford Colour Press Ltd., Gosport, Hampshire.

*Inter-Varsity Press publishes Christian books that are true to the Bible and that
communicate the gospel, develop discipleship and strengthen the church for its
mission in the world.*

*Inter-Varsity Press is closely linked with the Universities and Colleges Christian
Fellowship, a student movement connecting Christian Unions in universities
and colleges throughout Great Britain, and a member movement of the
International Fellowship of Evangelical Students. Website: www.uccf.org.uk*

Denzill Raymer and Colin Hemer
in memoriam

My soul is in anguish.
How long, O LORD, how long?
Psalm 6:3 NIV

Contents

Preface to the Second Edition

None of my other books has elicited as many moving letters from readers as this one. For the unavoidable reality is that if we live long enough, we will suffer—and this attempt to think about suffering and evil from within a biblical perspective helped some believers, at least, who were struggling through deep waters. So I am grateful that it is being republished in this revised edition.

The structure of the argument has not changed. Many of the illustrations have been brought up to date, and a number of other improvements have been attempted. Discussion of AIDS, for instance, needs not only updated statistics, but a number of other substantial changes. The NIV has been replaced by the TNIV.

Yet I have tried to preserve the level of discussion of the first edition, along with the balance of Scripture. Indeed, if you want to plunge into the biblical and theological material right away, skip chapter 2: not every reader wants to survey "false steps" before beginning to think through what the Bible says. Regardless of where you start, my hope and prayer is that this short volume will help a new generation of Christians, and others who may wish to listen in, think through questions all of us must face in this broken, beautiful, and twisted world.

D. A. Carson
Trinity Evangelical Divinity School

Preface to the First Edition

I had better say right away what this book is not about. It is not a quick answer to difficult questions about suffering. Nor is it (except implicitly) a defense of the existence of God. It is not even the sort of book I would give to many people who are suffering inconsolable grief. Still less is it an academic discussion of philosophical problems.

So what is it about? It is, first of all, a book written by a Christian to help other Christians think about suffering and evil. That means, for instance, that I am not primarily addressing unbelievers who think that the problem of evil and pain is so intractable that it calls into question the very existence of God. There are excellent books that treat the subject from that perspective, but this is not one of them. If you are an unbeliever, you are welcome to listen in. Indeed, you may find the "world" you are entering so compelling that you will want to become a Christian. But you are not the reader I have in mind as I write.

Primarily, this is a book of preventative medicine. One of the major causes of devastating grief and confusion among Christians is that our expectations are false. We do not give the subject of evil and suffering the thought it deserves until we ourselves are confronted with tragedy. If by that point our beliefs—not well thought out but deeply ingrained—are largely out of step with the God who has disclosed himself in the Bible and supremely in Jesus, then the pain from the personal tragedy may be multiplied many times over as we begin to question the very foundations of our faith.

Of course, not all doubts and fears arise from false expectations based on questionable beliefs. At the intellectual level, a Christian may be as orthodox as the apostle Paul, yet so lack the apostle's spiritual maturity that when the first crisis hits all the orthodox "commitments" are again thrown into the melting pot. Nevertheless, it is hard to think of Christians agonizing over basic questions if their suffering has not, to say the least, been exacerbated by false expectations as to what God is like, what God does, what place suffering has in this world. For instance, pain may pose the question, "Why me?" That soon gives way to "Why are you punishing me?" or "Why are you picking on me?" And that is only a whisper from far bleaker thoughts, articulated or not: "Maybe you aren't a God of love. Maybe you are capricious. Maybe you aren't fair, let alone holy. Maybe you aren't there." C. S. Lewis could describe his conversion by the memorable title *Surprised by Joy*; most of us Christians ruefully admit that there are times when our faith is surprised by grief.

This book, then, is designed to help. It does not offer a comprehensive guide to the problem of suffering; it develops only a few themes, somewhat arbitrarily chosen according to what has been of help to me and to some of those to whom I minister. Quite frankly, this little book, as I have already hinted, may not be of assistance to those whose despair is so bleak that they cannot bring themselves to read, think, and pray. But I shall be satisfied if it helps some Christians establish patterns and habits of thought that are so strong that when the hardest questions batter the soul there is less wavering and more faith, joy, and hope.

Because this is a book for general readers, I have largely avoided bibliographies and technical discussions. By and large, the books and articles I mention are those that I actually cite. Despite my best efforts, chapter 11 is a little difficult. If it is too daunting, skip it; but if you can absorb it, make the effort, for I am persuaded that the biblical truths outlined there have enormous potential for stabilizing the faith of God's people.

Much of the material in these pages was first developed for talks in America, Australia, the United Kingdom, and Kenya. I am grateful to many people for the questions they put to me, questions that have helped me to be more careful than I would have been, and to try extra hard to produce a book that would heal and nurture, and not merely inform. That I have not always succeeded is embarrassingly clear to me; if I have succeeded at all it is because I owe much to the probing of others, especially those who have suffered far, far more than I and whose lives have set an example for the Lord's glory and his people's good.

Pain and suffering often generate a profound sense of loneliness. We think we are cut off from everyone, we feel that no one can possibly understand. The truth is that it often helps to talk things over with other Christians. For that reason I have included a set of questions at the end of each chapter. Ideally they should be used in a study group. Reflecting on such questions in splendid isolation will not be nearly as therapeutic.

Soli Deo gloria.

D. A. Carson
Trinity Evangelical Divinity School

Part I

Thinking about Suffering and Evil

I

First Steps

Hard Cases

A pastor is cutting his front lawn. He looks up from his task just in time to see a heavy dump truck back out of his neighbor's driveway—right over the neighbor's eighteen-month-old son, who had been squatting behind the huge tires. The pastor accompanies the hysterical mother and ashen father to the hospital in the ambulance. There is no hope for the little boy; he has been crushed almost beyond recognition.

Where is God?

After five years of marriage, Jane wakes up in the night to find her husband Dan poking her, and pointing to his mouth. As she hauls herself out of sleep, she realizes that her husband has awakened to find he cannot speak, and is badly frightened. A quick phone call to the doctor issues in a swift trip to the hospital. The next day, the surgeons operate for cancer of the brain. They cannot get much of it. The trauma of the surgery is worse: it wipes out all learned memory. Dan no longer knows how to read and write; he cannot recognize his infant son. Yet somehow the operation has administered such a shock that the cancer stops growing. Dan's personality, however, has been altered; he is frustrated, angry, irritable, and needs someone to watch him twenty-four hours a day. After three years of minimal recovery, the cancer starts its insidious growing again, and kills Dan four months later.

Where is God?

A rural family with six children, four of them hemophiliacs, serves the Lord with joy and discipline. Then the AIDS crisis hits. Unknown to doctors and patients alike, the nation's blood supply is contaminated.

The four hemophiliacs must constantly tap into that supply. Two contract AIDS and are dead within three years. The third has tested HIV-positive; it is only a matter of time before the patient exhibits clinical symptoms, suffers, and dies. The fourth, age thirty, himself the father of three, has refused to be tested, but he knows that the chances are overwhelming that he too is a carrier, and that he will shortly leave his wife a widow and his children fatherless. He has almost no insurance, and no insurer will now give him the time of day.

Where is God?

I wish I could say I made up these stories. I didn't; they are about people I know. Only names and minor details have been changed. And all of us could tell our own stories. A colleague of mine and his wife served as foster parents for close to three decades. At one point they took in twin boys, just eighteen months old. This was the twins' sixth home. They were judged irremediably impaired (wrongly, as it turned out). They had been battered for crying in at least two homes, with the result that when they went to bed the first night in their new home they wept themselves to sleep without making a sound.

Where was God?

And then of course there are highly public catastrophes. Terrorists fly airplanes into the World Trade towers and into the Pentagon. The deaths of almost three thousand people are somehow made more shocking by the sight, on television, of people leaping from the ninety-fifth floor to escape the flames fed by jet fuel, by the spectacle of hundred-floor structures collapsing on themselves. A tsunami of gigantic proportions, caused by shifting plates in the ocean floor off the coast of Aceh in northwest Indonesia, causes horrific damage in several countries, and kills about 300,000 men, women, and children.

Where is God?

The truth of the matter is that all we have to do is live long enough, and we will suffer. Our loved ones will die; we ourselves will be afflicted with some disease or other. Midlife often brings its own pressures—disappointments, sense of failure, decreasing physical strength, infidelity. Parents frequently go through enormous heartache in rearing their children. My own mother was mugged at the age of 72. As a result, she fell and hit her head on the curb. Her family noticed mental deterioration and personality change within weeks; she was diagnosed with Alzheimer's and went through all the predictable stages of that wretched disease. She died nine years later. Live long enough and the infirmities of old age eventually catch up with you, compounded by the fact that all your friends have gone and left you alone.

And these things represent the suffering that takes place in relatively stable societies. Add war, racism, genocide, grinding poverty, starvation.

Even television does not adequately portray the reality. The first thing to assault me on my first trip to a really poor Third World country was the stench.

There is now a vast literature on the Holocaust, in which 6 million Jews were systematically exterminated. Much of this literature treats the Holocaust as an aberration, a singularity that we must never permit to happen again, a horrific brutality that destroys meaning. We are told that we must not compare it with other orgies of violence lest we trivialize it. Yet the sad truth is far worse: in the twentieth century alone it is only one of a string of similar holocausts. Already 40 million people worldwide are infected with HIV. How many will die depends on how long it will take to develop an effective vaccine—but since there are about 5 million new infections a year, even the most conservative estimates put the total number who will die from AIDS in the tens of millions. Twenty to 50 million Chinese died under Chairman Mao. The same percentage of Cambodians died under Pol Pot as Jews under Hitler. We do not know how many Soviet citizens died under Stalin, but most historians put the number of Ukrainian deaths alone at about 20 million. The suffering inflicted by Idi Amin is incalculable. Almost a million Hutus and Tutsis were slaughtered in Rwanda.

What shall we say about "natural" disasters? Each year hundreds of thousands die of starvation; millions suffer from malnutrition. Twenty-five thousand died in the earthquake in Mexico City; two hundred thousand perished in a similar disaster in China—that is, two-thirds of the deaths in the more recent tsunami. And how many so-called natural disasters, especially starvation, are the result of uncontrollable "natural" forces, such as drought, and how many stem in part from evil structures that human beings have created—despotic governments, tribal warfare, unfair trading practices, unqualified avarice?

In any and all of these tragedies, in all of this pain, where is God?

It is a question frequently asked in the Bible itself. The psalmists, Jeremiah, Job, Habakkuk, Elijah—all find the apparent triumph of evil more than they can handle. "Why does the way of the wicked prosper? Why do all the faithless live at ease?" (Jer. 12:1). "Why do the wicked live on, growing old and increasing in power?" (Job 21:7).

Hard Thinking

For some people, the question is almost exclusively an intellectual one. If God is both omnipotent and perfectly good, how can he permit such evil? If he is willing but not able to check the suffering, then he is not omnipotent; if he is able but unwilling, he is not perfectly good.

The implication is that the very existence of evil calls into question the existence of God.

For others it is not the mere existence of evil that is the problem, but its abundance. It is *gratuitous* evil that is so shocking. One might argue that the presence of some evil is not damaging to faith, on the assumption that God leaves people free to rebel. But how can this sort of theory account for "natural" disasters, for the sheer quantity of suffering that bears no clear relation to good and bad people, to age and experience, to unambiguous punishment?

There are excellent books that address these intellectual questions. One of the more thought-provoking ones for the ordinary reader is the little volume by C. S. Lewis, *The Problem of Pain*.[1] Few will agree with all his arguments, but more will prove sympathetic to his later testimony, *A Grief Observed*,[2] written at the time his wife died. In recent years several Christian scholars have advanced highly sophisticated defenses of the rationality of Christian belief even in the presence of evil,[3] and these have gained a fair bit of credibility in the marketplace of ideas. Occasionally in this book I will find it necessary to have recourse to such arguments; but they are not my chief focus.

The reason is pretty clear. The fact is that many believers are never troubled by such matters. There are millions of ordinary Christians who hold that God is omnipotent, that God is perfectly good, and that suffering abounds in the world. At many stages of their experience as Christians, they do not feel that there *is* a problem. They have brief theological answers that satisfy them: suffering is the result of sin; free will means that God has to leave people to make their own mistakes; heaven and hell will set the record straight. Or perhaps they have not really had to think about these matters much at all. They know God loves them, and that is enough. Why bother your head about things you cannot understand, let alone improve?

And then something takes place in their own life that jolts them to the core. Perhaps it is a first-year university course in philosophy. Perhaps it is an extraordinarily painful personal bereavement. Your father dies; your child contracts MS. Your spouse walks out with another partner. The job on which you had set your life's hopes slips away and is offered to someone else. You are stricken with a terminal disease. You drift into depression, the slough of despond. Your Christian witness proves not

---

1. C. S. Lewis, *The Problem of Pain* (New York: Macmillan, 1962).
2. C. S. Lewis, *A Grief Observed* (London: Faber, 1966).
3. See Alvin J. Plantinga, *God, Freedom and Evil* (Grand Rapids: Eerdmans, 1974). For useful surveys, see Stephen T. Davis, "The Problem of Pain in Recent Philosophy," *Review and Expositor* 82 (1985): 535–48; Ronald H. Nash, *Faith and Reason: Searching for a Rational Faith* (Grand Rapids: Zondervan, 1988), 175–221.

only fruitless, but offensive to all your friends and colleagues. You lose your job, and with it your house and life savings. Suddenly, questions about suffering become vital.

In other words, profound anxiety about suffering and evil is person-dependent. This can be made clear by a simple model.[4] Suppose John holds a set of beliefs that we shall call S. S may be consistent or inconsistent: for our purposes, it makes no difference. S is simply what John believes. Then, for some reason, to this set of beliefs John adds the rider R, which states that S is inconsistent. John now holds $S + R$ to be true, but this new set (call it S_0) is intrinsically unstable. John has fallen into an "epistemic dilemma": he must either find a reason to drop his belief in R, thus replacing his new set S_0 with his old set S, or he must change some elements in S, or drop some of them, so that R no longer applies. By dropping some of these beliefs, his old set S becomes, say, S_1. Again, whether S is truly consistent or not is for our purposes irrelevant. The point is that S_0 (the sum of $S + R$) is intrinsically unstable and the cause of endless anxiety. Sooner or later John will feel enormous pressure either to retreat to S (thus dropping R) or to rearrange his beliefs into S_1 (thus rendering R irrelevant).

We can fill this out with a hard example. Suppose John is an orthodox believer. His set S includes beliefs about the goodness of God, his power, and so forth. Then John travels in the Third World for a few months, for the first time in his life, and witnesses something of the scale of human suffering. Gradually he adopts R. He does not see how his beliefs about God and the world can be consistent. This causes enormous anguish. On the long haul, either he will come to see that R is invalid, and drop it (thus reverting to his traditional beliefs), or, under pressure from R, he will change some of the elements of S to make a slightly modified set, S_1: he still believes in the existence and goodness of God, say, but not in his omnipotence.

In one sense, this model is altogether too cerebral, too rationalistic. In my experience, most Christians who suddenly become aware of the problem of suffering and evil simultaneously face a set of other pressures as well. Perhaps prayerlessness plays a part; perhaps the believer is afraid of losing the confidence and friendship of other Christians, and therefore bottles up questions without talking them out. Perhaps there are significant spiritual battles going on of which the believer is only dimly self-conscious. Sometimes depression ensues, which may be caused by a chemical imbalance; or lack of sleep compounds despair. Digestive problems, insomnia, and headaches may follow, circling back to make the original set of questions about evil and suffering all the more severe.

4. Adapted from George I. Mavrodes, *Belief in God* (New York: Random, 1970).

But even though all these related problems may intrude, at the heart of this sort of problem is the rider *R*—the dawning conviction that there is something wrong with one's belief system somewhere. And that is why it is important for Christians to have as stable a set of beliefs as possible on these matters *before* a personal tragedy or a fresh experience of life challenges them to adopt that painful *R*.

Two more factors must be understood.

1. Even if you never adopt that *R*—the conviction that your belief system is inconsistent—into the structure of your thought, that does not mean that you see *exactly how* the set of beliefs I have called *S* really does hold together. In other words, you may think your belief system is logically consistent without being able to specify exactly *how* it is logically consistent. You may allow all sorts of room for mystery. For instance, you may think that God is omnipotent, that God is good, that evil exists in the world, and that these beliefs, though consistent, hang together in a mysterious way you do not pretend to understand. There is nothing intrinsically illogical about such a step. But in my experience, if you locate what is mysterious at the wrong place, sooner or later the mistake will come back to haunt you. I shall take this matter up again in chapter 11.

2. More importantly, even if your set *S* of beliefs is not troubled with a rider *R* to the effect that *S* is inconsistent, it does not necessarily follow that *S* itself will offer you much consolation when you are suffering. The *presence* of the rider will cause you additional pain; the *absence* of the rider does not assure you of additional comfort. For the truth of the matter is that naked beliefs offer little consolation under the worst experiences of suffering and evil.

To put this in the terms of Christian experience: in the dark hours of suffering, Christians want more than the assurance that their beliefs are consistent. They draw comfort only from the living Lord himself, from the Spirit whom he has graciously given, from a renewed grasp, a felt experience, of the love of God in Christ Jesus (Eph. 3:14–21). That is not to say, however, that the set of beliefs is irrelevant. It is to say that, in addition to holding that Christian beliefs are true and consistent, the Christian, to find comfort in them, must learn how to *use* them. Christian beliefs are not to be stacked in the warehouse of the mind; they are to be handled and applied to the challenges of life and discipleship. Otherwise they are incapable of bringing comfort and stability, godliness and courage, humility and joy, holiness and faith.

But before we go on to think through how various biblical emphases can serve as comforting bulwarks when evil and suffering threaten to swamp us, it may be worth pausing to warn against several vaunted shelters that are thoroughly insecure. Thoughtful Christians should avoid them: they promise security, but they are destructive.

Questions for Further Study

1. Compile your own list of suffering—both what you see in the world around you and what you yourself have suffered.
2. Does the problem of evil and suffering ever disturb you deeply? If not, why not? If so, why?
3. From your present understanding, how do you think God's sovereignty and goodness are to be reconciled with the presence of much evil and suffering in the world?
4. Have you ever gone through a period of asking disturbing questions about the love or power of God? What precipitated it? What was most important in helping you through it?
5. From what does the Christian draw deep comfort?

2

False Steps

False Steps Deriving from Ignorance and Arrogance

In 1988, in the wealthy community of Winnetka, some miles north of Chicago, an emotionally disturbed young woman entered an elementary school, bent on destruction. Handgun drawn, she shot and killed one pupil, wounded a couple of others, and, in a nearby house, severely wounded an adult who tried to stop her. Eventually she shot herself before the police closed in.

The community was horrified. Counselors spent hours with students at the school and with their parents. Highly emotional outbursts from parents and citizens were aired on radio and television. There were endless editorials on how this could and should have been prevented: what agencies failed the emotionally disturbed woman, how she should not have been able to obtain a handgun, which individuals failed to give warning to the authorities, and much more of the same. Some of the comment was doubtless cathartic.

1. *That sort of violence should occur only in black neighborhoods, in the slums, in the Third World, or among drug addicts; it is outrageous that it should happen in decent, white, upper-middle-class suburban areas.* Of course, no one was quite so crass as to put it this way; but that was the sentiment that perked along under some of the indignation. The assumption, of course, was that evil is or should be restricted to other people, especially to people without all the advantages we enjoy. There

was no acceptance of radical evil in the world, no recognition that it is part of the human dilemma, that it cannot be legislated or bought out of existence.

2. *I want to believe that my money can buy me security. I trust no one but myself and my resources; God is among the first I will blame if something goes amok.* Instantly there were discussions about security devices, security forces in all the schools, increasing the police force, and so forth. Regardless of the merits of individual suggestions, it was the attitude that was so astonishing: my money ought to secure my safety.

3. *The death of my child is far more important than the deaths by starvation of hundreds of children in Eastern and Central Africa every week.* In part, of course, this sort of distinction is inevitable. It is impossible to show as much concern for people who are no more than flickering images on a television set as for those with whom my entire life is entangled. The constant coverage of disasters by the media can lead to emotional burnout: I simply do not have the energy to care for so many wounded people, and so I care all the more intensely for my own.

Of course, this is nothing more than a reflection of the individual nature of grief. The Ethiopian widow who loses her son in a drought will not shed as many tears for earthquake victims in China as for her own son. One must not impose artificial standards: family and community ties are deep, and so the ruptures are the more painful. Even so, I could not help sensing that there was a problem of worldview. The grief was greater not just because the child was one of us, but because of who we are. Here was the promise of brightness, perhaps a Harvard career, of urbanity, wit, charm, wealth—all ruthlessly cut down. The loss was measured in terms of potential money, education, or influence, not in terms of what it means to destroy a creature made in the image of God. If that category had emerged, of course, it would have applied as much to the babies on the South Side of Chicago who are born with AIDS and who die before they go to school.

4. *Any notion of radical evil, of a fallen world, must be qualified by how good I am.* There was very little self-examination of the sort that might have asked the question: What kind of pressures might have brought me to the same desperate cruelty displayed by this young woman?

5. *Among those who were more religious, the prayers offered up for protection had to do almost exclusively with physical safety, property, and material well-being.* There was no tendency to learn lessons from this tragedy about the fragility of life, the shortness of our time here, the more important values of the kingdom. No one said, "This bizarre tragedy has helped me to remember that life is short, and therefore I must use whatever time God entrusts to me more responsibly and less selfishly

than I have been doing. It is about time I started laying up treasure in heaven, and not down here."

We want security; we want it desperately. But it has very little to do with the security of belonging to God, everything else being negotiable. Some time ago I bought a copy of Philip Yancey's thoughtful book, *Disappointment with God*. I could not help noticing that the publisher had pasted a yellow label on the dust jacket. This label reads, "100% Money Back Guarantee: If for any reason you are dissatisfied with 'Disappointment with God' return it postpaid (with the receipt) to Zondervan Publishing House for a complete refund." It appears that we are allowed to be disappointed with God, but not with books about disappointment with God.

In a sense, of course, these reactions to evil and suffering are not the formal outworking of a coherent system. In one sense, however, they are worse: they are untutored, personal responses to evil that takes place everywhere around me. And they are colored by independence and arrogance, tinged with fear that the high walls I have built up to protect myself may not be all that strong after all.

I am grateful that a few people in Winnetka sounded other notes. One should not in any case expect mature, Christian responses from a largely secular community. What is far more alarming is that these same sorts of responses sometimes find their way into the church. For a variety of reasons, Christians, too, display similar indignation, assuming that we *ought* to be immune from such evil and suffering. These reasons number at least five:

a. We may get the balance of Scripture wrong. We remember the wonderful triumphs of Joseph, Gideon, and David; we meditate continuously on the miraculous healing of the man born blind, or on the resurrection of Lazarus. We are less inclined to think through the sufferings of Jeremiah, the constant ailments of Timothy, the illness of Trophimus, or the thorn in Paul's flesh. A righteous man like Naboth perishes under trumped up charges (1 Kings 21). The "good guys" do not always win. We shall have occasion to return to such topics. For now it is enough to note that we may be infected by a pious version of the raw triumphalism that prevails in much of the surrounding culture because we have not taken care to follow the balance of Scripture.

b. We may succumb to the crush of the urgent. We think that if God is going to relieve our sufferings, he ought to do so immediately. Any delay vitiates his promises. We live in a fast-paced world, and we want God to respond with the same efficiency we expect from high-speed computers. We are not inclined to think through the delays in Scripture: Moses' forty years in the back side of the wilderness, the delay of twenty or more years before Joseph is vindicated, the anguish even of

the saints under the altar (Rev. 6:9–10). But God is not constrained by
our petty timetables. Committed though he is to his people's good, he
well understands that delays are not always bad. Moreover, if we walk
with God long enough, we begin to learn the lesson ourselves: we look
back from a longer perspective and start to appreciate that God's timing
is best. We may then marvel at our own impatience. We are too much
like children whose every request is stamped with "Now!"

c. Some of us thoroughly misunderstand a number of important texts.
For instance, Romans 8:28 reads: "And we know that in all things God
works for the good of those who love him, who have been called according to his purpose." If we interpret *the good* of those who love him" in
selfish, materialistic ways, we shall entirely miss the point of the passage. In the context, it is the *bad* things of the world that are befalling
God's people, part of the groaning of the entire universe still given over
to death and decay (8:22ff.), and climaxing in the persecution of God's
people (8:35ff.). What the passage promises us, then, is that *in the midst*
of such misery we may be assured that God is at work "for the good of
those who love him." That sort of promise has to be taken on faith—faith
that is strong because of the proof God has already given us of his love
for us, the proof that is nothing less than the gift of his Son (8:31–32).
There is nothing in the text that promises us an easy time, or a quick
way out of the groanings to which the entire universe gives vent.

d. Some of us have absorbed a form of theology with all the answers.
We can offer standard answers to every problem that comes along, especially if the problem is afflicting some other person. Our certainty
and dogmatism give us such assurance, our systematic theology is so
well articulated, that we leave precious little scope for mystery, awe,
unknowns. Then, when we ourselves face devastating catastrophe, and
we find that the certainties we have propounded with such confidence
offer us little relief, our despair is the bleaker: we begin to question the
most basic elements of our faith. Had we recognized that in addition to
great certainties there are great gaps in our comprehension, perhaps we
would have been less torn up to find that the mere certainties proved
inadequate in our own hour of need.

It becomes important, then, to decide just where the mysteries and
the certainties are. Christianity that is nothing but certainties quickly
becomes haughty and arrogant, rigid and unbending. Worse, it leaves the
Christian open to the most excruciating doubt when the vicissitudes of
life finally knock out the supporting pillars. The God of such Christianity is just not big enough to be trusted when you are up to your neck
in the muck of pain and defeat. Conversely, Christianity that is nothing
but mystery leaves nothing to proclaim, and makes faith indistinguish-
able from blind credulity. Part of our task in this book, then, must be to

emphasize some of those things that ought to be firm points of assurance for Christians, and to probe a little around the edges of the deep mysteries.

e. Above all, many of us have not adequately reflected on the cross. We have been used to thinking of the cross as the means of our salvation; we have not thought much about what it means to take up our cross and die daily, or to fill up the sufferings of Christ.

For these and other reasons, we Christians may respond to pain and suffering in much the same way our pagan neighbors do. We must take steps to overcome our ignorance of God's Word on these matters, and to drain away the arrogance we display that suggests we should be exempt from such constraints.

Even so, these false steps are personal and idiosyncratic, however common. The next set of false steps I shall mention result from fundamentally non-Christian structures of thought.

False Steps Deriving from a Non-Christian Worldview

Atheism and a Mechanistic Universe

There are many variations on this worldview. The basic problem with it, as far as the subject of this book is concerned, is how to avoid depreciating evil. If there is no God and no criterion of goodness outside the universe itself; if all that happens is simply the wastage of evolution, the chance bumping of atomic and subatomic particles, what rational person should feel any outrage before ostensible "evils" at all?

Atheism holds no attractions to the committed believer. What we must see, however, for our own peace of mind, is that it offers no solution to the problem of evil. It "resolves" the problem by saying, in effect, that evil is not there. Christian witness must press the matter home: atheism has often challenged Christianity with the problem of evil, but its own version of the same problem is surely less believable, as we look back on the incredibly violent twentieth century, than any difficulty that must be faced by Christians.

God as Less than Omnipotent

As we shall see in a moment, some Christians also adopt this position. But I shall argue that it is not only biblically indefensible, but generates far more problems than it resolves.

But we must pause for some clarification of terms. To say that God is omnipotent is not to say that God can do absolutely anything. Most

Christian thinkers rightly distinguish between what is *physically* impossible and what is *logically* impossible. The latter simply does not fall within the range of omnipotence, and this for the very good reason that what it describes is incoherent. It is logically contradictory to suppose that God can create two adjacent mountains without a valley between them, or to argue that God can draw a square circle, or to hold that God can create a stone that is too heavy for him to lift. All of these are pseudotasks; these logically impossible tasks are not on a par with physically impossible tasks. "A logically impossible action is not an action. It is what is described by a form of words which purport to describe an action, but do not describe anything which is coherent to suppose could be done."[1]

By confessing that God is omnipotent, then, we mean that God can do anything that is not logically impossible. Many have sought to "solve" the problem of evil by denying that God is omnipotent. God, they say, does not stand behind evil in any sense. If evil and suffering take place, it is because someone or something else did it. God not only did not do it, he could not stop it; for if he could have stopped it, and did not, then he is still party to it.

The most famous expression of this viewpoint in recent years is the widely circulated book by Harold Kushner, *When Bad Things Happen to Good People*.[2] Kushner lost his son, and his grief drove him to question his traditional Jewish faith. Though a rabbi, Kushner came to believe that God *could not* have prevented his son's death. He is frank: "I can worship a God who hates suffering but cannot eliminate it, more easily than I can worship a God who chooses to make children suffer and die."[3] Almost half a million copies of the hardcover edition were sold; the paperback edition soon topped one million. Clearly, Kushner had hit a nerve: people in pain were looking for answers, and many of them thought Kushner had provided one.

There are many variations on this "solution." One is to adopt some form of dualism, that is, the belief that there are two principles operating in the universe, a principle of good and a principle of evil; and neither has complete mastery over the other. This view is sometimes refined to make Satan either the personification of evil, or the personal evil genius behind evil, in exactly the same way that God is the genius behind good. The distinctive element in this worldview, however, is that neither Satan nor God is absolute; neither is omnipotent. Oddly enough, a similar result sometimes springs from monism: in the Star Wars saga, there is

1. Richard Swinburne, *The Coherence of Theism* (Oxford: Clarendon, 1977), 149.
2. Harold Kushner, *When Bad Things Happen to Good People* (New York: Schocken, 1981).
3. Ibid., 134.

one Force, but with a dark side and a good side. Which side of this one Force controls you is largely up to your own moral choices. But if there is only one Force, then the difference between good and evil sooner or later becomes muddied.

There are still other ways of eliminating God's omnipotence. Some insist, on philosophical grounds, that God himself is in certain ways bound by time. It would have been logically impossible, they say, for God to create a world which he could have known would be better than this one. God cannot infallibly know the future, for the future is undetermined. Inevitably, the entire created order is therefore something of an experiment. In this experiment, God grants certain absolute freedoms to human beings to see if they will develop *responsible* freedom.[4] Still others, influenced by a movement called "process theology," hold that God is limited and involved with human beings in the grand enterprise of trying to relieve evil and suffering. Any moral being has power of its own, and therefore it is impossible completely to control another moral being. God's lack of power is therefore not an imperfection; for, since controlling another being is impossible (in this view), God may be "almighty" but unable to perform the logically impossible.[5]

There is little point listing further refinements. From a Christian perspective, there are at least three problems. First of all, this vision of God simply cannot be made to square with Scripture. A summary of the biblical evidence will be presented later; at the moment, it is enough to say that this does not sound like the sort of God the wise man had in mind when he wrote, "In their hearts human beings plan their course, but the Lord establishes their steps" (Prov. 16:9).

The other two problems are no less serious. If God is not omnipotent, as the Bible insists, then how can believers be sure how the world will turn out? If dualism is right, then the odds are even that evil will ultimately triumph. If we are nothing but an experiment, God may someday have to acknowledge that the experiment has failed, and simply write us off. Indeed, some think that is exactly how God is presented in the account of the flood. If we point to other Scriptures where the certainty of God's triumph at the End is utterly unqualified, if we joyfully contemplate the prospect when the kingdom of this world becomes the kingdom of our Lord and of his Christ (Rev. 11:15), these opponents will say that there are mutually incompatible pictures of God in the Bible.[6] In constructing our theology, we have to choose those pictures that make the most sense

4. So George B. Wall, *Is God Really Good? Conversations with a Theodicist* (Washington, D.C.: University Press of America, 1983).

5. See David Griffin, *God, Power and Evil: A Process Theodicy* (Philadelphia: Westminster, 1976); Howard R. Burkle, *God, Suffering and Belief* (Nashville: Abingdon, 1977).

6. So Burton Z. Cooper, *Why, God?* (Atlanta: John Knox, 1988).

to us. But surely Christians with a high view of Scripture will want to ask how the various pictures of God are to be brought together. If we adopt only those elements with which we feel comfortable, we are in desperate danger of creating a god in our own image. And the particular god being advanced in this case cannot guarantee the future.

Most important of all, perhaps, is the fact that this sort of god cannot offer us any comfort. Belief in an omnipotent God brings with it all sorts of hard questions about how such a God, if he is good, can permit evil and suffering, but it also brings with it the promise of help, relief, an answer, an eschatological prospect. To abandon belief in the omnipotence of God may "solve" the problem of evil, but the cost is enormous: the resulting god is incapable of helping us. He may be able to give us quite a bit of sympathy, and even groan along with us; but he clearly cannot *help* us—not now, and not in the future. There is no point praying to such a god and asking for his help. He is already doing the best he can, poor chap, but he has reached the end of his resources. For all that one sympathizes with Kushner's search for a God he can respect, he has ended up with a god who cannot help.

The Deist's God

The difference between a deist and a theist must be appreciated. A theist believes there is a personal/transcendent God who is both Creator and providential Ruler. All Christians (in any biblical sense of the word) are theists (as are orthodox Jews, Muslims, and some others). A deist believes there is a transcendent god, and may hold that this god is a person, but denies that this god reveals himself personally. The deist thinks of god as the creator who set this universe on its present course, establishing its order and laws, and then let it go on its way, in much the same way as a watchmaker takes care to produce a well-designed and working mechanism but has no interest or control in his product once it has left his hand. This god is too "big" and transcendent to bother with little things like human beings and what we perceive to be "evil" and "suffering," in much the same way that we human beings do not give a lot of thought to whatever suffering and accidents may befall, say, slugs or head lice.

Once again, this view of God cannot be squared with the Bible. The God of the Bible is interested in each action and thought of each one of us, and nothing that transpires takes place outside the sweep of his sovereignty. The hairs of our head are numbered; not a sparrow falls to the ground without his sanction; he knows when I stand up and when I sit down; he turns the heart of the king in whatever direction he prefers. Moreover, he is *personal*: that is, he relates to us *as a person*. He is depicted not merely as a limitless reservoir of raw power, but as a person who loves, hates, speaks, responds, takes initiatives, and even suffers.

Like the god who is not omnipotent (if for different reasons), the deist's god is unable to offer any solace to those who suffer. The mother who has just lost her baby is unlikely to find comfort in a god who is so removed from her that she is in his eyes of no more consequence than a wounded centipede. The price of "resolving" the problem of evil by appealing to deism is appallingly high. Evil and suffering are so reduced that they mock our grief, and this god is so removed that he couldn't care less.

Pantheism

Once again, there are many variations. The heart of the matter, however, is that this structure of thought insists that "god" and the universe are one. There is no chasm between creator and created. All that is, is god; god is whatever is.

In this worldview, not only adopted by most Hindus but the working assumption of the entire New Age movement, god is not a transcendent "other" who is personal, who can come from beyond to help us. The entire universe belongs to one order. Within this universe, however, there are levels of attainment. What Christians see as sin or evil, pantheists are likely to see as imperfections in reality that need to be removed by progressive self-realization, progressive self-improvement. The goal of human beings is not to have their sins forgiven and to be reconciled to a God who holds them to account, but to spiral up the cycle of life, perhaps through reincarnation, but certainly through meditation, self-focus, self-improvement.

Once again, however, quite apart from the fact that this view of God cannot be reconciled with the God who has revealed himself in Scripture and in Jesus Christ, evil and suffering have again been relativized. In practice, this worldview often breeds formidable fatalism; it cannot easily breed moral outrage. The anguish of Job is senseless; the starkest cry of all, "My God! My God! Why have you forsaken me?" is nothing more than desperate proof of immaturity that refuses to accept things as they are.

But stolid detachment must not be confused with personal trust; self-improvement must not be confused with the pursuit of kingdom righteousness; and evil is too blisteringly awful to allow so light an escape.

False Steps Deriving from Sub-biblical Christianity

I had better register two confessions. First, the different kinds of false steps that I am delineating in this chapter are not mutually exclusive, and to that extent the three-part division I have imposed is artificial. For instance, a minority of Christians think that God is not omnipotent, even though the strongest expressions of that opinion come from outside the Christian camp. Almost any opinion can be linked with an attitude of ignorance and arrogance typical of the first set of false steps. But the division is useful in order to help us see what is most characteristic of certain approaches to the problem of evil and suffering.

Second, there is a long record of "theodicies" in the history of the church—that is, attempts to exonerate God as he is revealed in the Bible of any charge of wrongdoing, in light of the problem of evil and suffering. Many of these are now only of antiquarian interest; virtually no one adopts them anymore. They have been competently surveyed and evaluated by Henri Blocher,[7] and need not be mentioned here. But there are others that have been defended by devout believers that are still in play in contemporary discussion. Usually those who espouse them have no desire to depart from Scripture; indeed, in many cases they think that their "theodicy," their attempt to resolve the problem of evil and justify God, helps to defend the Bible by showing the sanity of faith, the rationality of faith.

The fact that I have placed them here, thereby labeling them "sub-biblical," is therefore very much a reflection of my own reading of the Bible. When I try to test these "solutions" by what I find in the Bible, I find them inadequate, reductionistic, sub-biblical. But I do not mean to suggest that those who espouse these opinions are necessarily trying to escape the constraints of Scripture. The biblical justification for my assessments will become clear in ensuing chapters; you will have to judge for yourself whether I have handled the Bible fairly.

God Is Not Omnipotent or Has Limited His Omnipotence

Among the common approaches to the problem of evil and suffering that many Christians espouse but which I find biblically and theologically unconvincing and pastorally unsatisfying, the first is the view that God either is not omnipotent, or for some reason limits his omnipotence. Relatively few Christians in the history of the church have argued that God is not intrinsically omnipotent. It is somewhat more common, as with Clark Pinnock and others,[8] to argue that God chose to make the

7. Henri Blocher, "Christian Thought on the Problem of Evil: Part II," *Churchman* 99 (1985): 101–30.

8. Clark Pinnock, in *Predestination and Free Will: Four Views of Divine Sovereignty*, ed. David Basinger and Randall Basinger (Downers Grove: InterVarsity, 1986), 141ff.; idem, *Most Moved Mover: A Theology of God's Openness* (Grand Rapids: Baker, 2001); Clark Pinnock, Richard Rice, John Sanders, William Hasker, and David Basinger, *The Openness of*

world with "significantly free" human beings, and thus intrinsically chose to limit both his own knowledge of what they would do and his own capacity to intervene. The biblical evidence will be scanned later; the theological weaknesses of this position are the same as those mentioned in the last section. At the end of the day, God is exonerated, but mystery is destroyed and so is God's ability to help.[9]

Considerably more subtle is the view that although God is omnipotent, he has limited himself or ordained evil within certain bounds, in order to achieve some greater good. For example, some say that God chooses to limit his power but not his knowledge. God knows what will take place, both good and evil, but chooses (for a variety of reasons) not to exercise his power to destroy the evil. But if God knows that a certain event will take place if he chooses *not* to act, and then in fact so chooses, it is hard to see how his restraint differs from absolute decree. In any case, we shall see that this is an inadequate way to explain many biblical texts.

God Has Made Humans Totally Free

But the most common self-imposed divine limitation has to do with human freedom, and is worth separate consideration. I hasten to say that with some expressions of the "free-will defense" (FWD) I have no quarrel, and I shall draw the necessary distinctions later in this book. But as popularly presented, the FWD assumes that for human beings to be held morally accountable before God, they must be *absolutely* free: that is, their choices must be entirely free from divine constraint or necessity. At such points God is *absolutely* contingent: in other words, he is not in control, but is merely responding to the situation. If he were in control, it is argued, then human beings would not be "free," and therefore not morally responsible.

At this point, proponents differ. Some think that God not only chooses not to interfere, but, because he has assigned such awesome freedom to his creatures, he cannot even know in advance what they are going

God: A Biblical Challenge to the Traditional Understanding of God (Downers Grove: InterVarsity, 1994); and not least some of the voluminous writings of Gregory A. Boyd, including *God of the Possible: A Biblical Introduction to the Open View of God* (Grand Rapids: Baker, 2000); idem, *Satan and the Problem of Evil: Constructing a Trinitarian Warfare Theodicy* (Downers Grove: InterVarsity, 2001).

9. Among the many responses to the "openness" theology, the following might be mentioned: Bruce A. Ware, *God's Lesser Glory: The Diminished God of Open Theism* (Wheaton: Crossway, 2000); John Frame, *No Other God: A Response to Open Theism* (Phillipsburg: P & R Publishing, 2001); Douglas S. Huffman and Eric L. Johnson, eds., *God Under Fire: Modern Scholarship Reinvents God* (Grand Rapids: Zondervan, 2002).

to do.[10] Others, as we have seen, think that God has the knowledge but not (because of his self-limitation) the power.

We shall shortly see that this view simply does not do justice to the language of Scripture. That does not mean there is no "free will" in any sense; but free will must not be defined in such a fashion as to make God contingent. Moreover, in the stronger form, where God does not even know in advance what free choices human beings will make, it is hard to see why it is not possible that God could be finally thwarted. It is even possible, surely, that creatures with such free will could, much to God's surprise, break out in rebellion once again in the new heaven and the new earth.

Knowledge of Evil Is Necessary

But the weakest aspect of this theory lies in the fact that it is almost always linked with the sub-biblical notion that the knowledge of evil is necessary to knowledge of good. This very common view has to be probed a little, for it can be taken several ways. If this means that one must experience evil in the sense of performing it if knowledge of good is possible, then God, who has never performed evil, has no knowledge of good! If this means only that human beings would have to at least witness evil before they could have any real knowledge of the good, then surely it would have been possible, following the account of the fall, to observe Satan's evil without actually falling into sin. More importantly, does this mean that the angels who never fell were not really good until they had the opportunity to observe some evil?

But, as I have indicated, this notion that for good to be present there must be some knowledge of evil is most commonly linked to the FWD. The idea is that for human beings to become what they ought to be, they must make choices, face hurts, cope with suffering, taste evil, and then turn away from it. The justification of evil then largely lies in the assumption that the end justifies the means. We could not be people who truly love and obey God unless we are free; and that freedom entails failures, evil, suffering, whose existence is justified in that it is being used to make us mature. This fallen world is the region of soul making.[11]

As in so many of these theories, there is an element of truth in the analysis, an element we will try to unpack a little later. But this line of argument constitutes a poor explanation for the presence of evil and

10. Thus, Bruce R. Reichenbach, *Evil and a Good God* (New York: Fordham University Press, 1982), insists that God's knowledge logically cannot include "counterfactual conditionals" of free will. We shall see that Scripture specifically contradicts him.

11. Best known, perhaps, is John Hick, *Evil and the God of Love* (New York: Harper and Row, 1966).

suffering. If such absolute freedom is necessary if we are truly to love God, does this mean we will no longer love God in the new heaven and the new earth, when (presumably) we will no longer be able to sin? Or are we to think that even there we might sin? But if God can so arrange things that in the new heaven and the new earth we will love him wholly and truly and without failure, why could he not do so without taking the race through a fallen world? Why should it be only here, in this fallen world, that we must have absolute freedom to be able to grow?

A Final Reflection

One of the remarkable features about most of these proposed "solutions" is that they make no reference to Jesus Christ and his suffering, death, and resurrection. By and large, we are treated to theodicies of theism, not of *Christian* theism. I am not suggesting that because of Calvary we Christians have all the answers to the problem of evil and suffering. Far from it: a little farther on I shall point to where the mysteries of the problem lie. But surely the death and resurrection of Jesus cannot be ignored. Surely it must shape the configuration of the debate, rearrange the priorities, make the elements look a little different.

For instance, when we feel we have been suffering unjustly, we may cry for justice, outraged at injustice. But is it justice we really want? Why, then, the cross? If justice will suffice, Jesus died in vain. Or, to put it another way, if God had simply been "just" with Jesus, he would not have sent him to the cross. Is it simple "justice" we want?

What do we do with a God who loves us so much he sends his Son to bear that kind of suffering? How must these realities that lie at the very center of our faith bear on our understanding of the problem of evil and suffering? From any Christian perspective, our theoretical and practical approach to evil and suffering must fasten on the cross, or we are bound to take a false step.

Questions for Further Study

1. What are the three categories of "false steps" in this chapter? What are their distinguishing features?
2. Does your personal response to evil and suffering fit into one or more of these three categories? If so, which one(s)? Why?
3. As far as the problem of evil and suffering is concerned, what is the worst element in atheism?

4. What bearing does your answer to the previous question have on the fact that not infrequently people turn to God when they suffer?
5. Why is biblical Christianity a form of theism, not deism? What difference does this make for the problem of evil and suffering?
6. Will believers truly love God in the new heaven and the new earth? Will any of them be able *not* to love God at that point? What bearing does your answer have on whether absolute freedom is necessary for men and women to be able to love God?

Part 2

Parts of the Puzzle

Biblical Themes for Suffering People

This part of the book probes several biblical themes important to the problem of evil and suffering. These themes are not the only ones that are important; nor are they explored here as fully as they might be. My aim is to set out some of the basic structures of the Christian faith that bear on the problem, and show what relevance they have to the way we face the tears that all of us must shed.

None of these chapters provides a "solution" to the problem of suffering, certainly not a merely intellectual solution. Nevertheless, they explore parts of the puzzle, and help to build a picture that locates evil and suffering within a certain framework. We may not have enough of the parts of the puzzle to have a complete picture; we do have enough for the framework to be reasonably clear. Many (though certainly not all) of our difficulties with the problem of suffering arise from the fact that we ignore this biblical framework. The tragedy is that the suffering then becomes worse, for if this framework leaves large holes, it also provides the elements of support, of comfort, of hope. If you flee this framework because of what is still not known, you will not "solve" the problem of suffering, and you will sacrifice much of the comfort the gospel gives.

3

The Price of Sin

The Bible's "Story Line"

Sometimes we can get so close to something we cannot see it properly. Stand with your eyes one inch from a large tree and stare straight ahead for five minutes. Try to imagine what it would be like if you had never seen a tree before. Would this first exposure to a tree prove very enlightening? You must stand back a bit to appreciate the whole tree. That is not to say there is no place for minute examination of the bark or a leaf; but if that is all you examine, you lose sight of the tree.

So also with the study of Scripture. One can become so engrossed in the study of this verse or that book that the Bible's "plot," its story line, drops from view.

The Bible begins with God creating the heavens and the earth (Gen. 1–2). Repeatedly, God's verdict is that all of his handiwork is "very good." There is no sin and there is no suffering. The Garden of Eden brings forth food without the sweat of toil being mixed into the earth. But the first human rebellion (Gen. 3) marks the onset of suffering, toil, pain, and death. A mere two chapters later, we read the endlessly repeated and hauntingly pitiful refrain, "then he died . . . then he died . . . then he died . . . then he died."

The end of the Bible sees the ultimate reparation of the damage, "a new heaven and a new earth" (Rev. 21:1), "where righteousness dwells" (2 Pet. 3:13). "God's dwelling place is now among the people, and he will

39

dwell with them. They will be his people, and God himself will be with them and be their God. He will wipe every tear from their eyes. There will be no more death or mourning or crying or pain, for the old order of things has passed away" (Rev. 21:3–4). But if this marks the end of suffering, it also marks the end of sin: "Nothing impure will ever enter it, nor will anyone who does what is shameful or deceitful, but only those whose names are written in the Lamb's book of life" (Rev. 21:27).

Between the beginning and the end of the Bible, there is evil and there is suffering. But the point to be observed is that from the perspective of the Bible's large-scale story line, the two are profoundly related: evil is the primal cause of suffering, rebellion is the root of pain, sin is the source of death. Thus, when the prophet Isaiah looks forward to the time of unqualified blessing, he insists it will be a time of unqualified purity and profound knowledge of God. "They will beat their swords into plowshares and their spears into pruning hooks. Nation will not take up sword against nation, nor will they train for war anymore," he writes (Isa. 2:4). But this is linked to the larger vision: "In the last days the mountain of the Lord's temple will be established as the highest of the mountains; it will be exalted above the hills, and all nations will stream to it. Many peoples will come and say, 'Come, let us go up to the mountain of the Lord, to the house of the God of Jacob. He will teach us his ways, so that we may walk in his paths'" (Isa. 2:2–3). If it is true that "the wolf will live with the lamb, the leopard will lie down with the goat, the calf and the lion and the yearling together; and a little child will lead them" (Isa. 11:6), it is also true that "they will neither harm nor destroy on all my holy mountain, for the earth will be full of the knowledge of the Lord as the waters cover the sea" (Isa. 11:9).

All the other elements of the Bible's very rich and nuanced story line fit within this framework. The destruction of the flood and the covenant with Noah, the choice of Abraham and the covenant that bears his name, the rise of the Israelite nation and the revelation at Mount Sinai, and, ultimately, the coming of Jesus himself, and his death, resurrection, and exaltation—all have to do with the problem set by human rebellion and the terrible consequences of that rebellion. Paul understood the point: "the wages of sin is death" (Rom. 6:23).

From this perspective, the distinction that many make between moral evils and natural evils needs careful qualification. At one level, of course, a useful distinction may be made: there is a difference between, say, a rape and a destructive tornado, between a war caused by human avarice and an earthquake that no human being could either start or stop. Yet from another perspective, both kinds of evil, and the suffering caused by both kinds of evil, are the result of sin, of rebellion—and therefore of moral evil.

The Evil of Evil

Before trying to draw out the implications of this "story line" in the Bible, it is important to grasp just how vile all evil really is.

Even parts of secular society are beginning to appreciate this point. In the Western world, the twentieth century began with utopian optimism and gargantuan self-confidence. We ended it much more soberly: our resources are running out, our weapons of war are monstrous, the dictatorships of right and left have murdered tens of millions. The past century was host to two world wars and a lengthy cold one. Massive famine on a scale unimagined threatens to handle the population explosion by the most elemental and draconian of means. And some, at least, have recognized that the root of the evil lies *in us*.

"We have met the enemy, and he is us": this famous line from the Pogo cartoon strip is rather tellingly reinforced by an immensely revealing book of essays, *Facing Evil*. The authors are by no means of one mind; none displays a distinctly biblical framework for understanding evil. Indeed, the introduction begins by even refusing to define it. Nevertheless, many of the essayists make the point that the violence, the greed, the lust, the malice that operate on the institutional scale find their primal springs in the human heart. In a remarkable confession, actor Lee Marvin testifies:

> How did I feel when I saw myself on the screen? I found it very unpleasant recently when I saw a film of mine called *Point Blank*, which was a violent film. I remember; we made it for the violence. I was shocked at how violent it was. Of course, that was ten, fifteen, eighteen years ago. When I saw the film I literally almost could not stand up, I was so weak. I did *that?* I am capable of that kind of violence? See, *there* is the fright; and this is why I think guys back off eventually. They say, "No, I'm not going to put myself to those demons again." The demon being the self.[1]

But it is the Bible itself that most vehemently insists on the evil of evil. No biblical writer sanctions the pagan doublethink by which opposites somehow circle around each other and eventually coincide: "Woe to those who call evil good and good evil, who put darkness for light and light for darkness, who put bitter for sweet and sweet for bitter" (Isa. 5:20). Prophets and apostles agree on the exceeding hatefulness of sin. Evil is to be abhorred (Rom. 12:9), yet it suffuses all of us. Citing a cascade of texts, Paul writes, "'There is no one righteous, not even one; there is no one who understands; there is no one who seeks God. All have turned

---

1. Paul Woodruff and Harry Wilmer, eds., *Facing Evil: Light at the Core of Darkness* (LaSalle: Open Court, 1988), vii.

away, they have together become worthless; there is no one who does good, not even one.' 'Their throats are open graves; their tongues practice deceit.' 'The poison of vipers is on their lips.' 'Their mouths are full of cursing and bitterness.' 'Their feet are swift to shed blood; ruin and misery mark their ways, and the way of peace they do not know.' 'There is no fear of God before their eyes'" (Rom. 3:10–18).

The ultimate measure of evil is the wrath of God (Rom. 1:18ff.), and that wrath is so resolute that it issues in the cross. We are all "by nature deserving of wrath" (Eph. 2:3): apart from the cross, there is no hope for any of us.

In this primal sense, then, evil is evil because it is rebellion against God. Evil is the failure to do what God demands or the performance of what God forbids. Not to love God with heart and soul and mind and strength is a great evil, for God has demanded it; not to love our neighbor as ourself is a great evil, for the same reason. To covet someone's house or car or wife is a great evil, for God has forbidden covetousness; to nurture bitterness and self-pity is evil, for a similar reason. The dimensions of evil are thus established by the dimensions of God; the ugliness of evil is established by the beauty of God; the filth of evil is established by the purity of God; the selfishness of evil is established by the love of God.

Some confusion arises from the fact that we commonly use the word "evil" in two rather different ways. We may use it to refer to evil in the primal, moral sense just described: it is rebellion against God. Alternatively, we may use the word to refer to all the suffering, pain, and adversity that is properly the consequence of evil in the first sense. This latter "evil" is therefore part of the penalty of human rebellion. Is such penalty itself evil in the moral sense?

From a biblical perspective, the answer must be ambivalent. Certainly such calamities are experienced by human beings as great evils. Death itself is the last enemy (1 Cor. 15:26). War, worry, persecution, deprivation, famine, pillage, natural disasters—the Bible treats them as great afflictions, great evils. Yet, at least some of these things are not acts of rebellion; they are not evil in the primal sense. Moreover, from God's perspective these things, insofar as they exact penalty and restore justice, must be assessed as good.

We may go farther. In the peculiar way in which God's sovereignty operates (discussed in chap. 11), even morally evil things may not only have a good result but may be good in God's intent even if evil in human intent. Apart from the cross itself, one of the clearest examples is the treatment of Joseph. He was sold into slavery out of the malice of his brothers; their intent was wholly evil, and for years Joseph's experience was appalling. Yet he came to see that his brothers' intent was not the only one operating: "You intended to harm me," he told them, "but God intended it for good to accomplish what is now being done, the saving of many lives" (Gen. 50:20). If even the wrath of man can bring praise to God (Ps. 76:10), it is not because human wrath is intrinsically good (it "does not produce the righteousness that God desires" [James 1:20]), but because God turns the evil to his own glory.

Several themes are intertwined here, and one or two of them will be drawn out in later chapters. For the moment, it is important to see that the Bible as a whole treats evil and suffering with the enormous seriousness it deserves. At the most basic level, moral evil is to suffering what cause is to effect; yet suffering itself is so tied to the fallen order that it too is rightly thought of as evil, and experienced as such. How God exercises his sovereignty over such diverse evils is still to be explored.

The Goodness of God

Before applying these basic Christian truths to our experience of suffering, there is one more point that the Bible recognizes as a "given": the goodness of God. There is no darkness in God at all (1 John 1:5). "He is the Rock, his works are perfect, and all his ways are just. A faithful God who does no wrong, upright and just is he" (Deut. 32:4). If Nahum can say, "The LORD is a jealous and avenging God; the LORD takes vengeance and is filled with wrath," almost in the same breath he can insist, "The LORD is good, a refuge in times of trouble" (Nah. 1:2, 7). People will not be excused on the last day on the ground that God has somehow induced them to evil (James 1:13).

Once again, there are difficult texts, especially those dealing with the sovereign sway of God in the case of evil actions. We will closely examine some of these in chapter 11. For my present purposes it is enough to discern the basic outline of the biblical plot. The sovereign and utterly good God created a good universe. We human beings rebelled; rebellion is now so much a part of our makeup that we are all enmeshed in it. Every scrap of suffering we face turns on this fact. The Bible itself centers on how God takes action to reverse these dreadful effects and their root cause, sin itself; and the believer's hope is the new heaven and earth where neither sin nor sorrow will ever be experienced again.

Some Implications

From this, it follows that in any Christian understanding of God and the world, Kushner's famous title is profoundly misleading. *When Bad Things Happen to Good People* assumes the world is populated largely by "good people." The drift of the Bible's story line sees things differently: we are all caught up in rebellion, and therefore none of us belongs to the "good people." In any absolute sense, "good people" is an empty set.

I am not saying that this resolves the problem of evil and suffering, as if the proper admonition to everyone enmeshed in sorrow is a brutal "Stop complaining. You are only getting what you deserve." In many contexts the Bible speaks in relative ways of the righteous and the un- righteous. None of us is as evil as we might be. Even a Hitler might have kicked his dog one more time. Moreover, we often ask why, within this fallen world, some seem to prosper and have an easy time of it while others who are on any reckoning far better persons suffer enormously. Many other biblical truths need a little unpacking if such a sense of the inequity of things is to be alleviated.

Yet Christians undergoing pain and suffering will be well served by contemplating the Bible's story line and meditating on the price of sin. We live in an age where everyone is concerned about their "rights." But there is a profound sense in which our "rights" before God have been sacrificed by our sin. If in fact we believe that our sin properly deserves the wrath of God, then when we experience the sufferings of this world, all of them the consequences of human rebellion, we will be less quick to blame God and a lot quicker to recognize that we have no fundamental right to expect a life of unbroken ease and comfort. From the biblical perspective, it is because of the Lord's mercies that we are not consumed.

Most emphatically, this does not mean that every bit of suffering is the immediate consequence of a particular sin. That is a hideous piece of heresy, capable of inflicting untold mental anguish. It would mean that the people who suffer the most in this world must be those who have sinned the most in this world; and that is demonstrably untrue, both in the Bible and in experience. Some of the possible connections between a specific sin and a particular illness will be worked out in a later chapter. For the moment it is enough to observe that illness *can* be the direct result of a specific sin (as in the case of those described in 1 Cor. 11:27–34; or in the case of the man in John 5:1–15 who was paralyzed for thirty-eight years), but there is no *necessary* connection between a specific sin and a particular spell of suffering (e.g., the man born blind [John 9]).

Indeed, one of the functions of biblical teaching about rewards in heaven and degrees of punishment in hell—yet another topic to be probed farther on!—is that it explains in part why there is no equitable distribu- tion of punishments *here*. Some answers we are not going to receive here; we shall have to wait for the Lord's return before justice is completely done, and seen to be done.

Meanwhile, the consequences of human sin infest many of our experiences with some measure of pain. Such afflictions may be splashed onto the canvas of human history with a very broad brush. Thus God says to Jerusalem, "I am against you. I will draw my sword from its sheath and cut off from you both the righteous and the wicked" (Ezek. 21:3). In one sense, of course, no one is righteous (Rom. 3:10ff.); but that is not what the prophet means here. He means that when devastation descends on Jerusalem, the people who will suffer will include both those whose immediate sins have brought the city to this horrible punishment, and those who have not participated in the sins that have brought about the destruction of the nation.

War, plague, congenital birth defects, and many other afflictions are like that: they are not very discriminating. Therefore if we see them only as retaliation or retribution for specific sins, we shall be terribly confused when people who have not indulged in such sins suffer along with those who have. But if instead we see such suffering as, in the first place, the effluent of the fall, the result of a fallen world, the consequence of evil that is really evil and in which we ourselves all too frequently indulge, then however much we may grieve when we suffer, we will not be taken by surprise.

That is why most biblical writers are surprised neither by the prevalence of wickedness (except among the covenant people) nor by the suffering it occasions. In individual cases, of course, there is painful questioning as to why this person or people should suffer when others who are far more wicked are exempt from such affliction. The supreme example is Job, whose questioning is especially insightful. But on the whole, the biblical writers are surprised, not by punishment, but by the Lord's patience and forbearance. God does not punish the Amorites until their sin has reached full measure (Gen. 15:16). Again and again we are told that the Lord is long-suffering, slow to anger, and very merciful. Jonah's flight from his assignment to preach in Nineveh is prompted by his confidence that God is more forgiving than the prophet could ever be. Jonah wanted the barbaric city of Nineveh destroyed. "That is what I tried to forestall by fleeing to Tarshish," he protests. "I knew that you are a gracious and compassionate God, slow to anger and abounding in love, a God who relents from sending calamity" (Jon. 4:2). From this perspective, it would have made more sense to write a book full of wonder under the title *When Good Things Happen to Bad People*.

All the blessings that we enjoy are signs of God's patience and forbearance. Small wonder Paul can ask the rhetorical question, "Or do you show contempt for the riches of his kindness, forbearance and patience, not realizing that God's kindness is intended to lead you toward repentance?" (Rom. 2:4). It is the martyred saints who cry out, "How long, Sovereign

Lord, holy and true, until you judge the inhabitants of the earth and avenge our blood?" (Rev. 6:10); the Lord himself still quietly waits.

I suspect that the reason why it is so hard for many of us to live out these implications of our theology is that we do not deeply feel the truths we formally espouse. My creed may tell me I am a miserable sinner, that I deserve hell, that all that I enjoy in life is a gracious gift from God, that I am in no position to expect to escape suffering. But when it comes right down to it, I simply feel my own suffering is unfair.

That surely means that I have not really taken aboard the Bible's picture of my own guilt. I am most likely to absorb that reality, I think, not when I sit around contemplating my own sins (though periodic reviews of my sins of word, thought, and deed, not to mention my sins of omission, are wonderfully salutary), but when I glimpse a little more of who God is. It was the display of who God is that finally helped to settle Job's mind; it was the vision of God in the temple that prompted Isaiah to cry out, "Woe to me! . . . I am ruined! For I am a man of unclean lips, and I live among a people of unclean lips, and my eyes have seen the King, the LORD Almighty" (Isa. 6:5).

If we grasp a little better where we fit into the Bible's story line, how God looks at our sin, what our own rebellion rightly deserves, then although not all our questions about evil and suffering are answered, we are likely to face the wounding times with less resentment and indignation, and with more gratitude and trust, than would otherwise be the case.

Questions for Further Study

1. Articulate the Bible's "story line," its plot, in a few sentences.
2. What bearing does this story line have on the problem of evil and suffering?
3. From the Bible's perspective, what makes evil so evil?
4. At this point in your understanding, what would you say is the relation between suffering and sin?
5. What do you deserve from God? Have you received what you deserve? What have you received?

4

Social Evils, Poverty,
War, Natural Disasters

In this chapter, I will not attempt even an outline of what the Bible says on so many complicated topics as those indicated by the title. I make no effort to offer "solutions" to grinding poverty, nor will I address the special subject of the "holy wars" of the Old Testament (a subject reserved for a later chapter). My aim in this chapter is far more modest: to survey some of what the Bible says about the suffering caused by such evils, and to reflect a little on what that means for us today.

The evils discussed here are far from being an exhaustive list of what might be included in this chapter. One particular social evil not discussed here is AIDS. To treat that subject from a set of biblical values would take up too much space in this chapter, but because it is both complicated and attended by high emotions, I have devoted an appendix to it.

Evils Prevented—and Perpetrated—by the State

As a whole, the Scriptures recognize that civil authority restrains evil. Arguably, that is its primary purpose. The book of Judges, for instance, describing a period before order was imposed by the monarchy, relates the most appalling violence: accounts of wanton rape, murder, exploitation, and barbarity. In the midst of this narrative of savagery, the writer repeatedly inserts a line that becomes a driving refrain, and finally closes the book: "In those days Israel had no king; everyone did as they saw fit" (Judg. 21:25). Canonically, this prepares the way for the onset of the kingdom of Saul and the kingdom of David; morally, it recognizes that unless there is a responsible authority to curtail evil, individuals become more and more brazen in their greed, pillage, and violence. The Bible has no time for the view that the source of all evil is civil authority, or for the romantic utopian myth that individuals on their own, perhaps in some loose federation with "nature," would cure all the evils of society.

That is why Paul can trace the hand of God himself behind human government.

> Let everyone be subject to the governing authorities, for there is no authority except that which God has established. The authorities that exist have been established by God. Consequently, whoever rebels against the authority is rebelling against what God has instituted, and those who do so will bring judgment on themselves. For rulers hold no terror for those who do right, but for those who do wrong. Do you want to be free from fear of the one in authority? Then do what is right and you will be commended. For the one in authority is God's servant for your good. But if you do wrong, be afraid, for rulers do not bear the sword for no reason. They are God's servants, agents of wrath to bring punishment on the wrongdoer. Therefore, it is necessary to submit to the authorities, not only because of possible punishment but also as a matter of conscience. (Rom. 13:1–5)

It is important to see how strong Paul's language is here. He is not only saying that the state exerts force (it "bears the sword") to restrain evil, and that therefore one important motive for obeying the state is the fear of punishment, but that behind the state stands God himself. Therefore Christians learn to obey civil authority not only out of fear of punishment, but also out of their recognition that God himself stands behind the state. Obedience to the state becomes for them not merely a pragmatic question ("I don't want to go to jail"), but a moral question, a question of conscience.

On the other hand, the Bible sustains no Marxist myths about the beneficence of the state. After all, the state is operated by people, and people are fallen. If you put fallen people into positions of power, corruption is never far away; and since all of us are fallen, corruption is pervasive. For ancient Israel, God provided a covenant, a detailed agreement between the people and himself that included a great deal of law. Both the rulers and the people were pledged to obey these laws. As long as punishment was meted out to rulers or to people when the law was broken, corruption and the suffering it caused were at least kept under control.

Again and again, however, rulers came to power who were not held accountable for their actions. The first king of the northern nation after the split that took place in the wake of Solomon's death led the people into idolatry. His name became proverbial for evil. Later kings were frequently assessed against the measure of his sin: "So-and-so did evil in the sight of the Lord, like Jeroboam the son of Nebat."

Even a great monarch like David could be evil and petty. He seduced Bathsheba and arranged the brutal murder of her husband Uriah (2 Sam. 11). Wicked King Ahab coveted Naboth's vineyard, and his equally vile queen Jezebel arranged to have Naboth's integrity besmirched and his life taken by a judicial system that could be manipulated and bribed. What suffering did Naboth endure as he died from the stoning? What did his family face by way of poverty and disgrace?

But it is not just the state of the Old Testament covenant community that God views with the same ambivalence. After all, when Paul writes Romans 13, the state he has in mind is the Roman Empire. Paul has already learned from the Hebrew Scriptures that God is sovereign over *all* the nations. From all of them he expects justice; all of them he holds to account. "Righteousness exalts a nation, but sin condemns any people" (Prov. 14:34); it is by justice that any government gives a nation stability (Prov. 29:4).

God's concern for justice threatens wrath not only to the covenant nation (see the book of Amos), but to other nations as well—even those whom God has used to bring his own people to heel. Thus in Isaiah 10:5ff., God declares that Assyria is nothing but a tool in his hand to bring judgment upon his own people. However, since that is not the way the Assyrians themselves view things, they will be held to account. *They* think they are destroying nations by their own strength. Therefore, after God has used them to destroy his people, he will turn around and destroy them. Thus God's passion for justice extends beyond the covenant community.

In his first epistle, Peter tells slaves how they are to react when they suffer unjustly under a system that is intrinsically dehumanizing. Certainly the first-century Christians held no romantic notions about the integrity of the state: they had seen what the state did to their Master. By the end of the century, there had been enough outbreaks of persecution by local magistrates against Christians that the state could be painted in lurid colors: the state is a beast, a whore (so Revelation), when it claims the allegiance that rightly belongs to God alone.

Thus, while the Bible insists that both ideally and in practice the state restrains wickedness, it fully recognizes that the state may perpetrate it. That means that the state sometimes protects us from suffering, and sometimes causes it.

That has certainly been our experience throughout the past century. On the one hand, no one would want to live under the anarchic conditions that prevailed in, say, Uganda, after the collapse of the government following the flight of Idi Amin. But who would want to live under his regime, either? "Like a roaring lion or a charging bear is a wicked ruler over a helpless people" (Prov. 28:15).

Nor must we think that every form of brutalization and suffering must be physical. The Nazi regime did a number of good things from 1933 to 1939. But those good things were entirely vitiated by the subversion of almost the entire populace by a combination of controlled media, terror, and morally bankrupt wishful thinking. Institutional violence that causes profound suffering may be unleashed in every sector of life—in the economy, in the educational system, in the courts, in the military. And, as in private life, there are sins of omission as well as sins of commission.

It is because of this essentially ambivalent situation that many theologians read Romans 13:1–5, quoted above, as demanding only a *qualified* obedience. Insofar as the state is God's servant to execute justice, they say, so far are we to obey it, for conscience' sake. But where the state becomes an instrument of evil, it is to be opposed. At bottom, this is one of the most important rationales advanced by Christians everywhere who have become involved in revolutionary wars, including the American War of Independence.

The issues are complex, and this is not the place to probe them.[1] From the perspective of human suffering, however, four things have become clear from this survey:

1. The Bible is entirely realistic about the suffering that the state inflicts, and the suffering from which the state protects us. There is no reason for Christians to think that they or any other group should be exempt from the pain that arises from these sources.
2. The underlying assumption in biblical thought is the fallenness of humankind, our propensity for evil, the tragedy and the malice of a broken and rebelling world.
3. Despite whatever suffering we may have to endure from this quarter—whether from evils the state is called to curtail, or from the state itself—Christians will see themselves responsible to promote justice. They entertain no dreamy-eyed hope that utopia is possible down here. They acknowledge that even the best efforts are only palliatives: the final "cure" awaits the new heaven and the

---

1. I have discussed these things at greater length in D. A. Carson, *Love in Hard Places* (Wheaton: Crossway, 2002).

new earth, and the most telling reformation of society this side of glory comes about in massive, heaven-sent revival (as the history of the Great Awakening and its aftermath suggest). Even so, they find they cannot read, say, Amos, without urgently rediscovering the mandate to pursue justice.

4. The mysteries bound up with God's sovereignty have returned in another form. God stands behind the state, yet acknowledges the state frequently acts wickedly and holds it to account. This point will be explored more fully in chapter 11.

Kinds of Poverty

With great insight, the wise man Agur, son of Jakeh, writes, "[Give] me neither poverty nor riches, but give me only my daily bread. Otherwise, I may have too much and disown you and say, 'Who is the LORD?'" (Prov. 30:8–9).[2] Poverty may be eulogized in syrupy ballads and praised by the pseudo-pious, but deep poverty is never pleasant.

Indeed, what we mean by "poverty" is immensely variable. To live just under a government-specified "poverty line" is quite different from dying of starvation. Indeed, to live "just under the poverty line" may feel rather different in two dissimilar families. In the first, the father and mother love each other. They serve the Lord in a low-paying job where they feel they can exercise real ministry. Their modest (and rented) home is characterized by gratitude; their children are disciplined for ingratitude and shown by example how the Lord provides for his own. There is time to read and think and discuss. There is moral and emotional support (and sometimes material support as well) from the local church, and even an adventurous challenge to see how much can be invested in the "bank of heaven" (Matt. 6:19–21). I grew up in such a home. I did not find out how "poor" we were until I left home to go to university (funded by scholarships and part-time work; my parents certainly could not afford to send me).

In the second family of five, on the same income, there is one mother and four children, three of them by different men, none of whom lives there now (though there are men who frequently stay for a few nights or a few weeks). The "home" is squalid, provided by the state but not maintained, an apartment on the fourteenth floor of a ramshackle building where the elevators work sporadically and the stairwells smell of human urine and

2. By far the best treatment of this subject is now that of Craig L. Blomberg, *Neither Poverty Nor Riches: A Biblical Theology of Possessions*, NSBT (Leicester/Downers Grove: InterVarsity, 1999).

dog feces. There is no supporting church; the tightest societal groups that attract the children are street gangs. Drugs are more accessible than books; but books wouldn't help much anyway, since all four of the children are functional illiterates. The mother has never encouraged study (after all, she can barely read herself), and the school is a disgrace. The cynical apathy of the mother is palpable, the rage of the children no less so.

It becomes clear rather quickly that there are different kinds of "poverty" in the world. God knows I did not grow up "poor" in any useful sense of the word, regardless of what government "poverty lines" pronounce.

We may probe more deeply. We sometimes reflect on "the problem of the poor in Christian theology" or the like, and fail to see that many aspects of this "problem" are distinctly modern.[3] Marxist analysis may identify the poor as those who are economically deprived from want of power. Some studies begin by assuming that in the Old Testament the poor are the landless. Almost all of them assume that poverty is always an evil, though from a biblical perspective that is not always the case; in fact, poverty is sometimes superior to other alternatives. And even where we have rightly understood the text of Scripture, how the Bible's meaning is to be applied to the present day is not always easy to determine.

These warnings are not meant to make the task so difficult that nothing whatever can be learned from Scripture. Rather, it is to acknowledge that with the gap between the rich and the poor widening in the modern world there is increasing pressure to think these issues through, and these pressures are at least potentially corrosive of clear thought.

At the risk of oversimplification, then, we may distinguish at least six kinds of poverty exemplified in Scripture, and try to think our way through the relevance of each to the topic of this book.

The Unfortunate Poor

Some people are poor because of unfortunate circumstances. Perhaps the breadwinner has been inflicted with a debilitating and incurable disease. Perhaps successive years of drought have brought penury. One thinks of Ruth and her mother-in-law Naomi. Drought drove Naomi and her family out of Judah into Moab; three tragic deaths sent her back, along with her widowed daughter-in-law.

In times of upheaval it is usually the poor who suffer most. "The wealth of the rich is their fortified city, but poverty is the ruin of the poor" (Prov. 10:15).

3. I am indebted to T. R. Hobbs, "Reflections on 'the Poor' and the Old Testament," *Expository Times* 100 (1989): 291–95, for some of what follows.

In a fallen world there will always be people whose poverty is the result of tragedy. We face, again, the mystery of providence, something I shall discuss later. But there can be little doubt how Christians ought to respond when they observe such poverty. From a biblical perspective, such poverty should not in the first place evoke philosophical speculation, still less self-righteous fatalism, but compassion and material support. "There will always be poor people in the land," God declares. "Therefore I command you to be openhanded toward those of your people who are poor and needy in your land" (Deut. 15:11). "When you are harvesting in your field and you overlook a sheaf, do not go back to get it. Leave it for the foreigner, the fatherless and the widow, so that the LORD your God may bless you in all the work of your hands. When you beat the olives from your trees, do not go over the branches a second time. Leave what remains for the foreigner, the fatherless and the widow. When you harvest the grapes in your vineyard, do not go over the vines again. Leave what remains for the alien, the fatherless and the widow. Remember that you were slaves in Egypt. That is why I command you to do this" (Deut. 24:19–22). In a society of day laborers, wages were to be paid promptly (Lev. 19:13). Whether observed more in the breach than in practice, the Mosaic law stipulated that every third year a tenth of agricultural produce was to be set aside for the poor and the Levites (Deut. 26:12ff.). In the seventh year, when fields were to lie fallow, the poor were permitted to live on their produce (Exod. 23:10–11). Ruth and Naomi benefited from the integrity of Boaz who observed such laws as these.

However great the mysteries of providence, it will not do to throw up our hands in philosophical despair and satiate our greed. The God of the Bible is the God in whose image each of us, rich and poor, has been created. That is why it is written, "Whoever mocks the poor shows contempt for their Maker; whoever gloats over disaster will not go unpunished" (Prov. 17:5).

The Oppressed Poor

Probably this is the most frequently mentioned category in the Old Testament. Such poverty stems from the thoughtless or malicious exploitation of others. "An unplowed field produces food for the poor, but injustice sweeps it away" (Prov. 13:23). One thinks again of Naboth, and of Uriah. The prophets can inveigh against the monopolistic greed that squeezes out the little man: "Woe to you who add house to house and join field to field till no space is left and you live alone in the land" (Isa. 5:8).

The profoundly dehumanizing effects of all poverty are perhaps increased with this kind, for cynicism is added to all the other evils. It is doubtful if anyone has ever been more cynical than the writer of Ecclesiastes as he projects the perspective of a man who simply observes what takes place "under the sun":

> I saw the tears of the oppressed—and they have no comforter; power was on the side of their oppressors—and they have no comforter. And I declared that the dead, who had already died, are happier than the living, who are still alive. But better than both is the one who has not yet been, who has not seen the evil that is done under the sun. . . . If you see the poor oppressed in a district, and justice and rights denied, do not be surprised at such things; for one official is eyed by a higher one, and over them both are others higher still. The increase from the land is taken by all; the king himself profits from the fields. Those who love money never have enough; those who love wealth are never satisfied with their income. This too is meaningless. (Eccles. 4:1–3; 5:8–10)

Here poverty is the direct result of sin—someone else's sin. As in the first kind of poverty, sin is involved, but now not as the background that attracts judgment on a fallen world but as immediate oppression. There may still be some question as to why God "allows" such evil, but there can be little doubt that the evil itself is the work of human beings. If we human beings are morally responsible creatures—and we are—we had better look to ourselves first.

In many cases, the most that an individual can offer to victims of oppression is compassion mingled with charity. But what the poor really need in these cases is justice; and where we can provide it, we ought to do so. "The righteous care about justice for the poor; but the wicked have no such concern" (Prov. 29:7). "Speak up and judge fairly; defend the rights of the poor and needy" (Prov. 31:9).

It might be better if we spent less time debating the problem of poverty from the perspective of theodicy, and more time remembering that we must give an account to the God of justice: "The poor and the oppressor have this in common: The LORD gives sight to the eyes of both. If a king judges the poor with fairness, his throne will be established forever" (Prov. 29:13–14).

The Lazy Poor

Although the book of Proverbs features most kinds of poverty, this kind is especially prominent. "A sluggard's appetite is never filled, but the desires of the diligent are fully satisfied. . . . Whoever disregards discipline comes to poverty and shame, but whoever heeds correction is honored" (Prov. 13:4, 18). "All hard work brings a profit, but mere talk leads only to poverty" (Prov. 14:23). "Laziness brings on deep sleep, and the shiftless goes hungry" (Prov. 19:15). Sometimes laziness is coupled with other vices: "Do not join those who drink too much wine or gorge themselves on meat, for drunkards and gluttons become poor, and drowsiness clothes them in rags" (Prov. 23:20–21). The poverty of the younger son in Jesus' parable of the lost son (Luke 15:11–16) was the result of his own decadent self-indulgence.

This is an area where sweeping generalizations are almost always out of place, where judgments must be made on a case-by-case basis. People who cannot find work, suffering layoffs in a major recession, may become so discouraged that they drift to drink and laziness, even though they did not start that way. They remain responsible for their attitudes, but there can be no reasonable doubt that losing their jobs has contributed not a little to the breakdown in their moral fiber. At the same time, there is more and more evidence that mere handouts in such cases, even when motivated by the deepest compassion, are not what is needed. Such charity may breed a sense of dependence that proves debilitating. If large numbers of people in any cultural group experience this same thing, that group is on its way toward long-term structural poverty.

Meanwhile, subtler forms of laziness can do desperate damage to a nation. Where we demand more and more money for less and less work, where there is neither pride in labor nor integrity in performing a full day's labor for a full day's pay, where there is no concern for the competitive productivity that must prevail if an industry is to compete in the international marketplace, there too will the fruit of laziness ultimately manifest itself in doomed industries, massive unemployment, and a decaying culture.

Once again, the sin factor is strong. Personal laziness and lack of discipline are offenses before God. Where idleness has been stimulated by loss of employment, the sins of others may also be involved (the second kind of poverty), or even the unfortunate circumstance, as when a coal face runs out and forces a lot of miners out of work (the first kind of poverty). Insofar as sheer personal laziness is at stake, however, the Bible does not encourage us to sit around and point a finger at God. It urges repentance and diligence: "Lazy hands make for poverty, but diligent hands bring wealth" (Prov. 10:4).

The Poor Who Are Dependent on the Punished

What do we make of the children of King Saul and of Jonathan, who spent years in relative penury until David discharged his vow to Jonathan and sought out Mephibosheth with the express aim of doing him good? If a man is executed for his own sin—murder, say, or treason—his family may well face poverty as a result. How shall we view such suffering?

In part, this is a specific form of the first kind of poverty, that is, poverty springing from calamity, from misfortune. But this is not the misfortune of so-called natural disasters, but of someone else's sin. Yet it is not the sin of oppression, in which some are made poor by being exploited or oppressed by others. Rather, someone else's sin and consequent punishment have effected such a change in the circumstance of dependents that poverty is the result.

What this pattern shows is that sin has an insidious effect on others *even when they are not the intended victims*. Unlike, say, rape or murder or robbery, where the one who suffers most is the oppressor's *intended* victim, here the one who suffers most may be personally innocent of the culprit's crimes and is certainly not the culprit's intended victim, yet nevertheless is drawn into the web of effects brought about by the culprit's sin.

Indeed, if we cast the net of suffering beyond poverty to include other forms of pain and injustice, this category looms large. Whatever the guilt of those who knowingly transmit the AIDS virus by their sexual promiscuity, no blame can attach itself to those who contract the disease because they are hemophiliacs who need transfusions from the nation's blood supply. The sins of others are often visited on the innocent. This is true not only of the sin itself but also of the attendant judgment. Elijah is told that in his day God had reserved seven thousand men and women in Israel who had never bowed the knee to Baal (1 Kings 19:18). Did none of these fall into poverty during the three-year drought?

Our response to such suffering, whether we experience it ourselves or observe it in others, can never be glib. For although it is true that such suffering is perpetrated by human agents, it is in some ways harder to accept than when one is the immediate victim of an oppressor. There the stark barbarity of a fallen world and of our place in it may be painful, but our very proximity to the evil makes a lurid kind of "sense." When we are one step removed, the sheer injustice of it all seems magnified.

Yet that is the nature of sin; it has always been the nature of sin. Sin has effects that billow outward from perpetrator and immediate victim. A little yeast affects the entire lump of dough (1 Cor. 5:6); a little evil can have disastrous consequences far beyond the little circle in which it was committed.

I am not suggesting that this truth offers great comfort to those who suffer in this way. It should, however, help the Christian to understand the nature of evil a little better, and therefore to avoid being surprised when such things occur. There may be specific things we can do: we may be able to foster justice, or offer help to those unfairly disadvantaged by the spin-off effects of evil. But we must enlarge our grasp of what it means to live in a fallen world, so that when such things occur we are not devastated because we have cherished false expectations. The Bible does not tell us that life in this world will be fair. Evil and sin are not Victorian gentlemen; they do not play fair. We ourselves are part of this evil world order, and it is only because of the Lord's mercies that we are not consumed.

The Voluntarily Poor

We need spend little time on this group, except to note their existence. Insofar as they have *chosen* their own poverty, their poverty can scarcely be viewed as a problem to be solved.

I am not talking merely about the generous. All Christians are called to generosity, to magnanimity. Indeed, in many instances God openly blesses such generosity: "One person gives freely, yet gains even more; another withholds unduly, but comes to poverty" (Prov. 11:24). Rather, I am talking about the voluntary poverty where believers choose to sell all they have and give their money to the Lord's work, making themselves largely free from worldly care as they serve the Lord Christ to the very best of their strength. Impelled by the Spirit, many of the first believers adopted just such a stance (Acts 2:44–45).

Clearly, it is not sin that has landed these believers in their poverty; at least, it is not these believers' own sin. Their case is not unlike that of their Master: his voluntary laying aside of his glory to attach himself to the human race (John 17:5; Phil. 2:6ff.) was not the result of personal sin, but of personal self-abnegation. Even so, in both instances the voluntary steps would not have been taken, would not have been necessary, were it not for the sin of others.

There are subtle traps associated with such poverty. One is pride; another is love for a reputation for holiness and selflessness rather than a love for holiness and selflessness in their own right. Ananias and Sapphira (Acts 5) exemplify this vice to perfection.

Of all possible responses to those who choose this form of self-denial, perhaps the least appropriate is pity. If they have chosen this course out of largely pure motives, they will not want your pity, and may despise it; if they have chosen this course out of impure motives, your pity provides them with a dangerous temptation.

The Poor in Spirit

"Blessed are the poor in spirit," Jesus said, "for theirs is the kingdom of heaven. Blessed are those who mourn, for they will be comforted.

Blessed are the meek, for they will inherit the earth" (Matt. 5:3–5). "These are the ones I look on with favor: those who are humble and contrite in spirit, and who tremble at my word" (Isa. 66:2).

Once again, as with the last kind of poverty, people who belong to this category do not need our sympathy or succor. Even so, it is worth pausing to reflect on why poverty is used as the controlling metaphor.

Already in the Old Testament, some Hebrew words for "the poor" refer to those who because of sustained economic privation and social distress have confidence only in God (e.g., Pss. 37:14; 40:17; 69:28–29, 32–33; Prov. 16:19; 29:23; Isa. 61:1). "For a king to speak repeatedly of himself as 'poor and needy' (or similar expressions; cf. Pss. 40:17; 69:29; 70:5; 86:1; 109:22) is somewhat anomalous if not downright silly, unless it is understood that he is not speaking in terms of possessions, but of status and honor. In fact, in the psalms named the threat to the king is that those who wish him harm 'seek his life,' and his response to them is that they, not he, will be 'put to shame.'"[4] Here the "wealth" from which the king is in fear of being stripped is not primarily material possessions, but honor, status, even life itself.

In the intertestamental period, when so many of the wealthy and powerful were also the most corrupt and spiritually compromised (certainly not a unique period of history!), many writers could almost equate being "poor" and being "righteous."[5] This is not because grinding poverty is an intrinsic good. But if it helps someone come to God and ask for mercy, the intrinsic evil may in God's providence turn out to be a means of grace. "Poverty of spirit" may in many instances begin with poverty; if it leads to self-confessed bankruptcy of spirit and a humble plea to God for help, it may function as a great boon.

Old Testament writers are quick to point out that there are worse things than poverty; it is Western materialism that doubts it. "Better a dry crust with peace and quiet than a house full of feasting, with strife" (Prov. 17:1). But there is a deeper factor: the rich and powerful are often so self-satisfied and boastful that they never feel their need of grace; and if they do feel it, they have so much of a front to maintain that they will never admit it. "The poor plead for mercy, but the rich answer harshly" (Prov. 18:23). The poor may therefore develop a vein of insight that the rich can never mine: "The rich are wise in their own eyes; one who is poor and discerning sees how deluded they are" (Prov. 28:11). Small wonder that Jesus repeatedly emphasizes how hard it is for rich people to enter the kingdom; small wonder that he can cast the opening of his public

---

4. Ibid., 293.

5. For evidence, see D. A. Carson, "Matthew," in *The Expositor's Bible Commentary*, ed. Frank E. Gaebelein (Grand Rapids: Zondervan, 1984), 8:131–32.

ministry in the prophetic words of Isaiah 61: "The Spirit of the Lord is on me, because he has anointed me to proclaim good news to the poor. He has sent me to proclaim freedom for the prisoners and recovery of sight for the blind, to set the oppressed free, to proclaim the year of the Lord's favor" (Luke 4:18–19).

The poor in spirit, then, like Mary the mother of Jesus (Luke 1:46–55), turn to the Lord in their need, and find him to be bountiful in mercy.

And this, perhaps, gives us one of the most important perspectives that we can grasp. We have been thinking through how we are to look at poverty, our own or that of others. We have glimpsed just a little of the enormous biblical emphasis on compassion and justice, and viewed yet again the mystery of providence that resides behind so many aspects of the problem of evil and suffering. But if we expend all our energies pondering providence and wondering how to exonerate God, we may lose sight of the obvious. If at some point we stop worrying about whether God can vindicate himself this time, and start worrying about how *we* ought to be responding, under the God of the Bible, to this or that case of suffering, we may learn a little earlier to call upon the Lord for help, not for self-justification; in faith, not in bitterness. That we come to an end of ourselves will then be an incentive to sue God for grace, rather than an incentive to curse God and die.

But this reflection is not meant to minimize anyone's pain and confusion. Its implications must still be set against the background of other biblical values and truths.

Wars and Natural Disasters

Several years ago, Peter Craigie wrote a valuable little book entitled *The Problem of War in the Old Testament.*[6] Yet we must ask, "*Is* there a problem of war in the Old Testament?"

Certainly the Israelites think there is a problem of war when they lose. Habakkuk and others find a profound problem in war when a more evil nation triumphs over a less evil nation. Mighty empires are held accountable for their rapacity and barbarism in conquest. Yet in the Old Testament there is no theoretical reflection at all on the question, "Why is this a world in which there are wars?" It is simply assumed that wars will settle certain forms of disputes. The people of God constitute a nation that defends itself by going to war, and sees displayed God's

6. Peter Craigie, *The Problem of War in the Old Testament* (Grand Rapids: Eerdmans, 1978). See also Tremper Longman III and Daniel G. Reid, *God Is a Warrior* (Grand Rapids: Zondervan, 1995).

hand of strength where there is victory. It is *our* generation that sees a
"problem" with war, brought about in part by a century of brutal conflict
in which high-tech military prowess has mown down millions of young
soldiers, decimated entire nations, and now threatens the entire planet
with a nuclear holocaust.

Within the canon, the move from the old covenant to the new, from
the locus of the people of God as a nation to the locus of the people of
God as an international assembly of men and women who call on the
name of the Lord (1 Cor. 1:2), means that God's people, *as the church*,
ought not defend their interests as the people of God by appeal to the
sword.

Even so, the New Testament, no less than the Old, is simply not shocked
by the presence of wars. Jesus himself announces that wars will persist
until he returns: "You will hear of wars and rumors of wars, but see to it
that you are not alarmed. Such things must happen, but the end is still
to come. Nation will rise against nation, and kingdom against kingdom"
(Matt. 24:6–7a). Something similar can be said about natural disasters:
"There will be famines and earthquakes in various places" (Matt. 24:7b).
We are not to be surprised: "All these are the beginning of birth pains"
(Matt. 24:8).[7]

None of this means that we should treat any particular war as inevitable, or that we should be complacent about suffering caused by wars
and natural disasters. There may be many responsible steps to take as
we work at the role of being peacemakers. It does mean, however, that
wars do not take God by surprise, and should not take us by surprise
either. If our faith threatens to dissolve because of the very presence of
such wars, it may owe something to the fact that we have not entered
very deeply into what Scripture actually says. Neither the Old nor the
New Testament treats war as if it were a good thing, a manly sport (as
did many Victorians). But neither Testament is surprised by war; and
neither offers any hope that wars will cease before Jesus comes again.
It is simply assumed that this is a fallen world where such evils can only
be expected.

How, then, should we Christians train our minds to look on wars and
disasters? One of the most helpful passages is Luke 13:1–5. It is worth
citing at length:

> Now there were some present at that time who told Jesus about the Gali-
> leans whose blood Pilate had mixed with their sacrifices. Jesus answered,
> "Do you think that these Galileans were worse sinners than all the other
> Galileans because they suffered this way? I tell you, no! But unless you

7. Which, if I am not mistaken, refers to the entire period of suffering between the
first and second advents. See Carson, "Matthew," 8:488ff., esp. p. 498.

repent, you too will all perish. Or those eighteen who died when the tower in Siloam fell on them—do you think they were more guilty than all the others living in Jerusalem? I tell you, no! But unless you repent, you too will all perish."

This is a remarkable passage. There are a number of important lessons in it.

First, Jesus does not assume that those who suffered under Pilate, or those who were killed in the collapse of the tower, did not deserve their fate. Indeed, the fact that he can tell his contemporaries that unless *they* repent they too will perish shows that Jesus assumes that all death is in one way or another the result of sin, and therefore deserved.

Second, Jesus does insist that death by such means is no evidence whatsoever that those who suffer in this way are any more wicked than those who escape such a fate. The assumption seems to be that all deserve to die. If some die under a barbarous governor, and others in a tragic accident, it is no more than they deserve. But that does not mean that others deserve any less. Rather, the implication is that it is only God's mercy that has kept them alive. There is certainly no moral superiority on their part.

Third, Jesus treats wars and natural disasters not as agenda items in a discussion of the mysterious ways of God, but as incentives to repentance. It is as if he is saying that God uses disaster as a megaphone to call attention to our guilt and destination, to the imminence of his righteous judgment if he sees no repentance. This is an argument developed at great length in Amos 4. Disaster is a call to repentance. Jesus might have added (as he does elsewhere) that peace and tranquility, which we do not deserve, show us God's goodness and forbearance.

It is a mark of our lostness that we invert these two. We think we deserve the times of blessing and prosperity, and that the times of war and disaster are not only unfair but come perilously close to calling into question God's goodness or his power—even, perhaps, his very existence. Jesus simply does not see it that way. If we are to adopt his mind, we have some fundamental realignments to make in our assessment of ourselves.

Not long ago I was moved when I heard a missionary serving in Medellin, Colombia, give his assessment of the volatile and dangerous situation in that city. Known throughout the world as the capital of the drug barons, violence had taken over as the drug czars challenged the very government of the country. This missionary gave a level-headed assessment of the situation in which he and his family were serving, and then added a few more sentences. He said, in effect, "The root problem is greed, greed for money and the material blessings and power money can buy. But the truth of the matter is that we are all party to that sin. It is extremely important for us to capitalize on the situation by recognizing our own faces in the faces of the drug runners, to confess our own sins and to call men and women to repentance of sins that are merely less disguised among the drug barons."

That missionary was applying to his own situation the teaching of Jesus in Luke 13:1–5.

Questions for Further Study

1. To what extent does the civil authority in your country restrain evil? To what extent does it perpetrate evil?
2. Should a Christian disobey the state? If so, under what circumstances? Are there any circumstances when a Christian should rebel against the state? If so, what are they?
3. What four conclusions does this chapter draw from its discussion of the evils and suffering the state both restrains and perpetrates? What guidance do they give us as to how we should respond when we witness such things?
4. Give contemporary examples of the kinds of poverty detailed in this chapter. What should be our response to each?
5. From the biblical perspective, what is the greatest danger in being wealthy? What is the potential good that is linked with poverty (even though extreme poverty is itself a great evil)? How do your answers apply to you?
6. Summarize in your own words what Jesus says in Luke 13 about oppression and natural disasters. Do you respond to such tragedies the way Jesus says you should? How can you develop in your own life the perspectives and values that Jesus mandates?

5

The Suffering People of God

Despite the best efforts of the proponents of the health and wealth gospel, the fact is that Christians get old and wrinkled. They contract cancer and heart disease, become deaf and blind, and eventually die. In many parts of the world Christians have to face the blight of famine, the scourge of war, the subtle coercion of corruption. This is not to say that God does not sometimes intervene on behalf of his people in remarkable ways. It is to say, rather, that we, too, live in a fallen world and cannot escape participation in its evil and suffering. If you doubt this, you are (1) ignorant of what many Christians around the world have to face daily; (2) not old enough yet, for certainly if you live long enough you too will suffer; (3) kidding yourself; or (4) some combination of the above.

But there are some sufferings that are peculiar to the people of God. Those who track such things tell us that there have been more Christian martyrs in the past century than in the previous nineteen centuries combined. Of course, this owes a great deal to the incredible growth in world population during the last century and a half. Even so, Christians in the West, largely untroubled by official persecution, must become aware that we are something of an anomaly. And in the West, subtle anti-Christian pressures are increasing. Sometimes we are aware of them and sometimes we are not.

In this chapter I want to reflect on the kinds of suffering that are peculiar to the people of God, and to think through how we ought to respond to them.

Suffering Peculiar to the People of God: Discipline

Probably the most dominant form of suffering that is peculiar to God's people, according to the Bible, is the discipline that God himself metes out.

The theme is strong in both Testaments. One of the most striking passages is found in Hebrews 12:5–12 (part of which cites Prov. 3:11–12):

> And have you completely forgotten this word of encouragement that addresses you as children? It says, "My son, do not make light of the Lord's discipline, and do not lose heart when he rebukes you, because the Lord disciplines those he loves, and he chastens everyone he accepts as his child." Endure hardship as discipline; God is treating you as his children. For what children are not disciplined by their father? If you are not disciplined—and everyone undergoes discipline—then you are not legitimate children at all. Moreover, we have all had parents who disciplined us and we respected them for it. How much more should we submit to the Father of spirits and live! Our parents disciplined us for a little while as they thought best; but God disciplines us for our good, that we may share in his holiness. No discipline seems pleasant at the time, but painful. Later on, however, it produces a harvest of righteousness and peace for those who have been trained by it. Therefore, strengthen your feeble arms and weak knees.

These verses are remarkable in several ways.

First, the context shows that the discipline the author has in mind is designed to help Christians combat sin. The verse that introduces this passage finds the author rebuking his readers: "In your struggle against sin, you have not yet resisted to the point of shedding your blood" (Heb. 12:4). In other words, he writes, their efforts to combat sin in their lives have not yet produced any martyrs; so what are they complaining about?

Second, the author designates the cited passage from Proverbs as a "word of encouragement." Of course, when you stop to think of it, the prospect of discipline *must* be encouraging to those who genuinely want to please their heavenly Father. If he disciplines those he loves, and punishes those he accepts as his children, then to chafe unduly under such punishment is to betray our immaturity—or even, finally, to call into question our desire to grow in conformity to our heavenly Father. That is one of the reasons why Paul can delight in weakness and infirmity: he knows such things curtail his pride (2 Cor. 12:7–9) and are the precursor to wonderful experiences of the Lord's grace.

Third, this discipline is for our good: "God disciplines us for our good, that we may share in his holiness" (Heb. 12:10); and "without holiness no one will see the Lord" (Heb. 12:14). The burden of much of the Epistle to the Hebrews is that it is dangerously possible to start well, to make a fine show of Christian life and strength, but that only Christian faith that perseveres to the end is genuine: "We are his house, if indeed we hold firmly to our confidence and the hope in which we glory. . . . We have come to share in Christ, if indeed we hold firmly till the end our original conviction" (Heb. 3:6, 14). That is why God lovingly exercises discipline: he is training us to persevere.

Fourth, this is so much a part of God's way with his people that if any live without God's discipline in their lives their status as the children of God is called into question. Such people show themselves to be "not legitimate children at all" (Heb. 12:8).

The diversity of God's discipline is not spelled out here. Scanning the narratives of Scripture enlightens us: God's discipline may include war, plague, illness, rebuke, ill-defined and rather personal "thorns," bereavement, loss of status, personal opposition, and much else beside.

The difficulty is that many of these things are themselves evils, and in other contexts can be portrayed as the effluent of a fallen world or the work of the devil. Thus Paul has no doubt that his "thorn in my flesh" is simultaneously "a messenger of Satan" and something that God himself sent Paul to keep him from becoming conceited (2 Cor. 12:7). It is extremely important that we come to terms with these ambiguities. If we do not, we will constantly be assigning this little bit of our life and circumstances exclusively to the devil, and some other little bit exclusively to God. We may then unwittingly live our lives as if we were in a dualistic universe, with neither good nor evil quite strong enough to claim our allegiance; or we may conclude that, because some circumstance in our life is demonstrably evil, we must assume that God, being good, *must* remove it in response to a prayer of faith. If this evil does not disappear, then either we are disappointed with God or crushed because our faith is so bankrupt.

In reality, we *never* escape God's sovereignty. Part of learning to live as faithful children of the sovereign God is therefore tied to trusting him when he can at best be only dimly discerned behind events and circumstances that the Bible itself is quick to label evil. The mystery of providence thus returns in another form; we will explore it a little more in chapter 11. But for the moment, it is important to see that at least some of God's means of discipline, all designed for our good, can simultaneously be viewed as calamitous evils.

For instance, prolonged suffering from chronic illness is certainly not a "good" thing, yet rightly accepted it can breed patience, teach discipline of prayer, generate compassion for others who suffer, engender some reflection and self-knowledge that knocks out cockiness and the arrogance of condescending impatience. I know couples who ended up on the mission field because they lost their children, preachers who learned to care when they were first themselves bereaved, senior saints whose Christian influence swelled enormously after they lost all of their children in tragic circumstances.

I do not claim to know whether each of these instances should be viewed as examples of God's fatherly discipline. I rather imagine that there was a mixture. It is the uncertainty of reading what is going on that sometimes breeds pain. Is the particular blow I am facing God's way of telling me to change something? Or is it a form of discipline designed to toughen me or soften me to make me more useful? Or is it part of the heritage of all sons and daughters of Adam who live this side of the parousia, unrelated to discipline but part of God's mysterious providence in a fallen world?

But must we always decide? If a little self-examination shows us how to improve, we ought to improve. But there are times when all that the Christian can responsibly do is to trust his heavenly Father in the midst of the darkness and pain. This, too, we need to think about some more, and set within a larger framework (see chaps. 11 and 12). Even so, we need to see that discipline, this particular "part of the puzzle," is not unrelated to the rest of the puzzle. Nor is it a complete "solution" to the problem of evil and suffering. On the other hand, it is an important part, and one too little thought about by most Christians in the Western world, where discipline is frequently in short supply, not least in the church.

There is a fifth point that emerges from Hebrews 12. The author frankly acknowledges that "no discipline seems pleasant at the time, but painful" (v. 11). In other words, even though Christians have accepted all that this passage has taught, when they actually *experience* the next dose of discipline it will not be a pleasant experience. All the correct theology in the world will not make a spanking sting less, or make a brutal round of toughening-up exercises fun. Yet it does help to know that there is light at the end of the tunnel, even if you cannot yet see it; to know that God is in control and is committed to his people's good, even though it still does not look like that to you. The suffering is no less real, but perhaps it is less debilitating when the larger perspective is kept in mind. Like the boy who is getting a spanking for breaking his sister's Alice band in a fit of rage, so the discipline God metes out hurts, and causes us to wail. But if the boy's Daddy is good, loving, and even-handed, the boy himself is made secure by the expression of love in discipline, and ultimately grows to appreciate his father's wisdom. Additionally, of course, the boy learns the important lesson that there are consequences to behavior. So we too learn to trust our heavenly Father and rely on his wisdom to take us through paths we never would have chosen for ourselves, while learning life lessons we would not have learned any other way.

Many of these points can be illustrated from the Bible. For instance, this mixture of faith and anguish frequently surfaces in the psalms. David writes: "LORD, do not rebuke me in your anger or discipline me in your wrath. Have mercy on me, LORD, for I am faint; heal me, LORD, for my bones are in agony. My soul is in deep anguish. How long, LORD, how long?" (Ps. 6:1–3). Whether the agony in his bones is a physical malady or not, the psalmist recognizes that what he is facing is nothing less than the discipline of God. That discipline extends to anguish in soul, to the mockery of his enemies (v. 10), and even to the threat of death (v. 5).

It is overwhelmingly important to reflect on the fact that this psalm and dozens of similar ones are included in Scripture. There is no attempt in Scripture to whitewash the anguish of God's people when they undergo suffering. They argue with God, they complain to God, they weep before God. Theirs is not a faith that leads to dry-eyed stoicism, but a faith so robust it wrestles with God.

Much of Western spirituality is deficient on both scores: where faith triumphs in adversity, we expect it to be manifest in unmoved resignation, and where faith fails the failure is displayed in doubt that questions the integrity and possibly even the existence of God.

David points to a better way. He does not display stoic resignation, nor does he betray doubt that God exists. Even when he feels abandoned by God, his sense of isolation issues in an emotional pursuit of the God who, in his view, is slow to answer. David's suffering leads him to frank pleading with God, to confession, to tears. "My soul is in deep anguish," he says: he does not worry whether this might be viewed as rather letting down the side. "Turn, LORD, and deliver me; save me because of your unfailing love" (Ps. 6:4): he pleads God's character when he cannot plead his own. "I am worn out from my groaning. All night long I flood my bed with weeping and drench my couch with tears" (Ps. 6:6): he frankly appeals to the Lord's pity.

But on the other hand, when David breaks through to a new level of confidence, it is not cast in abstract resignation to a mysterious providence. Rather, David wins a renewed knowledge of God, and an assurance that God has heard him and will in fact help: "Away from me, all you who do evil, for the LORD has heard my weeping. The LORD has heard my cry for mercy; the LORD accepts my prayer. All my enemies will be overwhelmed with shame and anguish; they will turn back and suddenly be put to shame" (Ps. 6:8–10). This is a man who is not pursuing a merely intellectual theodicy or a fatalistic resignation. It is a man who wants to know God, to know God experientially. This is a man who can elsewhere write, "You, God, are my God, earnestly I seek you; I thirst for you, my whole being longs for you, in a dry and parched land where there is no water. . . . Because your love is better than life, my lips will glorify you. . . . I will be fully satisfied as with the richest of foods; with singing lips my mouth will praise you" (Ps. 63:1, 3, 5).

The prophecy of Habakkuk may serve as another illustration of discipline, an illustration that highlights many of the same lessons. For a start, the book preserves the same kind of frank exchange between a suffering believer and God. The prophet despairs because of the wickedness of his nation, and the apparent silence of heaven: "How long, LORD, must I call for help, but you do not listen? Or cry out to you, 'Violence!' but you do not save? Why do you make me look at injustice? Why do you tolerate wrongdoing? Destruction and violence are before me; there is strife, and conflict abounds. Therefore the law is paralyzed, and justice never prevails. The wicked hem in the righteous, so that justice is perverted" (Hab. 1:2–4).

Perhaps Habakkuk expected God to raise up a great prophet or a just and powerful king. Perhaps he hoped for a period of sweeping revival. But, in fact, the Lord's answer drives him to distraction. "Look at the nations and watch—and be utterly amazed," the Lord replies. "For I am going to do something in your days that you would not believe, even if you were told" (Hab. 1:5). And what is this astonishing thing? God is going to send the Babylonians to punish his covenant people. Even though God himself describes the Babylonians as "ruthless and impetuous people" who "come bent on violence" and "are a law to themselves," he insists that he himself is raising them up for this task (Hab. 1:6ff.).

Habakkuk is aghast. He understands what God has said: "You, LORD, you have appointed them to execute judgment; you, my Rock, have ordained them to punish" (Hab. 1:12). But why should the God whose "eyes are too pure to look on evil" and who "cannot tolerate wrong" permit his own covenant community, as rebellious as they are, to be chastened by a still more sinful people? It seems massively unfair. Granted you are so pure, Habakkuk tells God, "Why then do you tolerate the treacherous? Why are you silent while the wicked swallow up those more righteous than themselves?" (Hab. 1:13).

There are many elements in the Lord's reply to his servant Habakkuk. Perhaps the dominant one is the blistering denunciation of sin. Calamitous woes are pronounced on those who pile up stolen goods, who build their realms with unjust gain, who foster drunkenness, revelry, and shame, who succumb to quintessential idolatry—the worship of what human beings make with their own hands (Hab. 2). The ranting and the boasting and the idolatry are desperately out of place before this God: "The LORD is in his holy temple; let all the earth be silent before him" (Hab. 2:20).

This response from the Lord cuts both ways. On the one hand, it provides a reason why Israel must be punished: their sin deserves it. But on the other hand, it also threatens the Babylonians who will punish Israel: their sins too are remembered by God, and he will hold them to account. The end of the story is not played out with the chastening of Israel. Justice will be served all round; it will be done, and will be seen to be done.

Habakkuk may not like all that he hears; but he understands. He still begs God to intervene with the saving works he has displayed in the past: "LORD, I have heard of your fame; I stand in awe of your deeds, LORD. Renew them in our day, in our time make them known; in wrath remember mercy" (Hab. 3:2). Then, after reviewing in poetic terms the terrible displays of God's wrath in the past, Habakkuk makes three commitments.

First, he resolves to take the long view, in the assurance that God's justice will prevail over the oppressors, even though the oppressors are instruments in God's hands to punish the covenant community: "I heard and my heart pounded, my lips quivered at the sound; decay crept into my bones, and my legs trembled. Yet I will wait patiently for the day of calamity to come on the nation invading us" (Hab. 3:16). By "taking the long view" I mean that Habakkuk can more easily accept that punishments will be meted out on the short term by a nation yet more evil and violent, if he is assured that all nations, including the oppressor that will administer the chastening, will ultimately be held to account. Peter expresses much the same thought (though he turns it to a different end): "For it is time for judgment to begin with God's household; and if it begins with us, what will the outcome be for those who do not obey the gospel of God?" (1 Pet. 4:17). Habakkuk's resolution thus anticipates the direction we must take in this book: some of our sufferings appear a little different if we view them from the vantage of the End.

Second, Habakkuk resolves that, however great the privation he must suffer along with the covenant community, he will delight the more in God. It is almost as if the threatened loss of all material blessings and security drives him to enjoyment of God: there is nothing and no one else to rely on, and therefore nothing to mask the enjoyment of God that ought to be the believer's focus. "Though the fig tree does not bud," he writes, "and there are no grapes on the vines, though the olive crop fails and the fields produce no food, though there are no sheep in the pen and no cattle in the stalls, yet I will rejoice in the LORD, I will be joyful in God my Savior" (Hab. 3:17–18). Firm resolve this may be; grim resolution it is not. It is the resolution of one whose eyes have been opened to see where his delight should have been in the first place. God's discipline, displayed in calamitous punishment of the nation, becomes a means of grace, if not for the entire nation, then at least for Habakkuk and those who join his train.

William Cowper (1731–1800) meditated long on these verses from Habakkuk:

> Sometimes a light surprises
> The Christian while he sings;
> It is the Lord who rises
> With healing in His wings;
> When comforts are declining,
> He grants the soul again
> A season of clear shining,
> To cheer it after rain.
>
> Though vine nor fig-tree neither
> Their wonted fruit should bear,
> Though all the field should wither,
> Nor flocks nor herds be there,
> Yet, God the same abiding,
> His praise shall tune my voice,
> For, while in Him confiding,
> I cannot but rejoice.

Third, Habakkuk commits himself to praise, not complaint: "The Sovereign LORD is my strength; he makes my feet like the feet of a deer, he enables me to tread the heights" (Hab. 3:19). This is not stoicism; it is the sacrifice of praise (cf. Heb. 13:15). It is not merely the power of positive thinking in religious guise, nor is it a Pollyanna-style optimism (after all, Habakkuk's circumstances and prospects have not changed). Rather, this commitment to praise is simultaneously the fruit of determined obedience to respond aright to the God who is there, and an un-self-conscious paean of worship that stems from a deeper grasp of who this God is.

In the Bible, then, the dominant form of suffering peculiar to God's people is discipline. We should glance at one more passage, for here such discipline is tied both to what it means to be a Christian, and to the kind of character it produces.

In Romans 5, Paul begins to draw out some of the implications of the doctrine of justification by faith. Justification has a certain primacy in his thought—not that it is necessarily the key around which all other Christian teaching turns, but that it is the entrance point into Christian life and discipleship. "Therefore, since we have been justified through faith"—that is the given—"we have peace with God through our Lord Jesus Christ" (Rom. 5:1). Such peace with God is to be desired above all things. As Paul has taken pains to prove at the beginning of the book, we are all by nature and choice under the wrath of God, and the drama of the Epistle to the Romans, like the drama of the Bible as a whole, is how rebels who attract only the wrath of God can be reconciled to him. The answer is in the gospel of Jesus Christ, the good news of his coming, death, and resurrection. God sent him to die in our place, "so as to be just and the one who justifies those who have faith in Jesus" (Rom. 3:26). Because of what Christ has borne, those who trust him are "justified": they are declared just by the holy God himself, not because they are, or because their sins do not matter, but because Christ has stood in their place. And the consequence of having been "justified through faith," Paul writes, is that "we have peace with God through our Lord Jesus Christ."

All of this is the work of God's grace, the unmerited favor which, despite his wrath, he mercifully bestows on needy sinners like me. It is through Jesus, Paul goes on to say, that "we have gained access by faith into this grace in which we now stand." This, surely, is cause for unbounded joy. It means we are not only reconciled to God here and now, but that one day we shall see him in his unshielded glory. That, I think, is what Paul means when he adds, "And we boast in the hope of the glory of God" (Rom. 5:2). The word "hope" does not here suggest mere possibility, but certain prospect: our boast is in the prospect of one day seeing the glory of God.

So sweeping a vision changes all our priorities. Maximal comfort in this fallen world is now low on the agenda. The real question is how our current circumstances are tied to our faith in Jesus Christ, our peace with God, and our prospect of seeing him. So Paul insists that we rejoice not only in the hope of the glory of God, but "we also glory *in our sufferings*, because we know that suffering produces perseverance; perseverance, character; and character, hope" (Rom. 5:3–4, emphasis added).

Here, then, is a philosophy of suffering, a perspective that ties it both to the salvation we now enjoy and to the consummation of that salvation when the glory of God is fully revealed. Like the discipline of physical training, suffering produces perseverance. This is not a universal rule, for suffering can evoke muttering and unbelief. But when suffering is mingled with the faith of verses 1–2, and with delight in being reconciled to God, it then produces perseverance. The staying power of our faith is neither demonstrated nor developed until it is tested by suffering.

But as perseverance mushrooms, "character" is formed. The word "character" suggests "provedness," the kind of maturity that is attained by being "proved" or "tested," like a metal refined by fire. And as character or "provedness" is formed, hope blossoms: our anticipation of the glory of God (v. 2) is nurtured and strengthened. This hope "does not put us to shame" (v. 5)—i.e., it is not illusory, and so it will never leave us in the lurch, ashamed of our foolish beliefs. Far from it! The object of this hope is certain, and already the hope is reinforced and proves satisfying "because God's love has been poured out into our hearts through the Holy Spirit, who has been given us" (v. 5). This mention of the Holy Spirit anticipates the full discussion Paul offers in Romans 8. Here he is alluding to a theme he frequently develops: the Holy Spirit is given to the believer as the down payment and guarantee of the full inheritance that will one day be ours. This Holy Spirit is the agent who pours God's love into our hearts: this is *felt* Christianity, and Paul elsewhere shows that this experience of the richness of God's love is an essential part of Christian maturity, something for which to pray (cf. Eph. 3:14–21, esp. vv. 17b–19). Such experience of the love of God is not yet the perfection of the vision of God; but it is fully satisfying, and strengthens hope, and places our sufferings in a light where they make a certain existential "sense."

There is a certain kind of maturity that can be attained only through the discipline of suffering. "During the days of Jesus' life on earth, he offered up prayers and petitions with fervent cries and tears to the one who could save him from death, and he was heard because of his reverent submission. Son though he was, *he learned obedience from what he suffered* and, once made perfect, he became the source of eternal salvation for all who obey him" (Heb. 5:7–9, emphasis added). The idea is not that Jesus was *dis*obedient before he suffered, but that in his incarnate state he too had to learn lessons of obedience, levels of obedience, that could only be attained through suffering. In this sense he grew to "perfection": not that he was morally imperfect before his sufferings, but that the fullness, the perfection of his identity with the human race and of his human, temporal obedience to his heavenly Father could be attained only through the fires of suffering. This "perfection" he achieved, not only with the result that "he became the source of eternal salvation for all who obey him," but also with the result that he is able "to sympathize with our weaknesses" since he "has been tempted in every way, just as we are—yet he did not sin" (Heb. 4:15). If even Jesus "learned obedience from what he suffered," what ghastly misapprehension is it—or arrogance!—that assumes we should be exempt?

Indeed, it is the set of values articulated in Romans 5 and the example of Jesus adumbrated in Hebrews 2 that accounts for the strong language of the apostle Paul in Philippians 3. He weighs up everything the world offers, sets it against all that he has in Christ Jesus, and concludes: "I consider everything a loss because of the surpassing worth of knowing Christ Jesus my Lord, for whose sake I have lost all things. I consider them garbage, that I may gain Christ and be found in him, not having a righteousness of my own that comes from the law, but that which is through faith in Christ—the righteousness that comes from God on the basis of faith" (Phil. 3:8–9). But this is not a static attainment; Paul is committed to growth in his knowledge of Christ Jesus. So he adds: "I want to know Christ—yes, to know the power of his resurrection *and participation in his sufferings, becoming like him in his death*, and so, somehow, attaining to the resurrection from the dead" (Phil. 3:10–11, emphasis added).

How we handle the suffering of testing and discipline therefore depends not a little on what we focus on. On a trip to Australia, I met an Anglican bishop who had been mightily used in evangelism and church planting in three African nations. He was sometimes referred to as "the apostle to Tanzania." After he "retired" from his missionary work in Africa, he set up a seminary in the United States. But when I met him, his suffering from Parkinson's disease was so advanced that he could no longer talk. He could communicate, just barely, by printing out block letters in a wavering hand that was almost indecipherable. He often had to draw a word three or four times for me to understand him.

We "talked" about a number of matters close to his heart—at least, I did the "talking," and tried to ask most of my questions in a form where he could signal merely yes or no. In the short time I spent with him, I sensed a man of unshaken faith, and so I had the audacity to ask him how he was coping with his illness. After decades of immensely productive activity, how was he dealing with his own suffering, with the temptation to feel he was now useless and fruitless? He penned his answer twice before I could make it out: THERE IS NO FUTURE IN FRUSTRATION. That bishop understood Romans 5 and Hebrews 12.

Suffering Peculiar to the People of God: Opposition and Persecution

As I have already suggested, it is not always possible or even desirable to differentiate between suffering understood as discipline and suffering that stems from opposition and persecution. Nevertheless the Bible itself encourages us to think that in some cases, at least, the distinction should be made; and then a slightly different array of perspectives comes into play as we grapple with the suffering such evil inflicts.

What I have in mind in this section is the kind of opposition against and persecution of the people of God that arises *just because they are the people of God*, with all that this identity means in conviction and conduct. Because after Sinai the covenant community in the Old Testament constituted a nation, it is not always possible to discern when the motive other nations had for opposing the community was religious and when it was simply political or economic. Probably many observers at the time did not make such distinctions very easily anyway. When the Assyrians swept down on Israel or the Babylonians on Judah, they were bent on furthering their expansionist policies. They were, in a word, imperialists, not an ancient version of the Spanish Inquisition. That *some* political and military opposition was motivated by hatred of the Jews' religion is clear. Perhaps it came to a head in the brutality of Antiochus Epiphanes, whose regime precipitated the Maccabean revolt almost two centuries before Jesus. But the distinctions cannot always be drawn.

On the other hand, at the personal level there is ample evidence of the sense of pressure that attended godly individuals who faced the evil of those who opposed them. The psalms are preeminent in reporting the responses of believers when they faced such attacks. "Give me relief from my distress; have mercy on me and hear my prayer," David prays (Ps. 4:1). Then he turns to his attackers and says, "How long will you men turn my glory into shame? How long will you love delusions and seek false gods? Know that the LORD has set apart his faithful servant for himself; the LORD hears when I call to him" (Ps. 4:2–3). Elsewhere he takes the long view: "Those who are pregnant with evil conceive trouble and give birth to disillusionment. Those who dig a hole and scoop it out fall into the pit they have made. The trouble they cause recoils on them; their violence comes down on their own heads" (Ps. 7:14–16; cf. Matt. 26:52). Not a few psalms center on the monarch's struggle with evil, deceitful, and violent men.

But it is under the new covenant that the theme of the suffering people of God comes into its own. This is partly because they no longer constitute a nation, and so opposition against them can no longer be construed as a merely political confrontation, nation against nation. More importantly, the object of Christian faith is a *crucified* Messiah; and, as we shall see, he has set the pattern for his followers. Further, he has already inaugurated the kingdom of God, and this kingdom actually engenders a clash of loyalties wherever any institution or authority—home, government, job, popular philosophy—intolerantly claims allegiance that belongs to God alone. This is what Jesus means when he says that he did not come to bring peace to the earth, but a sword (Matt. 10:34).

Suffering the opprobrium of the world is bound up with what it means to be a Christian. Perhaps the most famous passage in this connection is Mark 8:34–38: "Whoever wants to be my disciple must deny themselves and take up their cross and follow me. For whoever wants to save their life will lose it, but whoever loses their life for me and for the gospel will save it. What good is it for you to gain the whole world, yet forfeit your soul? Or what can you give in exchange for your soul? If any of you are ashamed of me and my words in this adulterous and sinful generation, the Son of Man will be ashamed of you when he comes in his Father's glory with the holy angels."

Without embarking on a full-scale exposition of this passage, it is nevertheless worth pausing to note several things.

First, "to take up one's cross" does not mean to put up with some relatively minor irritant, like a crabby in-law or a runny nose. Crucifixion was the form of execution reserved for the most despised and evil of criminals. No Roman citizen could be crucified without the sanction of the emperor; that form of death was reserved for slaves and non-citizens. After sentence was passed, the victim was scourged with the most severe of the three Roman levels of beating (the *verberatio*[1]), and then the cross-member was lashed to his arms and shoulders so that he could carry it out to the place of execution. There the cross-member was fastened to the upright member of the cross, already sunk in the ground. Thus, for anyone to "take up their cross" was to go to the place of painful, shameful execution.

To use that expression in a metaphorical sense is not to strip it of its force. Jesus means that his followers must die to self-interest, declare themselves dead to the glories and attractions of this world, and be prepared for suffering, even the most ignominious suffering. And in this, we are doing no more than following Jesus, for that is the way he went—without the advantage of hiding behind metaphorical language.

Second, the alternative is to forfeit one's soul. It is to gain the approval of the "world" and Jesus' disapproval. The confrontation between, on the one hand, Jesus and his kingdom, and, on the other, the world he has come to redeem, is so total that one necessarily sides with one or the other. The irony is that those who "lose" their lives by this "crucifixion" thereby find their lives. They discover what they had always denied before: they belong to God by creation, and they can never find themselves, never be fulfilled, never realize their potential, unless they abandon self-interest and abandon themselves to God. But as long as that takes place in this rebellious and self-focused world, suffering and opposition are inevitable.

Third, Jesus casts this confrontation in terms of Christian witness. If anyone is ashamed of Jesus and his words "in this adulterous and sinful generation," Jesus will be ashamed of that person when he returns at the end of the age: he will say, in effect, "I never knew you. Away from me, you evildoers!" (Matt. 7:23). Thus, real Christianity cannot forever be hidden: it will manifest itself in attestation of Jesus and his words before a world that is wholly opposed to his claims.

1. See the discussion on John 19:1 in D. A. Carson, *The Gospel of John* (Leicester: Inter-Varsity; Grand Rapids: Eerdmans, 1991).

That is why Paul elsewhere warns, "In fact, everyone who wants to live a godly life in Christ Jesus will be persecuted" (2 Tim. 3:12). Of course, Paul has in mind the first-century Roman Empire. He did not envisage modern Western democracies which to some extent have inherited a Christian worldview. Even so, appearances can be deceiving. That Christian heritage has become so attenuated, has been so thoroughly diluted or compromised, that Christians now face all sorts of subtle pressures in many sectors of business, sport, industry, and public service. A police officer's promotion is held up because he will not allow himself to be corrupted; a Jewish family holds a funeral for their son who has become a Christian; parents stage a wailing scene when their son, a prized surgeon, decides to enter the ministry instead; the media conspire to present most Christians as either irrelevant or as wimps. It is beginning to cost something to be a Christian; and perhaps the church will be purer for it.

In one church I know, a medical doctor, formerly a missionary, was appointed to the board of elders. Some time later he had an affair, divorced his wife, abandoned his children, and separated himself from any form of biblical Christianity. Countless attempts were made to rehabilitate him; doubtless some of these attempts were wise, and some were unwise.

But the most thoughtful assessment of the mess came three years later, from one of the leaders in the church. He suggested that this doctor, who came from a Christian home and had done all the "right" things, had never had to make a decision that cost him anything. Everything was too easy; at every point he had been supported and praised. Even his missionary career was bound up with his own specialty interests in medicine. Then, when some troubles opened up in his marriage (as they open up in most marriages at one time or another), and an attractive alternative presented herself, this doctor had no moral center on which to depend. He had never, for the sake of Christ, made a decision that cost him something; and he wasn't about to start now. In hindsight, it is not even clear that his profession of faith was real, for real professions of faith manifest themselves in a principial death to self-interest, in a principial commitment to the cause of Christ and his gospel.

I am far from suggesting that every divorce proves a person is a non-Christian. Christians sin; those who claim they do not are self-deceived, and make God out to be a liar (1 John 1:4ff.). But in this case (and it is not unique), it is hard to find even one area of this man's life, one major incident in his life (so far as his life is known), where professed allegiance cost him anything.

That is not normal. It may be common (as spurious believers are regrettably common); but it is not normal. What is normal is taking up one's cross and following Jesus; it is recognizing that in this fallen world, "everyone who wants to live a godly life in Christ Jesus will be persecuted." That is inevitable; decisions are made; the cost is cheerfully borne; and iron is bred into the soul. Moreover, for Christians living in most parts of the world, this would not have to be explained at such length: it would be obvious. Imagine ponderously explaining these things to Christians in Sudan, China, the northern islands of Indonesia, Saudi Arabia, Bangladesh!

It is not as if Jesus did not warn us. He repeatedly advised would-be disciples to count the cost (Luke 9:57–62; 14:25–34). He told his disciples to expect opposition not only during their trainee missions, but in the longer vista of their extended ministries (e.g., Matt. 10:11–42). This passage is moving; it deserves to be read and reread—along with *Foxe's Book of Martyrs* and many contemporary reports of Christian suffering. Few such reports are more moving than the recent account of the killing fields of Cambodia.[2] The principle is clear: "If the world hates you, keep in mind that it hated me first. If you belonged to the world, it would love you as its own. As it is, you do not belong to the world, but I have chosen you out of the world. That is why the world hates you. . . . If they persecuted me, they will persecute you also. If they obeyed my teaching, they will obey yours also" (John 15:18, 20).

It is not surprising, then, that when the apostles suffered their first flogging, they had a framework to make sense of it. As a result, they "left the Sanhedrin, rejoicing because they had been counted worthy of suffering disgrace for the Name" (Acts 5:41). The first Christian martyr died emulating his Master: "Lord, do not hold this sin against them" (Acts 7:60).

Peter learned the lesson well. The same Peter who wanted to draw a sword in Gethsemane and fight it out (John 18:10–11) had to learn that he would one day glorify God by his own death in martyrdom (John 21:18–19). He learned the lesson well enough that he could pass it on to others. He wrote,

> Dear friends, do not be surprised at the fiery ordeal that has come on you to test you, as though something strange were happening to you. But rejoice inasmuch as you participate in the sufferings of Christ, so that you may be overjoyed when his glory is revealed. If you are insulted because of the name of Christ, you are blessed, for the Spirit of glory and of God rests on you. If you suffer, it should not be as a murderer or thief or any other kind of criminal, or even as a meddler. However, if you suffer as a Christian, do not be ashamed, but praise God that you bear that name. . . . So then, those who suffer according to God's will should commit themselves to their faithful Creator and continue to do good. (1 Pet. 4:12–16, 19)

2. See Don Cormack, *Killing Fields, Living Fields* (London: Monarch Books, 1997).

Paul is firmer yet: "For it has been *granted* to you on behalf of Christ not only to believe on him, but also to suffer for him, since you are going through the same struggle you saw I had, and now hear that I still have" (Phil. 1:29–30, emphasis added). Here is suffering as *privilege*, a grace *granted*. By this means, according to Jesus, we align ourselves with the prophets (Matt. 5:12).

There is a parental and pastoral implication to all this. Sometimes we want to protect our children or our flock from too many things. For instance, we sometimes try to protect them from the caustic scorn of peers who have little time for Christian values. After all, we console ourselves, the Bible says much about earning a good reputation with outsiders. But that reputation is for integrity, kindness, love; it is never to be won at the expense of silence. I look at my children, and I wish for them enough opposition to make them strong, enough insults to make them choose, enough hard decisions to make them see that following Jesus brings with it a cost—a cost eminently worth it, but still a cost. A church that is merely comfortable, that never evangelizes, never encourages its people to stand on the front line, will never be strong, never be grateful, never be able to sort out profoundly Christian priorities.

It is only in the context of suffering that Christians can learn what it means to be "more than conquerors." This phrase does not come in a context suggestive of a "higher Christian life," a superior brand of Christianity that triumphantly lives above nasty little things like doubt or discouragement or defeat or depression. Rather, it comes in a context where Christians are *attacked*. "Who shall separate us from the love of Christ?" Paul asks with rhetorical flourish. "Shall trouble or hardship or persecution or famine or nakedness or danger or sword? As it is written: 'For your sake we face death all day long; we are considered as sheep to be slaughtered.' No, in all these things we are *more than conquerors* through him who loved us" (Rom. 8:35–37, emphasis added). How could it be otherwise? "If God is for us, who can be against us? He who did not spare his own Son, but gave him up for us all—how will he not also, along with him, graciously give us all things?" (Rom. 8:31–32)—which in the context does not suggest all material things we greedily covet, but all things needed to complete our salvation and bring us safely to the consummation of the new heaven and the new earth, when all who have been called and justified will also be glorified. With supreme confidence stemming from faith in a sovereign God who cannot fail in any of his promises, Paul concludes, "I am convinced that neither death nor life, neither angels nor demons, neither the present nor the future, nor any powers, neither height nor depth, nor anything else in all creation, will be able to separate us from the love of God that is in Christ Jesus our Lord" (Rom. 8:38–39). And that is assurance enough.

Suffering Peculiar to the Leaders of the People of God

In many societies of the world, the leaders are so much above the people they lead that efforts are made (by themselves or their courtiers) to exempt them from the troubles of the lesser breeds.

Not so among the people of God. Here it is frequently the leaders who are called to suffer the most. How could it be otherwise? We serve a crucified Messiah.

The pattern is already established in the Old Testament. True, God raised up many men and women of sterling character and leadership ability, and to some of them he gave great honor and wealth. In no case where we have much knowledge, however, was such blessing free from great responsibility or great opposition, or (more frequently) both. Most of the prophets faced opposition that would have shattered others; not a few lost their lives. According to extrabiblical tradition, aged Isaiah was sawn in two when he tried to hide in a hollow tree. And it is not for nothing that we refer to Jeremiah as "the weeping prophet."

Jeremiah did not want to be a prophet. One can understand why: if his experience sets the standard, one would have to be a masochist to volunteer. His message was disbelieved; he was mocked by the high and mighty and by the low and ungainly (Jer. 37:2). He was charged with disturbing the peace; he was beaten and put in the ancient equivalent of a straitjacket (Jer. 20). Later he was charged with treason for insisting, on God's instructions, that standing against the Babylonians was futile and dangerous. He was incarcerated in a miserable dungeon; only the intervention of Zedekiah eventually brought him to less inhospitable constraints. More than once his life was at risk.

Jeremiah survives the fall and sack of Jerusalem, but there is only anguish in being right. Repeatedly God actually forbids Jeremiah to pray for his people (7:16; 11:14; 14:11). God forbids the prophet to marry or have children (Jer. 16), a desperately painful decree in an age when almost everyone got married. This was to serve as a sign of the coming judgment, when fathers, mothers, and children would die. For the same illustrative purposes, Jeremiah is not permitted to mourn or to offer condolences, in anticipation of the time when so many would die that there would be no time or energy to grieve or offer succor. He is forbidden to attend a feast, for in the day of judgment all gaiety will be silenced. And when he is asked why any disaster should befall the covenant people of God, he must deliver one uncompromising and unpopular message: "'It is because your ancestors forsook me,' declares the LORD, 'and followed other gods and served and worshiped them. They forsook me and did not keep my law. But you have behaved more wickedly than your ancestors. See how all of you are following the stubbornness of your evil hearts instead of obeying me'" (Jer. 16:11–12). Thus in his suffering and life, Jeremiah serves as a sign of his own message.

Of course, not every prophet is called to live in such bleak times. But suffering has been so much a part of so many of the most remarkable Christian leaders, both in the New Testament and in the history of the church, that it deserves a closer look.

What we find is that there is a theological tie between suffering and Christian leadership. In fact, at least three connections are discernible.

The first is not peculiar to the New Testament, but is common to both Testaments. It is simply a particular manifestation of what was discussed in the first section of this chapter: suffering tempers believers and is part of God's discipline. Whether we think of Moses' banishment for forty years to the back side of the desert, or of Paul's exhortation to Timothy to endure hardness as a good soldier of Jesus Christ, the assumption is the same: if God disciplines all his children, then the leaders of those children must not expect any less, and can frequently count on a little more. Many a great preacher has suffered prolonged affliction, doubtless part of the Lord's merciful tempering of character. C. H. Spurgeon, for instance, in addition to various chronic ailments, fought deep bouts of depression all his life.

The second link turns on the fact that aggressive witness in an opposing world is likely to bring down peculiar pressures on those who lead the church in such witness. Under dictatorial regimes, pastors and evangelists are the ones most frequently incarcerated and killed. To read Paul's list of sufferings in 2 Corinthians 11:23ff. reminds us of this point. According to tradition, eleven of the twelve apostles (including Mathias, who replaced Judas Iscariot) were martyred. Genuine Christian leaders do not lead from the rear.

Small wonder, then, that when the Corinthians pride themselves on all they have attained in Christ, Paul has to remind them of how the apostles themselves live.

> Already you have all you want! Already you have become rich! You have begun to reign [Were they arguing that because they were children of the heavenly King they were already princes and should live like princes?]— and that without us! . . . For it seems to me that God has put us apostles on display at the end of the procession, like those condemned to die in the arena. [The analogy, of course, is drawn from Roman processions of captured peoples, where the captives were serried into ranks according to their status. The lowest classes brought up the rear, eating everyone

else's dust, and were consigned to the pits to fight to the death with wild animals or trained gladiators for the amusement of Roman citizens who flocked to the bleachers to watch.] We have been made a spectacle to the whole universe, to angels as well as to human beings. We are fools for Christ, but you are so wise in Christ! We are weak, but you are strong! You are honored, we are dishonored! To this very hour we go hungry and thirsty, we are in rags, we are brutally treated, we are homeless. We work hard with our own hands [something respected teachers did not do in polite Greco-Roman circles in the first century]. When we are cursed, we bless; when we are persecuted, we endure it; when we are slandered, we answer kindly. We have become the scum of the earth, the garbage of the world—right up to this moment. (1 Cor. 4:8–13[3])

The third link is more remarkable yet. The most mature Christian leaders want to absorb an additional share of sufferings so that their flocks may correspondingly be spared some suffering. In this, they imitate Christ. "I rejoice in *what I am suffering for you*, and I fill up in my flesh what is still lacking in regard to Christ's afflictions, *for the sake of his body, which is the church*" (Col. 1:24, emphasis added). Elsewhere Paul writes: "We are hard pressed on every side, but not crushed; perplexed, but not in despair; persecuted, but not abandoned; struck down, but not destroyed. We always carry around in our body the death of Jesus, so that the life of Jesus may also be revealed in our body. For we who are alive are always being given over to death for Jesus' sake, *so that his life may also be revealed in our mortal body*. So then, death is at work in us, *but life is at work in you*" (2 Cor. 4:8–12, emphasis added).

Now the connections are clearer. The more the leaders are afflicted with weakness, suffering, perplexity, and persecution, the more it is evident that their vitality is nothing other than the life of Jesus. This has enormously positive spiritual effects on the rest of the church. The leaders' death means the church's life.

This is why the best Christian leadership cannot simply be appointed. It is forged by God himself in the fires of suffering, taught in the school of tears. There are no shortcuts.

Questions for Further Study

1. What are God's purposes in disciplining his children?

3. See Scott J. Hafemann, *Suffering and the Spirit: An Exegetical Study of II Cor. 2:14–3:3 within the Context of the Corinthian Correspondence*, WUNT 19 (Tübingen: J. C. B. Mohr [Paul Siebeck], 1986).

2. Give practical examples from your own life of such discipline; or, if you are a young Christian with little experience, give examples from the lives of Christians you have observed.

3. What kind of faith does David (among others) display in his laments to God, when he faces suffering? How does his frankness of expression and appeal compare with your own?

4. Does God really answer Habakkuk's questions?

5. Explain Romans 5:1–5 in your own words. How should this passage be applied in your life?

6. What opposition have you experienced because you are a Christian?

7. Has it done you any harm—or any good?

8. What does it mean to "take up your cross" and follow Jesus? What does it mean at the practical level in your life?

9. Give reasons why Christian leaders often (though certainly not always) suffer more than other Christians in the New Testament.

10. Do you want to be a Christian leader?

6

Curses and Holy Wars—and Hell

Arise, LORD, in your anger; rise up against the rage of my enemies (Ps. 7:6). May his days be few; may another take his place of leadership. May his children be fatherless and his wife a widow. May his children be wandering beggars; may they be driven from their ruined homes. . . . May no one extend kindness to him or take pity on his fatherless children (Ps. 109:8–12). Daughter Babylon, doomed to destruction, happy are those who repay you for what you have done to us. Happy are those who seize your infants and dash them against the rocks (Ps. 137:8–9).

When you march up to attack a city, make its people an offer of peace. If they accept and open their gates, all the people in it shall be subject to forced labor and shall work for you. If they refuse to make peace and they engage you in battle, lay siege to that city. When the LORD your God delivers it into your hand, put to the sword all the men in it. As for the women, the children, the livestock and everything else in the city, you may take these as plunder for yourselves. And you may use the plunder the LORD your God gives you from your enemies. This is how you are to treat all the cities that are at a distance from you and do not belong to the nations nearby.

However, in the cities of the nations the LORD your God is giving you as an inheritance, do not leave alive anything that breathes. Completely destroy them—the Hittites, Amorites, Canaanites, Perizzites, Hivites and Jebusites—as the LORD your God has commanded you. Otherwise, they will teach you to follow all the detestable things they do in worshiping their gods, and you will sin against the LORD your God (Deut. 20:10–18).

As the weeds are pulled up and burned in the fire, so it will be at the
end of the age. The Son of Man will send out his angels, and they will weed
out of his kingdom everything that causes sin and all who do evil. They
will throw them into the blazing furnace, where there will be weeping and
gnashing of teeth (Matt. 13:40–42).

A few years ago, my wife and I brought a middle-aged lady connected
with our family to church with us. She fancied herself religious, indeed
a Christian, although she rarely attended church, except for Christmas
and Easter. It so happened that the pastor of our church was beginning a series of sermons on the prophecy of Hosea. In the course of
his address, he read lengthy excerpts from Hosea, full of rather explicit
language about adultery, whoredom, nakedness, shame, and the like.
This lady was rather subdued when she left the service with us. The
silence continued in the car on the way home. Finally, she asked, "How
different is the Bible you use in your church from the one we use in
our church?"

We finally figured out what she was driving at. She simply did not
believe that all the things she had heard that morning from Hosea could
actually be found in "her" Bible. It took no little effort to persuade her
otherwise.

I wonder what her response would have been had the reading been
the passages with which this chapter begins.

The truth of the matter is that most Christians (let alone non-Chris-
tians) are uncomfortable with such passages. We hear the curses, and
we wonder what possible place they can have in a book that tells us to
turn the other cheek, to remember that vengeance belongs exclusively to
the Lord, to love our enemies and to pray for those who use us shame-
fully. We read the passages that not only describe but mandate genocide,
and remember that when genocide takes place today there is either an
international furor or perhaps a war crimes tribunal. We read of hell,
and we are attracted to interpretations that relativize the threat (Will
hell be real, but finally empty? Will it destroy its residents, so that their
torment will not last forever?).

Some of us avoid the difficulties by passing over such passages in our
Bible reading as quickly as we can. Some of us would rather "spiritual-
ize" all references to cursing and war, and perhaps unwittingly switch to
another set of categories occupied with justice and the triumph of God.
Even where such a switch is legitimate at the level of *applying* Scripture,
we must first come to grips with the fact that real people die in Old
Testament genocide. Still others of us first think seriously about such
matters when our friends and loved ones are affected. What exactly was
I to say to the young woman who came and asked for help and comfort

after her father had recently died and, as far as she could tell, went to hell? *Her own father!*

I do not claim to have all the answers in such matters. But there is little doubt that some people, more sensitive, perhaps, than others, find these teachings and passages in the Bible sometimes cause them enormous distress. As part of the "framework" for looking at these things I find it helpful to weigh these realities of Scripture against six factors that the Bible itself calls us to take into account.

The Perception of the Problem

When Peter Craigie wrote the little book I alluded to in chapter 4, *The Problem of War in the Old Testament,*[1] he was careful to point out that the "problem" to which his title refers is *our* problem when we read the Old Testament. That is another way of conceding, of course, that by itself his title is potentially misleading: it might suggest that the Old Testament writers themselves find a "problem" in war. As we have seen, the fact is they do not. Indeed, one biblical writer can say, "Praise be to the LORD my Rock, who trains my hands for war, my fingers for battle" (Ps. 144:1).

If Saul refuses to obey the Lord by utterly destroying the Amalekites, it is not because he claims some sort of superior moral compunction, but because he arbitrarily opts to preserve the life of King Agag and the best of the sheep and cattle (1 Sam. 15). His excuse—that cattle, at least, were kept aside to be offered to the Lord in sacrifice—brings this withering denunciation: "Does the LORD delight in burnt offerings and sacrifices as much as in obeying the LORD? To obey is better than sacrifice, and to heed is better than the fat of rams. For rebellion is like the sin of divination, and arrogance like the evil of idolatry. Because you have rejected the word of the LORD, he has rejected you as king" (1 Sam. 15:22–23). In other words, it is not the command to commit genocide that shocks Samuel; it is the rebellion that refuses to commit it.

Something similar could be said about the cries for vengeance and the biblical teaching on hell. As horrific as the descriptions of hell are, the stunning truth of the matter is that most of them come from the lips of Jesus. He has far more to say about hell than anyone else in the Bible.

Surely that must give us pause. We must dare to ask ourselves if our own moral sensibilities have somehow been misdirected, misfocused. Is it possible that our severest problems about these forms of suffering

---

1. Peter Craigie, *The Problem of War in the Old Testament* (Grand Rapids: Eerdmans, 1978).

owe more to the pluralism of our age than to any ostensible superiority in moral judgment on our part? Is it possible that part, at least, of our horror at hell owes something to our inability (or refusal?) to look at sin from God's perspective?

Why is it that we are comfortable with evangelical clichés about God "loving the sinner but hating the sin," when within the first fifty psalms alone there are fourteen passages where God is explicitly said to hate the sinner, or to be angry with the sinner, or the like?[2]

I am not for a moment suggesting there is no truth at all in the cliché; the question will be explored a little in chapter 10. Still less am I suggesting that we would be justified in going out today and committing genocide. The horrible slogan of some militarists, "The fight against communism is the fight for God" (which I heard one preacher actually say), is too blind for words. Mercifully, this sort of demagoguery is now largely passé, owing primarily to the demise of the Soviet empire. (Can one imagine the apostle Paul thundering, "The fight against the Roman Empire is the fight for God"?) This is not to assert the moral equivalency of both sides in every armed conflict—whether World War II or the current war on terror. It is merely to observe two things: (1) One of the fundamental differences brought about by the new covenant is the fact that the locus of the people of God under this covenant no longer constitutes a nation, but an international community not to be identified with any nation. This means that the loyalty of Christians to their state must always be conditional. (2) Even if the state has the right—indeed, the obligation—to use the sword in defense of justice, we had better recognize the propensity of all states, and of all individuals in it, to demonstrate that power in this fallen world is corrupting, with violence too easily becoming the first resort rather than the last resort.

Even so, after all caveats have been entered, the distance between our perception of where the problem lies and the perceptions of the biblical writers is one of the most sobering considerations for those who take the Bible seriously. It is one more indication that we have given ourselves to thinking great thoughts about human beings and small thoughts about God.

How does rebellion appear to One so incomparably transcendent that even the superpowers appear to his eyes like the fine dust in a balance? How does rebellion appear to One who measures our sin by the death of his Son?

---

2. I have discussed these matters at greater length in *The Difficult Doctrine of the Love of God* (Wheaton: Crossway, 2000).

The Rhetoric of Outrage

Not every expression of moral outrage is to be taken as concrete description, or even as considered desire.

Take, for instance, this malediction from Jeremiah, once again lamenting his unhappy lot: "Cursed be the day I was born! May the day my mother bore me not be blessed! Cursed be the man who brought my father the news, who made him very glad, saying, 'A child is born to you—a son!' May that man be like the towns the Lord overthrew without pity. May he hear wailing in the morning, a battle cry at noon. For he did not kill me in the womb, with my mother as my grave, her womb enlarged forever. Why did I ever come out of the womb to see trouble and sorrow and to end my days in shame?" (Jer. 20:14–18).

The general thrust of these verses is clear: Jeremiah is so miserable that he wishes he were dead—or, better yet, that he had never been born. But does that mean he is placing a well-considered curse on the head of the poor chap unlucky enough to have brought the news of Jeremiah's birth to Jeremiah's father? Does Jeremiah *really* want his mother to be forever pregnant? Only the crassest literalist could read the text in this way.

To cut the passage from the text on the ground that it is irresponsible would be a great loss, for the vividness of the outrage would be diluted were it replaced by a bland abstraction such as "Jeremiah is deeply disturbed," or by mere literalism such as "Jeremiah wishes he had never been born." Jeremiah makes us *feel* the heat of his indignation; cautious literalism could not achieve so much.

It follows that we must ask whether some of the malediction language in the psalms is in the same way not the language of considered address but the rhetoric of outrage. Its purpose is not to inform but to ignite; it has little in common with cool discourse, a great deal in common with a sudden scream. It does not establish military policy; it vents confusion and terror when "haunts of violence fill the dark places of the land" (Ps. 74:20).

Related to this is how these cries of outrage fit into the larger context of the man and his message. Jeremiah was sometimes gently rebuked by the Lord for his understandable but bitter self-pity; David was not permitted to build the temple because, unlike his son Solomon, he was a warrior who had shed blood (1 Chron. 28:3). The anticipation of the consummation of history, when people "will beat their swords into plowshares and their spears into pruning hooks," when "nation will not take up sword against nation, nor will they train for war anymore" (Isa. 2:4), provides ample evidence that war is not treated as a neutral thing, still less an intrinsically good thing. Rather, war, cries of vengeance, and mass deaths are themselves to be set against the backdrop of a fallen

world where evil must be restrained, where evil inflicted evokes cries of
outraged despair and candid calls for exacting justice.

The Influence of the Old Covenant

Under the old covenant, the covenant that God made with the people
of Israel at Mount Sinai through his servant Moses, the locus of the
people of God was a nation. Other nations enjoyed God's forbearance
and blessings, sometimes even his forgiveness (e.g., Nineveh in the time
of Jonah); but Israel was the covenant people of God. And Israel was a
nation—in time, two nations.

Further, although God was Israel's King, he operated through media-
tors: his vassal king in the Davidic line, his priests from the tribe of Levi,
and prophets raised up for the occasion. They represented the people
to God; they represented God to the people. When they sinned, they
brought down the people with them; when they were courageous and
righteous, in some measure they reformed the people for whom they
were responsible.

Because the people of God constituted a nation, it was impossible to
dissociate God's blessing on the people from the welfare of the nation,
or God's judgment of the people from the decline of the nation, or the
spiritual and moral purity of the people from the religious integrity
of the nation, or the compassion of the people from the charity of the
nation.

That means that the easy distinctions we make between the civil and
the religious, between the political and the moral, could not possibly
exist. The covenant people of God constituted a nation; the nation was
a theocracy. Its fundamental laws were God's laws, its officers God's
appointees.

Ideally, therefore, political decisions, court decisions, legislative decisions—all should have reflected the mind of God, and this in a political
context. When judicial punishment was being meted out, in theory at least
(and sometimes in practice) it was punishment from God himself.

But that was also true (again, in theory, and sometimes in practice) of
Israel's wars. Israel's enemies were God's enemies. Israel was told when
and where she was allowed to fight. And not a little of the destruction
that took place as Israel entered the promised land was understood to
be a terrible judgment on the wickedness of the people already living
there. Had not God said that Israel had to remain in Egypt, and not
return to Canaan, until the sin of the Amorites had reached its full
measure (Gen. 15:16)? The rank idolatry had been compounded with
fertility-cult religion (people sleeping with cult priests and priestesses

to encourage the gods to copulate, in the hope of bringing fruitfulness to land and home) and even child sacrifice (as occurred when babies were offered, screaming, to the god Molech, whose stone bowl was heated by fire).

If God felt it was necessary to curb the evil of the world by obliterating most of the human race at the time of the flood (Gen. 6–9), and if by the same powerful word that effected that judgment "the present heavens and earth are reserved for fire, being kept for the day of judgment and destruction of the ungodly" (2 Pet. 3:7), is it so very surprising that God should inflict through his covenant people punishments of a similar sort, but on a much smaller scale?

By the same token, when the best of Israel's kings saw themselves surrounded by foes, they could not possibly think in merely military and political categories. The king was God's son; the king was God's vassal. His cause was just, because it was God's. It was entirely right that the king should turn to God and plead his cause and cry for justice; and if justice was forthcoming, then under the structures established by the old covenant that justice necessarily had national, political, and sometimes military overtones.

We may ask ourselves if God still works in similar fashion today. The answer is decidedly ambiguous. On the one hand, the answer must be negative: the locus of God's people under the new covenant is not a nation, and every attempt to establish a unified "Christian nation," where the respective boundaries of church and state are made to coalesce, has not only been misconceived but has resulted in disastrous failure. On the other hand, God is still the God of all the nations, acknowledged or not. Wars, as we have seen in an earlier chapter, can be looked at, from a Christian perspective, in several ways. But surely one of them is the perspective of judgment. Is it not worth pondering that most devastating, far-flung wars over the past century have been started and led by the most sophisticated, intellectually scintillating, "civilized," well-bred, technologically proficient nations, whose blindness, greed, ambition, and arrogance had already generated massive defection from the faith more commonly adopted by their fathers?

I do not mean to suggest that there were no discernible "rights" and "wrongs" in the Second World War. There can be little doubt that Germany started it, and for all the wrong reasons. But I remember Habakkuk: sometimes a more wicked nation is used by God to punish another nation, less wicked perhaps, but whose time for judgment, in God's providence, has arrived. When I read the record of the incredibly stupid decisions taken by the British Parliament and the French Cabinet in the seven-year period leading up to the war (for Hitler could have been stopped at several strategic junctures, as when he took over the Ruhr),

I wonder if God was blinding the eyes of some, to bring about the judgments that actually fell.

Of course, Christians must always be leery of claims that providence can be "read" in hindsight like an old-fashioned morality play. Still, most of us have swung too far the other way: we think along such naturalistic lines that we allow little room for God. We have certainly not taken to heart the biblical portrait of a God of justice, who holds all to account, both individuals and nations, and who sovereignly works out his purposes, sometimes behind the scenes in mysterious providences that use the evil machinations of mere mortals to raise up and put down entire nations and peoples.

This suggests that the most important response to the "problem" of holy wars in the Old Testament is not arrogant self-righteousness and shocked, condescending horror, but contrition, brokenness, intercession. Do we hear again the voice of the Master, "But unless you repent, you too will all perish" (Luke 13:5)?

The remaining three topics of this chapter may also help us to find our way.

Jesus' Teaching on Hell

If there is any subject that few Christians like to think about, this, surely, is it.

Yet it is Jesus, more than any other person in the New Testament, who gives us the most graphic details. He speaks of a fiery furnace, a place where there is weeping and gnashing of teeth, of people crying out for a drop of water to cool their tongues, a place of darkness, "outside" and away from the bliss enjoyed by God's people. He does not hesitate to draw the absolute disjunctive: "Then they will go away to eternal punishment, but the righteous to eternal life" (Matt. 25:46). He can speak of the resurrection of the just and of the unjust, and of the evil rising to be condemned (John 5:28–29). It is he who insists that the chasm between those who are in torment and those who are by Abraham's side is fixed and uncrossable.

Even if we note that many of these images are drawn from parables, even if we assume that the language is metaphorical, it is metaphorical language that has a referent; and if the metaphors are doing their job, they are evoking images of a horrible existence. And the shocking language Jesus uses is confirmed elsewhere in the New Testament.

There are several perspectives that help us come to terms with these texts.

First, on the whole Jesus himself is not shocked by the existence of hell, but by the hardness of people's hearts. As I have already suggested, that may tell us that we need to wrestle much more diligently with how God looks at sin, and the degree and degradation and moral offensiveness of the sin that he sees.

Second, there is no hint in the Bible that there is any repentance in hell. Like the rich man in the parable of the rich man and Lazarus (Luke 16:19–31), there may be a cry for relief, or even a plea that the surviving brothers be warned; but there is no hint of repentance. Indeed, there is one passage that suggests the opposite. In the final chapter of the Bible, the interpreting angel says to John, "Do not seal up the words of the prophecy of this scroll, because the time is near. Let those who do wrong continue to do wrong; let those who are vile continue to be vile; let those who do right continue to do right; and let those who are holy continue to be holy" (Rev. 22:10–11). In a sense, this pronouncement brings the judgment forward: those who will be found vile at the end may just as well continue to be vile now, for their time of mercy has passed. But the assumption, I think, is that just as those who are declared holy at the end, doubtless owing to the gospel of Jesus Christ, continue in holiness, indeed in the very consummation of holiness, so also those who are declared vile at the end, doubtless owing to their own rebellion and hardness of heart, continue in all that is vile, indeed in the very consummation of what is vile.

Perhaps, then, we should think of hell as a place where people continue to rebel, continue to insist on their own way, continue societal structures of prejudice and hate, continue to defy the living God. And as they continue to defy God, so he continues to punish them. And the cycle goes on and on and on.

After all, it is arguable that that is rather analogous to what goes on in the Old Testament—and today. "Who handed Jacob over to become loot, and Israel to the plunderers? Was it not the LORD, against whom we have sinned? For they would not follow his ways; they did not obey his law. So he poured out on them his burning anger, the violence of war. It enveloped them in flames, yet they did not understand; it consumed them, but they did not take it to heart" (Isa. 42:24–25).

In recent years, several notable evangelical scholars have publicly espoused the view that hell itself may exist forever, but that it will not be peopled forever. Although punishments may differ, eventually every resident will be destroyed, annihilated. The idea of eternal punishment, they say, is not biblical. And this interpretation, they suggest, eliminates a great moral problem: no one is punished eternally for finite, temporal sins.[3]

---

3. Those who have come out in support of some form or other of annihilationism, over against any notion of eternal self-conscious punishment, in fact do so for varied

These are difficult questions, and no one should speak too assuredly. But if it is wrong to adopt a merely traditional view of hell that is allegedly without adequate biblical warrant and that leads to insuperable moral problems (as annihilationists insist), it is surely no less wrong to abandon a long-standing interpretation of biblical texts on inadequate grounds that may give false assurance and comfort to some who need to be shaken by the sterner view. I doubt if any of us is equipped to assess what is an "appropriate" punishment for defiance of the holy and sovereign God, save God himself. And I am not quite certain what an "eternal" punishment is. In any case, if the reasoning I have sketched out is correct, the dilemma posed by the annihilationists is a false one. Quite apart from the fact that in my view their interpretation of individual texts is mistaken, there is not even any moral impetus for their view if in hell sinners go on sinning and receiving the recompense of their sin, refusing, always refusing, to bend the knee.

Third, we must always remember that the Bible does not present us with a God who chances upon neutral men and women and arbitrarily consigns some to heaven and some to hell. He takes guilty men and women, all of whom deserve his wrath, and in his great mercy and love he saves vast numbers of them. Had he saved only one, it would have been an act of grace; that he saves a vast host affirms still more unmistakably the uncharted reaches of that grace. From a biblical perspective, hell stands as a horrible witness to human defiance in the face of great grace.

Fourth, heaven would surely be hell to those who do not enjoy and desire the blessing of the unshielded presence of God.

Fifth, and perhaps most important of all, the God of the Bible is not unmoved by our suffering. He is slow to anger, abundant in mercy. The Jesus who delivers the terrible "woes" to the religious hypocrites of his day (Matt. 23) ends up weeping over the city of Jerusalem: "Jerusalem, Jerusalem, you who kill the prophets and stone those sent to you, how often I have longed to gather your children together, as a hen gathers her chicks under her wings, and you were not willing. Look, your house is left to you desolate" (Matt. 23:37–38). The stereotype of a "hell-fire preacher" really letting his hearers have it cannot be found in the Bible. Though the Bible speaks plainly, and sometimes in fury, it never does so without tears. And Christians can never forget that they too, like the rest, are by nature objects of wrath. They never warn others about the wrath

reasons. The issue is both important and complex but cannot be addressed here. I have briefly discussed some of the relevant passages in one of the chapters of *The Gagging of God: Christianity Confronts Pluralism* (Grand Rapids: Zondervan, 1996). See also Edward Fudge and Robert Peterson, *Two Views of Hell: A Biblical and Theological Dialogue* (Downers Grove: InterVarsity, 2000), and the bibliography that each author cites.

of God from a position of intrinsic superiority, but from the brokenness of experience and the relief of redemption they want to share.

The Nature of the Church's Discipline—and Cries

If we bring together the last two reflections—on the nature of the old covenant, and Jesus' teaching on hell—we are driven to a fresh point.

It is sometimes thought that although the Old Testament sanctions holy war and displays nasty tendencies to call down curses on God's enemies, the New Testament is morally and ethically superior, and leaves such traits behind.

It is true that the church, the locus of the new covenant people of God, is not to defend itself as the church, or to propagate the gospel, by resorting to arms. But that does not mean there is no discipline to be dispensed at all. Jesus lays down some simple procedures for disciplining a brother (Matt. 18:15–18); Paul leads the Corinthian church in the steps it needs to take to expel a professing Christian who is sleeping with his stepmother (1 Cor. 5:1ff.).

In fact, Christian discipline in the church can take many forms: gentle rebuke, encouragement, mutual confession, private confrontation, and more. The final sanction is excommunication: the church, with tears and self-examination, expels someone. In the New Testament, this final sanction is applied in only three areas: where there is major doctrinal deviation, where there is major and persistent moral turpitude, and where there is persistent, loveless divisiveness.

"Ah," someone objects, "that is merely *spiritual* discipline. In the Old Testament, there was *physical* discipline." But the words are no sooner uttered than all the New Testament teaching about hell rushes to mind and gives one pause. If the church judicially declares that someone is outside the pale of the people of God, then although the decision may be executed in the hope that this person will be saved on the day of the Lord (1 Cor. 5:5), the alternative possibility is horrific, and must be squarely faced.

As for the cries for vengeance, the Apocalypse provides stunning counterparts to the psalms. "How long, Sovereign Lord, holy and true, until you judge the inhabitants of the earth and avenge our blood?" (Rev. 6:10), cry those who had been slain because of the Word of God and the testimony they had maintained. "Give back to her [Babylon the Great] as she has given; pay her back double for what she has done. Pour her a double portion from her own cup. Give her as much torment and grief as the glory and luxury she gave herself. In her heart she boasts, 'I sit enthroned as queen. I am not a widow; I will never mourn.' Therefore in one day her plagues will overtake her: death, mourning and famine. She will be consumed by fire, for mighty is the Lord God who judges her" (Rev. 18:6–8). "Woe! Woe to you, great city, where all who had ships on the sea became rich through her wealth! . . . Rejoice over her, you heavens! Rejoice, you people of God! Rejoice, apostles and prophets! For God has judged her with the judgment she imposed on you" (Rev. 18:19–20). And there is much more of the same.

The factors we weighed when we considered similar Old Testament passages apply here as well. But the point to be made is that if we take seriously the eternal perspective that is laid out in the New Testament, then it simply will not do to write off the Old Testament witness as intrinsically harsher and therefore not something we need worry our heads about today. I think it is closer to the truth to say that in the coming of the Lord Jesus and the new covenant he sealed with his own blood, both the justice of God and the mercy of God appear in sharper relief than ever before, leaving us with correspondingly less excuse, and with greater grounds for praise and worship.

Worse Alternatives

I return to the young woman who asked me how she was to think of her father, who, as far as she knew, had gone to hell.

There were, of course, and are, many important things to say. I could say that none of us knows for certain what transpires between any person and God Almighty before that person is ushered into eternity. I could say that the final proof of the love and goodness of God is the cross. I could say that we know far too little of the new heaven and the new earth to have any idea what consciousness we shall there have of those who have chosen to live and die independently of God. I could add that there are times when, in the confusion, it sometimes helps to think of all that we know of the character of God and ask, with Abraham, the rhetorical question, "Will not the Judge of all the earth do right?" (Gen. 18:25).

All this I could say, and more. But it will not do to opt for a sub-biblical system, a *selectively* biblical system. Shall we opt for absolute universalism? Then what do we do with the countless texts that foreclose on this speculation? Does God treat those who trust his Son and those who disobey the Son the same way, even though his Word insists, "Whoever believes in the Son has eternal life, but whoever rejects the Son will not see life, for God's wrath remains on them" (John 3:36)? Shall we assume that truth and revelation are not the discriminating factors, but human sincerity? What purpose, then, the cross? And what value?

However hard some things are to understand, it is never helpful to start picking and choosing biblical truths we find congenial, as if the Bible is an open-shelved supermarket where we are at perfect liberty to choose only the chocolate bars. For the Christian, it is God's Word, and it is not negotiable. What answers we find may not be exhaustive, but they give us the God who is there, and who gives us some measure of comfort and assurance. The alternative is a god we manufacture, and who provides no comfort at all. Whatever comfort we feel is self-delusion, and it will be stripped away at the end when we give an account to the God who has spoken to us, not only in Scripture, but supremely in his Son Jesus Christ.

Questions for Further Study

1. When, if ever, is it appropriate for Christians to utter the pleas for vindication found in the psalms and in Revelation?
2. To what extent does our perception of something "wrong" in the cries for vindication, in the "holy wars" of the Old Testament, and in Jesus' teaching about hell, depend on our own estrangement from the way God thinks and looks at things?
3. When are expressions of moral outrage not much more than signs of bad temper and selfish vindictiveness, and when are they the rhetoric of pain, and truly God-directed?
4. What sanctions mentioned in this chapter *should not* be brought directly over from the old covenant to the new? Why not?
5. Does God change in his fundamental attitudes toward sin? What expressions of God's response to sin occur in both the Old Testament and the New?
6. What is hell? Summarize what you know of it.
7. Why is it best to trust God even when we do not have all the answers?

7

Illness, Death, Bereavement

All we have to do is live long enough, and we will be bereaved.

All we have to do is live long enough, and we will die.

In a fallen world, these points are immutable, yet grief and pain always catch us unawares. We know we are not immune, but there is a suppressed hope that pretends we are. And when our child dies, or our spouse; when we see a loved one wasting away from a painful disease, or observe a brilliant and courteous mind disintegrating before our eyes; when we ourselves suddenly face the most appalling pain or incapacity, with no prospect of relief, then our pretensions rush forward in another form: Why is God doing this? Though it is blasphemous to think it, our whole being cries out that this is unfair of him, that our grief and pain are disproportionate to our sin, that we have been abandoned.

In some ways, this chapter is one of the most difficult to write, for readers of any maturity will have already drunk from the flagon of grief, and will be looking for existential answers. Cries for vengeance, holy wars, hell—they are often one step removed from our experience, and therefore we look for merely intellectual and theoretical answers. But when we ourselves are weeping, we want comfort. Merely intellectual answers do not readily satisfy.

Doubtless it is true, for instance, that "in all things God works for the good of those who love him" (Rom. 8:28), but it is less than obvious that this should be quoted to the couple that has just lost their child in a road accident. If they know the Lord well, then perhaps, with time,

they themselves will cite the verse with renewed faith and understanding;
but it should not be thrust at them in the wrong way, or at the wrong
time, or without tears, lest it seem like a bit of cheap ritual, miserable
comfort, heartless proof texting.

Yet although I shall return to this question of pastoral comfort in chapter 13, it is important to try to establish Christian structures of thought
that are already "givens" *before* pain and bereavement strike. What I am
writing in this chapter is therefore not necessarily what I would say to
everyone who grieves. It is certainly part of what I teach to congregations,
with the aim that more Christians will be better prepared for suffering
when it comes. If you want to get a handle on the stages of grief, there are
fine books on that topic; if you are in the midst of pain, and clamoring
for immediate relief from suffering that seems unavoidable, like the air
we breathe, and inescapable, like the sky over our heads, you would be
far better off reading Psalms 23 and 90, not fewer than five or six times
a day. But if you are ready to train your mind to think biblically about
some difficult and sensitive topics, then these introductory reflections
(and that is all they are) may be of help to you.

Sin, Sickness, and Death

We have already seen how all suffering, not least sickness and death,
is tied to sin. If there had been no sin, there would have been no death,
and no illness, which is death's prelude. But the connections need to be
spelled out more precisely.

First, death must be seen, not as the supreme instance of a cosmic
lack of fairness, but as God's well-considered sentence against our sin.

Now this is not what the bereaved person wants to hear. I am aware
of the other considerations that must be factored into our understanding of death, and many of them are mentioned elsewhere in this book.
Yet this first point is so central to the Bible's perspective that we must
not evade it or shove it to the periphery of our thought, like a barely
tolerated pot consigned to the bottom of the garden.

Death is no accident; it is God's doing. Moses boldly writes, "You turn
people back to dust, saying, 'Return to dust, you mortals.' A thousand
years in your sight are like a day that has just gone by, or like a watch
in the night. Yet you sweep people away in the sleep of death—they are
like the new grass of the morning. In the morning it springs up new, but
by evening it is dry and withered" (Ps. 90:3–6). But this activity of God is
not merely a reflection of the distance between the infinite and the finite,
between the transcendent and the limited. Death is not here thought of
as the Almighty's way of toying with mere creatures; for Moses goes on to

explain, "We are consumed by your anger and terrified by your indignation. You have set our iniquities before you, our secret sins in the light of your presence. All our days pass away under your wrath; we finish our years with a moan. Our days may come to seventy years, or eighty, if our strength endures; yet the best of them are but trouble and sorrow, for they quickly pass, and we fly away. If only we knew the power of your anger! Your wrath is as great as the fear that is your due" (Ps. 90:7–11).

This perennial slide toward death is nothing other than the outworking of God's judicial sentence: "when you eat of it you will certainly die" (Gen. 2:17). It is always true that "the wages of sin is death" (Rom. 6:23).

But why death? Could there not have been some other punishment?

Death is God's limit on creatures whose sin is that they want to be gods (Gen. 3:4–5; Rom. 1:18–23). The true God is holy; he is unique, and cannot, by his very nature, tolerate those who try to relativize him. We are not gods; and by death we learn that we are only human. Our pretensions are destroyed. We are cut off, and all our yesterdays "are one with Nineveh and Tyre."

At the same time, we cry out against this limitation, not only because in our rebellion we still want to become gods, but because we have been made in the image of God. We are not mere mammals. We are persons. If we really believed that we are nothing more than accidental collections of atoms, moral outrage over anything would be irrational. But we want to live, even while our hubris means we have been cut off from him who alone gives life. That we are mammals means that our death has a physical side; that we are not merely mammals means that our death is God's determination to limit our arrogance.

This means that I am a responsible participant in my own death. Death is not simply something that happens to me. It happens to me because I am a sinner. In that sense I have caused death; I am death's subject, not just its object. In my transgression I have attracted the just wrath of God. And that wrath is not mere outworking of impersonal principles, still less the arbitrary demarcation between time and eternity, but God's personal and judicial reaction to the transgression in which I have responsibly indulged as a person.

Helmut Thielicke goes so far as to say, "In other words, a personal relation means that I must not complain against God when death comes. God is telling me something by it. In my death he is reacting to me. There is a message in it. I see God's hand and word aimed at me."[1]

I do not wish to be misunderstood. I am not saying that it is wrong to rage against death, or that Paul is wrong to treat death as "the last enemy"

---

1. Helmut Thielicke, *Living with Death*, trans. Geoffrey W. Bromiley (Grand Rapids: Eerdmans, 1983), 125.

(1 Cor. 15). The Bible everywhere assumes that those who are bereaved will grieve, and their grief is never belittled. Job grieves unbearably at the loss of his ten children (Job 1:20; 2:13); so does the widow of Nain who lost her son (Luke 7:11–13), and she attracts Jesus' compassion.[2] And to our grieving minds there seems an inequity when wicked men live out their seventy years while little children perish.

It is essential to grasp the theological point that stands at the heart of our lostness, and therefore of our redemption: death is, finally, the result of our sin, and therefore rage directed against God, as if he were unfair for passing the sentence that our sin deserved, is inherently foolish, as foolish as criticizing a judge for passing a just sentence on a bank robber. Our rage is better directed at the ugliness of death, the wretchedness of sin, our sense of betrayal and self-betrayal. It may be a venting of our profound loss and frustration. But thoughtful Christians will never lose sight of the origins of death, and therefore will not, at least on this ground, rage against God himself.

This theological point does *not* treat the kind of death, the time of death, the age of death, and the like. It does focus our minds on the origin of human death. And we must face up to our individual and corporate responsibility.

Second, illness and death can be the immediate judicial consequence of a specific sin. This goes beyond anything that has been said so far. We all sin; we all die. We are a race of sinners; we are a race of death. But in some instances, judicial sentence is executed immediately upon a specific sin. The thirty-eight-year paralysis of the man in John 5 is a case in point (see John 5:14). So is the leprosy of Gehazi (2 Kings 5:20–27); so are the deaths of Ananias and Sapphira (Acts 5); the painful end of Herod (Acts 12:19b–23); and the illness and deaths of some members in the Corinthian congregation (1 Cor. 11:27–32).

The conclusion to be drawn is not that the people who suffered in this way were the worst sinners of their times. Others died of leprosy who had not sinned in the manner of Gehazi; doubtless others extorted people for money in ways far more brutal and deceitful than what he deployed,

---

2. It is often argued that Jesus' tears at the tomb of Lazarus (John 11:35) support the same sort of respect for grief. In fact, this instance is harder to understand. We must probe *why* Jesus wept. It is hard to believe that he was crying because he felt the loss of his friend, when the story makes it clear that he knew he would raise Lazarus in just a few minutes' time. On that showing, confident smiles might have been more appropriate. Closer exegesis of the context shows Jesus was "deeply moved in spirit" (v. 33)—indeed, outraged—by the ravages of death and massive unbelief all around him. Indeed, "the same sin and death, the same unbelief, that prompted his outrage, also generated his grief. Those who follow Jesus as his disciples today do well to learn the same tension—that grief and compassion without outrage reduces to mere sentiment, while outrage without grief hardens into self-righteous arrogance and irascibility" (Carson, *John*).

yet were left unpunished. The conclusion, rather, is that sin merits such punishment. It is because of the Lord's mercies that we are not all instantly punished whenever we sin. If we were, the world would become a vast cemetery; none would be left to generate new human life.

And that means that God does not *owe* us a civilized seventy years. If for various reasons (only some of which we can discern) he chooses to hold someone to account immediately, he does not thereby become unjust. For our part, we cannot be certain that he will *not* call us to give an account of what we have done, long before we have reached the celebrated "three-score years and ten."

Third, illness and death are not necessarily the immediate judicial consequence of a specific sin. They are of course tied to our rebellious condition; they may not be tied to a particular sin. Indeed, there may be all sorts of more immediate links. Hezekiah's initial illness and impending death were, apparently, the Lord's way of ending his earthly pilgrimage (2 Kings 20:1). The man born blind (John 9) did not contract his congenital handicap for any specific sin that either he or his parents had committed. Paul can testify that it was an illness which, in the Lord's providence, directed him in the first instance to Galatia (Gal. 4:13): possibly it was malaria, contracted in the swampy lowlands, and "treated" in those days by retreating into the highlands. Timothy was afflicted with frequent illnesses (1 Tim. 5:23), and Paul told him to take frequent doses of wine to combat his ailments. On one of his last journeys, Paul had to press on and leave the ill Trophimus behind in Miletus (2 Tim. 4:20).

In none of these instances is illness or death linked to a specific sin; in several cases, such a link is expressly disavowed. In none is there any miraculous healing, except for the case of blindness in John 9, and that one is tied to the self-disclosure of Jesus, the manifestation of the glory of God—and even then only after the victim had suffered two or three decades of blindness, with all the distress that such an infliction incurred both for the beggar and his family.

Practically speaking, this means that it is almost always wrong, not to say pastorally insensitive and theologically stupid, to add to the distress of those who are suffering illness, impending death, or bereavement, by charging them with either: (a) some secret sin they have not confessed, or (b) inadequate faith, for otherwise they would certainly have been healed. The first charge wrongly assumes that there is always a link between a specific ailment and a specific sin; the second wrongly assumes that it is always God's will to heal any ailment, instantly, and that he is blocked from doing so only by inadequate or insufficient faith. The examples given vitiate both claims, and many of the chapters in this book show God may have other reasons for sanctioning illness and sorrow among his people. I shall address this question again, from a slightly different perspective, a little farther on in this chapter.

Fourth, there are some illnesses and deaths that are the consequences of sinful acts or behavior, where there is no supernatural judicial sentence but the "natural" outworking of cause and effect, under God's providence. How many illnesses are the direct cause of suppressed hatred, anger, jealousy, bitterness, guilt? How much high blood pressure, how many ulcers, how much colitis would be avoided if sinful attitudes were done away with? How many deaths are the result of gluttony? How many pollution-caused deaths occur because people care more for the bottom line than for other people? How many emotional problems have at their origin "dysfunctional families"—which is another way of saying that families, for a host of personal and societal reasons, are not functioning as God ordained them to? How many "emotional problems" or "mental breakdowns" owe something to a background where the individual never enjoyed the security of love and discipline in equal doses, or never felt forgiveness for some gross sin? What about syphilis and herpes? Although many AIDS sufferers have contracted the disease from a contaminated blood supply, is there *no* moral lesson to be observed where the disease most commonly circulates through sexual promiscuity and the use of illicit drugs?

The connections are not always easily or wisely drawn. There may be factors we know too little about. Certainly sinners, not least *forgiven* sinners, need to be very cautious how they point the finger at other sinners. Something like the AIDS crisis raises a host of complex moral and political issues, some of them explored in the appendix to this book. But it should be clear that sometimes God's judgment falls, not in supernatural display of horrifying power (as with Ananias and Sapphira), but in providential control of natural processes bound up with how the Lord God made the world in the first place. Eli's sons engaged in horrific sexual perversion because their father had never exercised discipline; Absalom murdered his half-brother Amnon and rebelled against David, with the consequent loss of thousands of lives, in large part because David never disciplined his sons, and handled the rape of his daughter Tamar so poorly. There may be painful consequences to our sins *in this life.*

Fifth, in other chapters I have tried to show that suffering and pain, including that which derives from illness and bereavement, may serve to bring about a good end, when they are mingled with faith. I have not argued that they are themselves simply "good things": in chapter 11 I shall try to scout around the edges of the mysteries of providence. But that the Bible insists that God disciplines his people—whether as chastening punishment or as the toughening up of a soldier—there can be little doubt; and millions of Christians have been enabled by God's grace to look back on terrible sorrow and thank God for what they have learned.

None of this means the sorrow is pleasant. None of this argues that the means of sorrow are all intrinsically "good." None of this means that this version of "the end justifies the means" constitutes a "solution" to the problem of evil and suffering. I am saying only that the good results that often take place must be borne in mind.

Moreover, it is not always possible analytically to disentangle this aspect of suffering from other aspects, and this means that, experientially, we may not easily perceive that what we are going through is accomplishing anything good, in us or in anyone else, until quite some time has elapsed. That is all the more reason to try to establish these structures or habits of thought firmly in our minds before days of affliction descend upon us.

Finally, there is an entailment in these reflections on the connections between sin and illness, bereavement and death. It may sound a bit shocking to those who have been bereft of children. It is not meant to comfort, merely to provide some perspective. I may put it like this: If we are all under sentence of death, then an *early* death is less shocking than is sometimes assumed. I could detail the friends and relatives I have lost, and their ages when they died. I know that I am shocked when someone young dies—much less than seventy, so full of promise and hope—especially if that person is close to me. Yet in light of the fact that we must all die, the exact timing, surely, is of relatively little consequence. If we are too shocked by "untimely" death (Is death ever "timely"?), may our reaction not owe something to the unvoiced assumption that we *ought* to live out a full span, that God somehow *owes* us that?

But he doesn't. It is because of the Lord's mercies that we are not consumed.

Accepting Death

I have already insisted that there is a proper sense in which we should be outraged by death.

But there is a cultural factor at work in the Western world that must be squarely faced. Death has become the last taboo. I can write about sex and breasts, discuss homosexuality in public, and debate the ethics of abortion, but I must not mention death in civilized company.

Corpses are whisked off to the undertakers' where family members will not see them until they have been "prepared." Even the bereaved themselves find candor difficult. Many is the grieving family that refuses to talk out its grief, even within the family—with incalculable loss of comfort and perspective. Meanwhile, incredible advances in medical science have convinced us we have the *right* to live.

The Puritans published sermons and books on how to die well; they cherished collected "last words" of Christians who had already gone to be with the Lord. But we find it exceedingly difficult to look death squarely in the face and talk about it.

Consider the following poem, written by Thomas Nashe (1567–1601), an Elizabethan author of no great repute who penned these lines, possibly his best, when he along with hundreds of thousands of others contracted the plague and lay on their deathbed:[3]

> Adieu, farewell earth's bliss,
> This world uncertain is;
> Fond are life's lustful joys,
> Death proves them all but toys,
> None from his darts can fly.
> I am sick, I must die.
>   Lord, have mercy on us!
>
> Rich men, trust not in wealth,
> Gold cannot buy you health;
> Physic himself must fade,
> All things to end are made.
> The plague fully swift goes by.
> I am sick, I must die.
>   Lord, have mercy on us!
>
> Beauty is but a flower
> Which wrinkles will devour;
> Brightness falls from the air,
> Queens have died young and fair,
> Dust hath closed Helen's eye.
> I am sick, I must die.
>   Lord, have mercy on us!
>
> Strength stoops unto the grave,
> Worms feed on Hector brave,
> Swords may not fight with fate,
> Earth still holds ope her gate.
> Come! Come! The bells do cry.
> I am sick, I must die.
>   Lord, have mercy on us!

3. I am grateful to Roy Clements for drawing this poem to my attention.

Haste, therefore, each degree,
To welcome destiny.
Heaven is our heritage,
Earth but a player's stage;
Mount we unto the sky.
I am sick, I must die.
    Lord, have mercy on us!

It is hard to imagine a modern writer facing death so openly. We are more likely to lionize Dylan Thomas's counsel to his dying father: "Rage, rage against the dying of the light." Indeed, after we have accepted our place in God's world and grasped the desperate realities of sin and its consequences, rage may be called for. But Dylan Thomas's rage is not called for. He still wants to be the center of the universe, and is frustrated to the point of rage that he cannot be. Contrast Nashe. His refrain faces reality openly: "I am sick, I must die." And he perceives that in God's universe there is only one possible prayer to follow this unavoidable reality: "Lord, have mercy on us!"

If we turn to Psalm 90, we discover that Moses draws the same lesson from the prospect of death. He sees that death is an expression of God's anger, itself God's response to our sin; he sees that death is therefore a divine limit on our hubris and is not to be thought about as something apart from God's message to us. But after concluding these reflections with the words already cited, "If only we knew the power of your anger! Your wrath is as great as the fear that is your due" (v. 11), he adds, "Teach us to number our days, that we may gain a heart of wisdom" (v. 12).

Here, then, is no futile flight from death. Moses stares at death, thinks through its relation to life, to sin, to God, and strives to understand what death means. And then he asks for wisdom to live his life in light of that death. He would have utterly scorned the modern mood that wants to live life as if death were not there waiting for us at the end. Moses wants us "to number our days," that is, to recognize the limit that is imposed on us, and to live with that limit in full view. Only in this way can we "gain a heart of wisdom."

The habit of looking at life "from the vantage of the End" I shall discuss more fully in the next chapter. It means, for instance, that we can no longer be quite so distressed if the wicked and ungodly opponent is rich and at ease, for it is written, "Do not be overawed when others grow rich, when the splendor of their houses increases; for they will take nothing with them when they die, their splendor will not descend with them" (Ps. 49:16–17); "life does not consist in an abundance of possessions" (Luke 12:15); and it is quite certain that "we brought nothing into the world, and we can take nothing out of it" (1 Tim. 6:7). Christians will learn to invest in the bank of heaven (Matt. 6:19–21): that is where both their treasure and their heart will reside.

Now let us suppose that your spouse comes home from a medical checkup with fearful news: there are signs that a vicious melanoma has taken hold. The hospital runs emergency tests during the next few days and the news comes back all bad: the prognosis is three months' survival at best, and all that modern medicine can do is mitigate the pain.

I do not want to minimize the staggering blow such news can administer to any family. There are many forms of practical comfort and support that thoughtful people can show. But it must be said that if you are a Christian who has thought about these things in advance, you will recognize that this sentence of death is no different in kind from what you and your spouse have lived under all your life; that you have been preparing for this day since your conversion; that you have already laid up treasure in heaven, and your heart is there. We are all under sentence of death; we are all terminal cases. The only additional factor is that in this case the sentence, barring a miracle, will certainly be carried out sooner than you had anticipated.

I am not pretending this bare truth is immensely comforting. Our comfort turns on other factors. But full acceptance of this truth can remove a fair bit of unnecessary shock and rebellion; for we will have escaped the modern Western mind-set that refuses to look at death, to plan for death, to live in the light of death, to expect death.

Things Worse Than Death

Some time ago I was told by my doctor that I had contracted a rather rare disease. The prognosis was uncertain: the disease varies in its power from being quite mild to being lethal. As the months went by, it became evident that my case fell into the mild end of the spectrum. But the news gave me occasion to think through my reaction to the prospect of my own demise. Three years ago I came down with a heart virus which was at first (wrongly) diagnosed as a serious heart attack. Once again, I could not escape thinking about my mortality.

The hardest part of dying, I decided, was leaving my wife and children. If the prognosis turned vicious, I decided, I would do everything I could with my remaining strength to make the transition as smooth as possible for my wife, and to leave the stamp of a Christian father on my children. But apart from that one tie, I could not think of a single reason why dying would be so bad a thing.

I confess, with some shame, that this assessment did not stem from prolonged meditation on the glories of living with Christ. With Paul, I believe, at least at the formal level, that "to live is Christ and to die is gain," that "to depart and be with Christ . . . is better by far" (Phil. 1:21, 23), but I suppose I am not spiritually mature enough for these realities to grip me incessantly. Sometimes they do; I do not perpetually live in their light.

But I remembered the fate of King Hezekiah (2 Kings 20; 2 Chron. 32:24–31; Isa. 38–39). When he was under sentence of death, he begged the Lord for fifteen more years, and received the extra span. And in the course of those fifteen years he blew his entire reputation for integrity in one incident prompted by foolish pride. Nor was his reputation alone at stake: the bearing his action had on the future of his nation was disastrous.

That is why I decided there are worse things than dying. I do not know how many times I have sung the words, "O let me never, never / Outlive my love for Thee," but I mean them. I would rather die than end up unfaithful to my wife; I would rather die than deny by a profligate life what I have taught in my books; I would rather die than deny or disown the gospel. God knows there are many things in my past of which I am deeply ashamed; I would not want such shame to multiply and bring dishonor to Christ in years to come. There are worse things than dying.

God's Megaphone

Earlier in this book (chap. 5), we looked at some passages that declare God's intention to discipline his children. We need to return to that theme, but to look at it from a slightly different perspective. We need to reflect a little on how it is that pain, suffering, and bereavement can function that way in the life of a believer. I must assume that the texts and reasoning of the earlier section are now a "given." You may want to review them before you move on.

There are at least three ways in which pain and suffering, rightly received in faith, will contribute to our growth as Christians.

First, in the words of Richard Baxter, "suffering so unbolts the door of the heart, that the Word hath easier entrance."[4] We can be so busy working, enjoying life, pursuing our careers, even "serving the Lord," that we no longer really reflect on his Word, or take time to pray, or sort out our priorities before him. The popular song, "He washed my eyes with tears, that I might see," may indulge in too much sentimental doggerel, but it expresses an important truth.

4. *The Saints' Everlasting Rest* (repr., Grand Rapids: Baker, 1978), 246.

But clearly, suffering does not always have that effect. Pain tends to make people better, or bitter. If we find it is developing in us a pattern of bitterness, we are in desperate straits. And one of the first steps to reverse such bitterness is to come before the Lord, broken and confused and hurt as we may be, and read his Word, seek his face, and ask him to provide the comfort that only he can. For in a fallen world, pain and suffering can be God's megaphone, to an individual or to a nation, distracting our attention from the selfishness of a life that functionally disowns God, no matter what we say in our creeds.

Second, illness, bereavement, and suffering actually shape us; they temper us; they mold us. We may not enjoy the process; but they transform us. As we have already seen, that truth is explicitly taught in Romans 5:1–5. Rightly accepted, pain cleanses us from self-centeredness, gives us insight into the nature of this fallen world, prepares us for death, makes us remember the sufferings of Christ and of others. The Welsh hymn-writer and evangelist William Williams testified that he had gained on his deathbed more knowledge of himself, and more knowledge of the goodness of God, than during the previous forty years of his life.[5]

Third, as a corollary to the previous point, experiences of suffering, illness, and bereavement engender compassion and empathy in us, and therefore make us better able to help others.

Some years ago, a couple I know who had between them never experienced a day's worth of illness in their lives, dismissed their young son's complaints about growing headaches. As his pleas grew louder and longer, they dismissed him the more firmly, telling him not to be a whining baby. When they finally decided to take him for medical help, the doctors discovered a brain tumor that had been growing for months. At one point it could have been removed without brain damage; by the time the parents sought help, the surgery required to save their son's life left him virtually blind. Of course, one cannot be sure, but it is hard not to wonder if the outcome would have been far happier if either of the parents had known anything of physical suffering themselves. This is not to blame them; it is to point out that sympathetic assessment of another's suffering, not to mention the offer of effective relief, is more likely to come from those who have suffered than from those who have not.

The apostle Paul understands the point: "Praise be to the God and Father of our Lord Jesus Christ, the Father of compassion and the God of all comfort," he writes, "who comforts us in all our troubles, *so that we can comfort those in any trouble with the comfort we ourselves receive*

    5. E. Houghton, *Christian Hymn-Writers* (Bridgend: Evangelical Press of Wales, 1982), 116.

from God" (2 Cor. 1:3–4, emphasis added). Moreover, this view of "trouble" is not just for apostles and other leaders. Rather, it is something that springs from the cross itself, and is to be passed on within the Christian community: "For just as we share abundantly in the sufferings of Christ, so also our comfort abounds through Christ. If we are distressed, it is for your comfort and salvation; if we are comforted, it is for your comfort, which produces in you patient endurance of the same sufferings we suffer. And our hope for you is firm, because we know that just as you share in our sufferings, so also you share in our comfort" (2 Cor. 1:5–7).

You do not have to serve as a pastor for many years before you find the people who can help others in grief; and they are almost always those who have grieved themselves. And that means that one of the things that can be held out to grieving or suffering believers is the prospect of being more fruitful than they could ever have imagined. The vine that bears fruit gets pruned, so it may bear more fruit (John 15). This is not a universal panacea; no single response to something as complex as evil and suffering can be. But it is a biblical perspective that cannot be overlooked. I have attended many funerals where people were converted; I have known many brokenhearted people who a few years later were the mainstays of a new generation of suffering and grieving people.

If our suffering unbolts our own heart to allow freer entrance by the Word of God, it also unbolts our heart to allow freer flow outward of empathetic love.

The Importance of Framework

In North America, most houses are built of wood-frame construction. As the framing of such houses determines their shape, so the framework of a theological discussion (largely) determines its emphases.

This is where I must say something about the "signs and wonders" movement associated with John Wimber. Wimber has gone to his reward, of course, but both the denomination he spawned, the Vineyard, and many other groups of churches have been heavily influenced by his theology. As I have discussed many aspects of the movement elsewhere, in connection with a sustained exposition of New Testament passages dealing with "charismatic" gifts,[6] I shall not go over the same material here. I am neither "anticharismatic" nor "anti-Wimber": doubtless the church has much to learn from both movements.

6. D. A. Carson, *Showing the Spirit: A Theological Exposition of 1 Corinthians 12–14* (Grand Rapids: Baker; Exeter: Paternoster, 1987), chap. 5.

My concern here, however, is to reflect a little on how Wimber's framework for discussion largely determines his outcome, and how that outcome would be a little different if he adopted a larger framework.

A simplification and condensation of his published views (I hope not an unfair one) might run something like this: Wimber holds that the inbreaking kingdom of God displayed in Jesus' ministry is still with us. Although the consummated kingdom has not yet arrived, the saving, transforming kingdom has already dawned, and Jesus is already reigning: all authority is his. Therefore just as works of power—exorcisms, healings, miracles of various sorts, including bringing people back from the dead—accompanied Jesus' preaching and evangelism, and were in fact integral parts of the demonstration of the presence and power of the kingdom, so also should it be today. The kingdom that has dawned and is already present among us should be demonstrated in works of power. These miraculous deeds add a certain credibility to the naked word: just as the people in Galilee were no less amazed at Jesus' authority over demons and over nature than at his words, so the combination of kingdom authority in deed with the proclamation of the authoritative word of the gospel is what is needed today. To be truly faithful to the Scriptures and to display the presence of the kingdom, there must be "power evangelism."

To this end Wimber and those who follow him devote some time at many meetings to healing, exorcisms in Jesus' name, and the like. Wimber is quite candid: he estimates that his "success rate" is about 2 percent, and he is careful to insist that there is no New Testament warrant for thinking that any individual ought to be healed or else charged with inadequate faith. In other words, the framework for his healing services is quite different from that of old-line charismatic theology. Indeed, I cheerfully insist that, apart from minor places where I might venture some disavowal, the basic structure of his understanding of the kingdom is biblically unimpeachable.

But—and it is a very important "but"—his framework is still not large enough. He has tried to establish a theology of healing and power encounter without a theology of suffering; he has a theology of victory without an adequate theology of the cross; he has a theology of life without proper reflection on the place of death. He sees the triumph of the kingdom when sickness is overthrown, and cannot see the triumph of the kingdom when people are transformed *in the midst* of sickness. He discusses God's power, but rarely wrestles with God's predilection for displaying his power in the context of continuing weakness. He encourages triumphant faith, but does not establish a broad enough grid to show that triumphant faith may be exactly what is displayed where there is raw perseverance in the face of incredible suffering. He rightly sees that sin and suffering are intrinsically evil, but he nowhere thinks through how a sovereign God in some way stands behind them, even on occasion using them as instruments of needed discipline. In short, Wimber's framework is not big enough.

I could go farther and suggest that his framework is not big enough even when analyzing the synoptic Gospels, from which his most important evidence springs. In particular:

1. It is quite dramatic to observe that when Jesus' intention is stated, or his initiative described, it is almost always the case that his teaching and preaching are in view, and not his healings (e.g., Mark 1:15, 21, 35–39; 2:2, 13; 3:14, 22–23; 4:1; 6:1–2, 34; 7:14; 8:31, 34; 9:30–31; 10:1; 12:1, 35).

2. By contrast, apart from one or two generalizing statements (e.g., Matt. 4:23), when Jesus heals individuals or casts out demons from them, then either the initiative is with the sufferer (e.g., Matt. 8:3–4; 9:20–22, 27–31; 17:14–18; Mark 1:23–26; Luke 7:1–10; John 4:46–54—including the initiative of the sufferer's friends, e.g., Matt. 9:27–31; 12:22; Mark 1:30–31, 32–34; 6:55–56), or, quite remarkably, Jesus may take the initiative with an individual after his purpose for being there is established on some other basis. In this latter category, we might include, for instance, the crippled woman of Luke 13:10–13 ("Jesus *was teaching* in one of the synagogues, and a woman was there. . . . *When Jesus saw her, he called her forward* . . ."); the paralyzed man of John 5 ("Jesus *went up to Jerusalem for one of the Jewish festivals*. . . . Here a great number of disabled people used to lie. . . . One who was there had been an invalid for thirty-eight years. *When Jesus saw him lying there and learned that he had been in this condition a long time,* he asked him . . ."); the man with the shriveled hand in Matthew 12:9–13 ("he *went into their synagogue,* and a man with a shriveled hand *was there* . . ."); and more of the same.

Now these observations must not be pushed too far. Certainly Jesus saw his healings as part of his messianic work (see Matt. 8:16–17; 11:5–6). Certainly in the trainee mission reported in Matthew 10, part of Jesus' charge to his disciples was to "heal the sick, raise the dead, cleanse those who have leprosy, drive out demons" (10:8)—though other specifics, such as what the disciples were not to bring with them (10:9–10) and the context of prolonged opposition and persecution (10:16–42), are often lost sight of. But it must be said that there is no record of Jesus himself holding a healing service, inviting people to be healed, or offering generalized prayers for healing and inviting people to come forward for a laying on of hands.

3. Where Jesus takes the initiative with an individual, it is never trivial and never ambiguous. There is no report of him saying, "I have a word from the Lord: there is someone here with a back pain, and God wants

to heal you"—or, worse, in one remarkable meeting, "someone with a pain in his toe." The only incident that comes close is the healing of the woman with a hemorrhage; and here, his famous challenge, "Who touched me?," took place *after the woman had already been healed,* and was in that sense already specified.

4. Although signs and wonders are sometimes cast in Scripture as elements that ought to compel faith (e.g., John 10:38), even then they are usually seen as an inferior means of faith (e.g., John 20:29); and often people are excoriated because of their pursuit of signs and wonders (e.g., Matt. 12:39; John 4:48). I do not find these diverse strands of biblical thought well integrated into Wimber's thinking.

In all these ways, then, Wimber's approach to pain and suffering is, in my judgment, cast within a framework so theologically narrow that although it initially seems impressive it not only ignores many contexts in the Gospels themselves, but fails to locate itself within a larger biblical framework that deals with the problem of evil and suffering and death more holistically.

Much more to be condemned is that form of theology that tells believers they *ought* to be healed, and that if they are not, it is because they lack faith. As far as I have been able to observe, those who propagate such theology die at no slower a rate than those who do not adhere to such theology. The sad fact is that this triumphalist theology is not only theologically ungrounded, it is pastorally cruel. Thoughtful Christians must come to grips not only with the truth that God can and sometimes does heal, but also with the truth that this side of Jesus' return "people are destined to die" (Heb. 9:27).

Suffering, Bereavement, and the Comfort of God

I have frequently hinted at this topic; it is time now to reflect on it more closely.

We have listened to parts of Moses' prayer in Psalm 90. After all the complaints, after his plea for wisdom in the light of God's anger and his own impending death, quite remarkably he prays, "Satisfy us in the morning with your unfailing love, that we may sing for joy and be glad all our days" (Ps. 90:14). In Psalm 102, where the afflicted psalmist details his sorrows and examines his imminent and premature death, what brings delight and comfort to him is his reflection on the enduring, changeless, faithful nature of God.

We ought to turn to God for comfort, naturally and spontaneously. If my son skinned his knee he ran into my arms with tears streaming down his face. He did not philosophize about whether his father cared;

he came for a cuddle. Of course, in some ways we are not children, and God's fatherhood is not exactly like my own. (In fact, mine is but a pale imitation of his: Eph. 3:15.) But we ought to be sufficiently childlike that we quickly turn to God for comfort when, metaphorically, we skin our knee. This is not a sign of immaturity; it is a sign of belonging. Indeed, if we do not instinctively turn to our heavenly Father, our reluctance may signal that we have let the relationship run so cold that our instinctive independence is grossly "unnatural"—that is, unspiritual.

It is exceedingly important to appreciate that the comfort God gives is real comfort. It is not mere stoicism expressed in some stony-faced assertion that God knows best—though confidence that God does know best may contribute to our comfort: that is still something to be explored. Now, however, I am not talking of merely "creedal comfort," but of personal comfort—the movement of God on the soul (for lack of a better way of phrasing it), a profound sense of his love, delight in his presence, the comfort of his care and wisdom. "The LORD is my light and my salvation—whom shall I fear? . . . One thing I ask from the LORD, this only do I seek: that I may dwell in the house of the LORD . . . and to seek him in his temple. For in the day of trouble he will keep me safe in his dwelling. . . . My heart says of you, 'Seek his face!' Your face, LORD, I will seek. . . . Though my father and mother forsake me, the LORD will receive me" (Ps. 27). "LORD, when you favored me, you made my royal mountain stand firm; but when you hid your face, I was dismayed" (Ps. 30:7). "I sought the LORD, and he answered me; he delivered me from all my fears" (Ps. 34:4). "Taste and see that the LORD is good; blessed are those who take refuge in him" (Ps. 34:8). God himself is the "very great reward" (Gen. 15:1) of his covenant people. It is not only in Nehemiah's day that the joy of the LORD is the strength of his people (Neh. 8:10). Paul prays that his Christian readers might grasp more and more in their own experience the limitless dimensions of God's love for them in Christ Jesus (Eph. 3:17b–19). The triune God makes himself present in the lives of his people by his Spirit (John 14:23), whom Jesus bequeaths to his own, along with copious peace (John 14:27) and joy (John 15:11) so that our hearts will be neither troubled nor afraid (John 14:27).

What we need, then, is the cultivation of this personal knowledge of God, for it will sustain us when every other pillar crumbles. And for this, we need the discipline of growing fervency in prayer, prolonged meditation on God as he has revealed himself in his Word, and the presence and power of the risen Christ working in us (Eph. 1:18ff.; 3:16–17a; Phil. 3:10) through his Spirit "so that Christ may dwell in our hearts through faith" (Eph. 3:17).

Death Transcended

When we who are Christians wrestle with questions about evil and suffering, and in particular illness and death, it is important that we do not too hastily appeal to what used to be called "the hereafter." We struggle *here*, and much of the comfort and perspective the Bible offers has little to do with any appeal to the End. It would be tragic if all such comfort and perspective were lost because we fled immediately in our thought to "the hereafter."

Nevertheless, the Bible does on occasion encourage us to look at illness, bereavement, and death from the perspective of the hope that is ours in Christ Jesus. The Bible does not encourage us to suppress our grief when loved ones die, but it does insist that we do not "grieve like the rest, who have no hope" (1 Thess. 4:13).

Anyone who has attended or officiated at many funerals knows the difference. I cannot describe the blank despair written large on the face and bearing of those who attend funerals where there is no gospel hope. In some traditions, the despair is magnified by unending wails and laments of mourners. But in decisively Christian funerals, where both the person who has died and those left behind to mourn know the Lord God in personal faith, the atmosphere is palpably different. The tears are still there; the grief is no less profound; the sense of personal loss may be devastating. But somehow, there is no grim despair. Indeed, some of the tears are shed because of the immensely moving impact of simple Christian witness standing up unbowed before the monstrous regimen of death. We grieve, but not "like the rest, who have no hope. We believe that Jesus died and rose again, and so we believe that God will bring with Jesus those who have fallen asleep in him" (1 Thess. 4:13–14).

Our ultimate hope is a new heaven and a new earth, where "God's dwelling place is now among the people, and he will dwell with them. They will be his people, and God himself will be with them and be their God. He will wipe every tear from their eyes. There will be no more death or mourning or crying or pain, for the old order of things has passed away" (Rev. 21:3–4).

Because death, as we have seen, is fundamentally God's imposed limitation on human arrogance, his stern "thus far, and no farther," the deepest terror of death is being cut off from him forever. But where there is reconciliation with God, where faith in the Son of God and his death on the cross has brought a man or woman into vital union with the living God himself, death no longer holds all its old threats. Death has not yet been abolished, but it has been stripped of its power. "The sting of death is sin, and the power of sin is the law" (1 Cor. 15:56); but where sin has been atoned for, and the curse of the law set aside by one who died in our place, we respond, "But thanks be to God! He gives us the victory through our Lord Jesus Christ" (1 Cor. 15:57).

"Hence the real point of death is no longer parting from, but home-going to. As death is deprived of its sting and poison, as it is no longer a personal fulfillment of God's wrath, it is only a biological mask that has no bearing on fellowship with the risen Lord."[7] Because Jesus is the resurrection and the life, the one who believes in him will live, even though he dies (John 11:25).

This truth must shape not only our approach to bereavement, but our assessment of illness and of our own approaching death. The more that a Christian lives in the consciousness of God's presence here, the easier it is to anticipate the unqualified delight that will be experienced in God's presence there.

In the past two or three years I have had to deal with several people with terminal illnesses who have been actively discouraged from thinking about death by well-intentioned but poorly informed brothers and sisters who try to deflect them from thinking along these lines. These would-be comforters try to distract them, or hold out the constant hope of healing, or keep them so occupied with matters in this world that they have neither the time nor the energy to think about the next world. They succeed only in robbing their loved ones of the enormous comforts of the gospel. The sad fact is that far too few Christians and Christian churches in the Western world are actively engaged in helping believers to die well. Distractions are a poor substitute for the comforts only Jesus can give, for the comforts that only gospel comforts can secure.

These gospel perspectives provide comfort not only to those who are dying, but to those who are bereaved. When we are bereaved, even bereaved of a young child, a close friend, a lifelong spouse, our sorrow turns, rightly, on *our* loss and loneliness, on the wrenching separation, on the frustration of hopes and plans, on our personal emptiness. But we do not sorrow because we think the loved one has disappeared into nothingness, or turned up in purgatory, or been absorbed into cosmic consciousness.

In September 1542, Magdalene, one of the daughters of Martin Luther, lay dying, her father weeping at her side. He asked her, "Magdalene, my dear little daughter, would you like to stay here with your father, or would you willingly go to your Father yonder?" Magdalene answered, "Darling father, as God wills." Luther wept, holding his daughter in his arms, praying that God might free her; and she died. As she was laid in her coffin, Martin Luther declared, "Darling Lena, you will rise and shine like a star, yea like the sun. . . . I am happy in spirit, but the flesh

7. Thielicke, *Living with Death*, 161.

is sorrowful and will not be content, the parting grieves me beyond measure. . . . I have sent a saint to heaven."[8]

We do not have to go so far back in the pages of history. I could tell you of the funeral service of a young woman, just twenty-three, herself the daughter of missionaries and already deeply committed to serving the Lord the same way. I could tell you of the memorial service of a pastor's wife who died suddenly in middle age, leaving her family utterly disoriented and distraught, but still able to sing:

> My hope is in the Lord,
> Who gave himself for me;
>
> For me, he died; for me he lives;
> And everlasting life and light he freely gives.

In fact, we begin to wonder if some pain and sorrow in this life is not used in God's providential hand to make us homesick for heaven, to detach us from this world, to prepare us for heaven, to draw our attention to himself and away from the world of merely physical things. In short, we begin to look at all of life's experiences, good and ill, from the vantage of the End.

But that is the topic of the next chapter.

Questions for Further Study

1. How are illness and death related to sin? List as many different connections as possible, giving biblical examples.
2. Why is death such a "taboo" subject of conversation for many Western Christians?
3. For a Christian, what things are worse than death?
4. Give illustrations of how people who have suffered have become richer, more compassionate, helping people?
5. What is needed to ensure that experiences of illness, suffering, and bereavement make us better people, not bitter people?
6. Does God owe us healing?
7. Is the consciousness of God's presence a growing delight for you, potentially of great importance in times of suffering? If not, why not?
8. Where is your "home"? In what ways do you live in the light of the new heaven and the new earth? What comfort does this prospect offer?

8. Cited in E. G. Rupp and B. Drewery, eds., *Martin Luther* (London: Edward Arnold, 1971), 162.

8

From the Vantage of the End

Christians remember that the Jesus who testifies to the contents of the book of Revelation promises, "Yes, I am coming soon," and the church replies, "Amen. Come, Lord Jesus" (Rev. 22:20). Christians live in the light of the End. Much of what we believe and much of the suffering we are prepared to endure derive their meaning from the prospect of vindication and resurrection. Without that prospect, without the reality that that prospect anticipates, Christianity does not make much sense, and neither do major planks in any Christian perspective on evil and suffering. "If only for this life we have hope in Christ, we are to be pitied more than all others" (1 Cor. 15:19).

The Kingdom Is Here! The Kingdom Is Coming!

Throughout the centuries of the church, it has proved difficult for many groups of believers to get the balance right between these two complementary truths: there is a sense in which the kingdom of God is here already, and there is a sense in which the kingdom has not yet come. Both facets of the truth have a bearing on how Christians should look at evil and suffering, though the emphasis in this chapter will be on the contribution made by the latter.

Perhaps I should begin by rapidly surveying the evidence. In various ways the Jews had looked forward for a long time to the coming kingdom of God, to the prospect of transformation and vindication that they were sure it would bring. Thus, when John the Baptizer began to preach, "Repent, for the kingdom of heaven has come near" (Matt. 3:2), his words were bound to cause a sensation and heighten the expectations of the crowds. Jesus opened his public ministry with the same pronouncement: "Repent, for the kingdom of heaven has come near" (Matt. 4:17; cf. Mark 1:15).

But how near is "near"? And does this mean "near in time," that is, "soon," or "physically near," "near at hand"? The ambiguity is picked up by Matthew. When John the Baptizer says these words, they are placed within the context of his announcement that he is preparing the way for another. That suggests a temporal nearness: it will not be long until the one to whom he is pointing will arrive on the scene. But when Jesus preaches the same message, Matthew associates Jesus' ministry with his return to Galilee, and with the fulfillment of the prophecy, "Galilee of the Gentiles—the people living in darkness have seen a great light; on those living in the land of the shadow of death a light has dawned" (Matt. 4:15–16; cf. Isa. 9:1–2). Moreover, Jesus' announcement is made right at the beginning of his ministry, and it leads to the demonstration of the kingdom's presence in miracles, mighty words of authority, and even the principial defeat of Satan and his cohorts.

It is not long before Jesus insists that some of those who listen to him will not taste death until they see that the kingdom of God has come with power (Mark 9:1). When he casts out demons, his opponents charge him with collaboration with occult powers (Matt. 12:24), but he himself insists, "But if it is by the Spirit of God that I drive out demons, then the kingdom of God has come upon you" (Matt. 12:28). The rendering "has come" may be slightly tendentious; but at the very least it signals a dawning so imminent that it cannot be further delayed.[1] In any case, Jesus' works of power are themselves anticipations of the cross (Matt. 8:16–17). His anticipation of the kingdom's coming leads up to what none of his contemporaries had envisaged: the death by crucifixion of the promised King of Israel, the Son of God, and his resurrection to immortal life in a transformed body—the first human being to conquer death.

Elsewhere, still relying on the sense of the physical nearness of the kingdom inherent in his own person, Jesus insists that the kingdom of God is in the midst of the people to whom he ministers (Luke 17:21). If I understand Matthew 11:12 aright, Jesus insists that throughout his ministry the kingdom is forcefully forging an advance.[2] As his word and

1. Chrys C. Caragounis, "Kingdom of God, Son of Man, and Jesus' Self-Understanding," *Tyndale Bulletin* 40 (1989): 3–23, 223–38.
2. See Carson, *Matthew*, 8:265–68.

power are passed on by his disciples in their trainee mission, Satan falls like lightning (Luke 10:18). Much of John's ironic account of the trial and death of Jesus turns on the fact that Jesus as the King is not like any other king, but that all the power of the mighty Roman Empire could not succeed in killing him if it did not have the sanction of the divine purpose. Jesus reigns, not by destroying the Roman troops, but (as the church fathers saw) from the cross. When Jesus tells one of the guerrilla fighters crucified with him, "Truly I tell you, today you will be with me in paradise," it is in response to that guerrilla's plea, "Jesus, remember me when you come into your kingdom" (Luke 23:42–43): the implication is that Jesus enters his reign that same day.

We are not surprised, then, to hear Paul reiterating to the Colossian Christians what they already know: God "has rescued us from the dominion of darkness and *brought us into the kingdom of the Son he loves*" (Col. 1:13, emphasis added). Indeed, in Paul's hands the expression "the kingdom of God" can refer to Christian experience (Rom. 14:17; 1 Cor. 4:20). Elsewhere, the New Testament assures us that already Christ "has made us to be a kingdom and priests to serve his God and Father" (Rev. 1:6).

References could be multiplied; but in fact it is just as important to hear the complementary strains. Many of Jesus' parables have to do with the kingdom of God, and not a few of them stress the delay before the kingdom is consummated, or the process before the final separation takes place. In such parables, even if "the kingdom" includes a reference to the long process or delay, it also includes the climax (e.g., Mark 4:26–29; Matt. 13:24–43; 24:36–25:46). Jesus looks forward to "the renewal of all things, when the Son of Man sits on his glorious throne" (Matt. 19:28). When Paul speaks of "inheriting the kingdom of God," he is referring to the consummated kingdom (e.g., 1 Cor. 6:9–10; Gal. 5:21b), the kingdom that flesh and blood cannot inherit (1 Cor. 15:50). If all of God's sovereignty is even now mediated through Jesus, Jesus is reigning—but he is doing so in the teeth of sustained opposition: he reigns until he has put all enemies under his feet, and utterly destroyed the last enemy, death itself (1 Cor. 15:25ff.). The ultimate hope of the Christian is the new heaven and the new earth, the Holy City, the new Jerusalem, the home of righteousness (2 Pet. 3:13; Rev. 21).

The New Testament writers find many ways to maintain the balance between the present and future facets of the kingdom of God. If Acts 2:16ff. insists that the Old Testament promises of the kingdom have been realized in the events of Pentecost, Acts 3:19–21 pictures Jesus remaining in heaven "until the time comes for God to restore everything." If the Epistle to the Hebrews can make the cross of Christ the climactic and complete sacrifice that ends all atoning sacrifices (9:26), two verses later it promises that Christ "will appear a second time, not to bear sin, but to bring salvation to those who are waiting for him" (v. 28). If Peter tells us that Christ has been revealed in these last times for our sake (1 Pet. 1:20)—a reference to Christ's first coming—he also assures us that we "through faith are shielded by God's power until the coming of the salvation that is ready to be revealed in the last time" (1 Pet. 1:5).

This tension between the "already" and the "not yet"—the kingdom has *already* arrived, and the kingdom has *not yet* come—is a commonplace of biblical thought. It has many important connections with other elements of Christian truth, but the one that interests us here is its bearing on evil and suffering. To put the matter in a nutshell: once the consummated kingdom has dawned, there will be no more evil or suffering among the Lord's people. But meanwhile, even though the kingdom of God has been inaugurated, evil and suffering are on the one hand said to be defeated in principle, and yet on the other are palpably present and in some ways can be expected to increase.

We can see this in passages like the parable of the weeds (Matt. 13:24–30, 36–43). In the parable, the farmer forbids his servants to pull up the weeds that an enemy has sown among the wheat. "Let both grow together until the harvest," he orders; and then the difference between the two kinds of plants will be obvious, and the separation absolute. When Jesus is pressed to explain his parable, he says that the wheat stands for "the people of the kingdom," while the weeds stand for "the people of the evil one." Both will grow together until the harvest, which "is the end of the age."

That is remarkable: both weeds and wheat grow together, in this period during which the kingdom has been inaugurated, but has not yet been consummated. Indeed, the Bible seems to see much contemporary iniquity as a pointer to a climactic outbreak of iniquity still to come: the secret power of lawlessness is already at work, even if temporarily restrained (2 Thess. 2:7). Elsewhere, the entire period between the first and second comings of Jesus can be viewed as "the last hour," at the end of which the antichrist breaks forth: "Dear children," John writes, "this is the last hour; and as you have heard that the antichrist is coming, even now many antichrists have come. This is how we know it is the last hour" (1 John 2:18). Jesus himself insists, "You will hear of wars and rumors of wars, but see to it that you are not alarmed. Such things must happen, but the end is still to come. Nation will rise against nation, and kingdom against kingdom. There will be famines and earthquakes in various places. All these are the beginning of birth pains" (Matt. 24:6–8). In other words, so many of the terrible evils and causes of suffering we have experienced in this century and in previous centuries serve as pointers to a climactic outbreak of iniquity still to come, here designated "birth pains." (The "birth pains of the Messiah" is a fairly common Jewish description of an outbreak of evil and rebellion just before the Messiah triumphantly sets up his kingdom.)

The wheat and the weeds grow together. The outworking of this truth should be intuitively obvious. On the one hand, the triumphant spread and growth of Christianity during the past twenty centuries, especially during the past two centuries, are nothing short of astonishing. Indeed, the figures for the last few decades take one's breath away. China had just over a million Protestants in 1949 when the Communists took over; today, there are perhaps 80 to 90 million. The number of Christians in Asia rose from 22 million in 1990 to over three hundred million in 2000. In the late 1970s there were only two thousand Christians in Cambodia; today, there are about one hundred fifty thousand. At one time, Mongolia was considered one of the most closed countries in the world: in 1989, there were only four known Christians. Today, there are about twenty thousand, worshiping in about six hundred churches and house churches. In 1959, there were only twenty-nine known Christians in Nepal; today there are about half a million. Korea has now sent out between twelve and fifteen thousand missionaries; Latin America has sent out about eight thousand. The number of churches in the Ukraine has jumped in the past ten years from two thousand to twelve thousand. One could easily draw attention to the rapid growth of the church in Romania, much of sub-Saharan Africa, Indonesia, and other countries.[3] Moreover, not a few historians judge that Christianity has been one of the dominant influences in the early shaping of modern science and in the rise of democratic forms of government; and these developments, for all their failures, have provided more people with relative wealth and freedom than at any time in the history of the world.

On the other hand, not everything is sweetness and light. In Europe, evangelicals constitute less than three percent of the population. In France, on any given weekend there are two-and-a-half to three times more Muslims worshiping than there are Catholics; in Vienna, there are more registered prostitutes than there are evangelicals; in Belgium, there are more Muslims than evangelicals. In Brazil alone, there are at least twelve million children living on the streets; in all of Latin America, perhaps forty million such minors (children under fifteen). Bangkok has become proverbial for its tens of thousands of child prostitutes, servicing plane loads of sex tourists, many from Japan and Germany. Around the world, the number of "evangelicals" who are genuinely converted is a

---

3. The numbers display the massive tilt of the confessing church away from the West toward the two-thirds world. See especially Philip Jenkins, *The Next Christendom: The Coming of Global Christianity* (New York: Oxford University Press, 2002).

matter of enormous doubt, judging by elementary conduct and behavior (recalling Jesus' blistering words in Matthew 7:21–23). Many parts of the world face enormous challenges from crime, poverty, deeply embedded political corruption, AIDS, violence, and tribalism. The rise of militant Islam, especially in Africa and the Middle East, combined with the re-shaping of global pressures this side of the fall of the Soviet block, has spawned numerous speculations about the potential for catastrophic violence in the twenty-first century, the end of which cannot yet be fore-seen.[4] Further, we have just escaped from the twentieth century, which of course witnessed brutal wars and repression on a global scale—global repetition of the merciless destruction of Genghis Khan. There is no particularly good reason for thinking that the present century will escape similar carnage. Moreover, in much of the Western world, Christianity has spun off an odious variety of apostate versions. The dignity of the human being predicated on creation in the image of God has become raw humanism, with God abolished and human beings raised to divine status. The biblical emphasis on historical development, on "before" and "after," on prophecy and fulfillment, on the notion of historical goal and purpose, has been warped into raw historicism, where the historical pro-cess itself is worshiped as god, interpreted through various secular grids. The kingdom of God has not only been politicized, but has been taken over by a worship of politics: our hopes, our confidence, our national discourse all turn on political developments, with very few seeking the face of God in such matters. The blessings of the kingdom have been twisted into hedonistic pleasure: you're a child of the King, we are told, so you should live like princes and princesses. This is worse than a return to paganism, for it is a return to paganism that is in self-conscious rebellion against biblical Christianity.

Thus the wheat and the weeds grow up together. It is of paramount importance that we Christians understand this, and grasp where we are in the sweep of God's purposes. We have a tendency, in the West, to read our Bibles and our Christian experience through notoriously individual-istic spectacles. This is as true when we wrestle with the problem of evil and suffering as in any other area of thought. Evil and suffering tend to become a "problem" when *I* suffer, when *we* suffer—or, alternatively, when we witness some particular suffering and project what we would feel under those circumstances. This is not mere empathy, which is good, but a projection of ourselves, as individuals, as the primary criterion for assessing what is going on and how to think of it—and that is surely itself evil.

4. The most important of these analyses remains that of Samuel P. Huntington, *The Clash of Civilizations and the Remaking of World Order* (New York: Simon & Schuster, 1996).

I am not for a moment suggesting that a mature understanding of biblical eschatology—that is, of the biblical disclosure of how the kingdom has come and has not yet arrived—will provide instant relief to pain, or "solve" all our intellectual doubts when we suffer. But it may help us to be a little less surprised by the prevalence of evil and suffering in the world, not least in this period between the "already" and the "not yet." Indeed, from a Christian perspective, if it were not so Christ and the writers of the New Testament would be proved liars. If we can get over our tendency to evaluate everything that transpires from a merely individualistic perspective, and glimpse at least a little of the broad movements of God in redemptive history, we may not only be a little less surprised when we suffer, we may also find that it is somewhat easier to "make sense" of suffering: at least some of it fits into a pattern that Jesus himself predicted.

The "already" or "realized" or "inaugurated" element of the kingdom also provides many kinds of comforting joys, some of which have already been mentioned in this book, and more of which is to come. But in the rest of this chapter, I want to look at the bearing of the "not yet" or "futuristic" facet of the kingdom on the way we respond to evil and suffering.

Justice Done—And Seen to Be Done

One of the most staggering characteristics of suffering is that, if measured exclusively by what takes place in this world, it is so often entirely disproportionate to the evil committed. In other words, if suffering is seen primarily as punishment, then intuitively one must conclude that where there is more evil there should be more punishment. Someone who is very wicked should suffer more than someone who is very self-denying, sacrificial, and caring. Hitler should suffer more than Mother Teresa; Stalin should be afflicted with more pain than Joni Eareckson Tada. Conversely, the person who does good should be blessed with more privileges and benefits than the one whose every thought is tinged with malice, lust, or greed.

To put the matter quite so crudely is enough to make any thoughtful person cry out with a host of "Yes, buts." Yes, we might say, but we must remember that some evil and malignity in this person or that person owes a great deal to a deprived childhood, a broken home, a cruel father, an inferior education: we cannot assume that the actual performance of more evil merits more punishment without also considering degrees of responsibility and opportunity. Yes, we might agree, the good person should receive extra blessings, but these "blessings" might not be material. Perhaps even in this world Mother Teresa has enjoyed more blessings than Hitler. Yes, we say, there should be some sort of proportionality between evil performed and suffering experienced, but we must not forget what was said earlier about the chastening purpose of some suffering. Not all suffering can be reduced to the punitive; some of it is educative, reforming, even redeeming. Yes, we agree, there ought to be some kind of proportionality, but the measurement of evil is a tricky thing: Jesus excoriated the "righteous" people of his day far more roundly than he condemned the outcasts and reprobates. In God's sight, is Idi Amin necessarily more wicked than the church leader who denies most of the basic truths of Christianity in the name of academic freedom, yet retains his senior seminary post or his bishopric, influencing generation after generation of budding preachers who in turn shape congregations that substantially transform the congregations into a conglomerate of superficial and spurious believers?

Yet even after we face all the difficulties in working out the proportionality of evil and suffering, on any showing there is all too little proportionality in this world. Babies starving to death, a fine wife and mother cut down by a disease as savage and as dehumanizing as Huntingdon's chorea, a missionary gang-raped: how do these stack up against wicked and greedy men living in luxury in penthouses and aboard yachts?

One of the reasons why the books of Job and Ecclesiastes play so important a role in Scripture is that they frankly acknowledge the irrationality and disproportionality of evil in this world. We shall look more closely at the book of Job in the next chapter. But one of the perspectives that helps is the prospect of a new heaven and a new earth—and hell. The entire totting up is not yet complete. Assessments of fairness and proportionality based solely on what takes place here and now, in this world, are bound to be premature at best, entirely misguided at worst.[5]

The point, then, is that the Bible insists that God is entirely just, and that therefore ultimately justice will be done, and will be seen to be done. Because this entails appealing to the End, that is, to what has not yet taken place, it involves walking by faith. Those who cannot wait for their answers, those who cannot trust God simply because he is a just God, will therefore find no comfort at all from the Bible's assurances on this point.

Perhaps it will prove most profitable to scan several biblical passages.

5. One of the great strengths of the book by J. Christian Beker, *Suffering and Hope* (Philadelphia: Fortress, 1987), is that it recognizes there can be no adequate Christian response to the problem of the disproportionality of evil and suffering in this world without appealing to the final apocalyptic vision of the biblical writers. See, e.g., p. 87.

Psalm 73

Asaph, the author of the psalm, begins with a general declaration of the goodness of God to the covenant community, at least to that part of it that meets one particular standard: "Surely God is good to Israel, to those who are pure in heart" (v. 1). "But as for me," Asaph says, looking back on a sad period in his own life, "my feet had almost slipped; I had nearly lost my foothold" (v. 2). What caused this lapse? "I envied the arrogant when I saw the prosperity of the wicked" (v. 3)—and envy is no sign of a pure heart!

What was it about the wicked that Asaph envied? The short answer is, almost everything. When one gets into that frame of mind, one is capable of generalizations that themselves are distortions, even when they preserve some truth. "They have no struggles; their bodies are healthy and strong" (v. 4), Asaph writes—which, doubtless, is often true, but by no means always. He goes on in his summary of the wicked: they are puffed up with pride because they suffer so little; they "clothe themselves with violence," their evil conceits "know no limits," they scoff, they are malicious, they threaten oppression, they lay claim to great piety while their tongues so manipulate affairs that they "take possession of the earth." They laugh at God himself, choosing to picture him as distant and unconcerned: "They say, 'How would God know? Does the Most High know anything?'" Asaph summarizes bitterly: "This is what the wicked are like—always free of care, they go on amassing wealth" (vv. 5–12).

This sort of rumination encourages a still more rebellious thought. It may be a fine creedal point to confess that God is good to those who are pure in heart (v. 1), but the evidence just outlined suggests it doesn't work that way: God seems to be quite good to the wicked. And that means that purity doesn't pay: "Surely in vain I have kept my heart pure and have washed my hands in innocence" (v. 13). Indeed, Asaph throws in a little self-pity for good measure: "All day long I have been afflicted, and every morning brings new punishments" (v. 14).

But all this, he insists, is what he *might* have said. Asaph does not in fact go quite that far. He is restrained, in the first instance, by the thought that such a step would betray his heritage with the covenant people of God, and could lead others astray: "If I had spoken out like that, I would have betrayed your children" (v. 15). But prolonged study and meditation provided no relief to the quandary into which his perceptions of the wicked had led him. It took something else: "When I tried to understand all this, it troubled me deeply till I entered the sanctuary of God; then I understood their final destiny" (vv. 16–17).

How much Asaph understood of final retribution after death is disputed. What is clear, however, is that as he returns to worship God and think about what God is like, he is prepared to take the long view, and trust a just God to work out his justice. That means Asaph can look at the present prosperity of the wicked, and still insist, "Surely you place them on slippery ground; you cast them down to ruin. How suddenly are they destroyed, completely swept away by terrors!" (vv. 18–19). Indeed, in God's sight, the wicked are insubstantial, inconsequential: "They are like a dream when one awakes; when you arise, Lord, you will despise them as fantasies" (v. 20). The thought is akin to the last verse of Psalm 1: "For the LORD watches over the way of the righteous, but the way of the wicked will be destroyed" (v. 6): not merely the wicked, but their way, so inconsequential are they. Like prints on a sandy beach that are obliterated by the incoming tide, so the heavy trace of wicked people, so appallingly evident to us now, will be swept aside by God himself.

Not to have seen this, Asaph now avers, was a reflection of his own bitterness, his own moral failure: "When my heart was grieved and my spirit embittered, I was senseless and ignorant; I was a brute beast before you" (vv. 21–22). But he has now not only learned a negative lesson—that God's justice catches up with the wicked—but two positive ones as well: it is better to be with God *now,* and this present relationship with God must also be assessed on the long term. Asaph writes: "Yet I am always with you; you hold me by my right hand. You guide me with your counsel, and afterward you will take me into glory" (vv. 23–24).

Although there are some who understand that last clause to mean that God will eventually crown the psalmist with glory *in this life,* that is, that God will vindicate him by raising him to a position of honor, it is better to take the text as in Today's New International Version. The thought is akin to Psalm 49:15: "But God will redeem me from the realm of the dead; he will surely take me to himself." In other words, if God cares so much for his people here, and establishes a personal relationship with his own, it is inconceivable that he will cancel it at death. That cannot be, and Asaph knows it: "You hold me by my right hand," he tells the Lord, "and afterward you will take me into glory."

It is the presence of God himself, whether on earth or in heaven, that is the key: "Whom have I in heaven but you? And earth has nothing I desire besides you" (v. 25). Gone is Asaph's former envy. If he but delights in God, the "advantages" of the prosperous wicked disappear before his eyes, both in this world and the next. Indeed, Asaph is now prepared to face physical affliction, if only he can enjoy the presence of God: "My flesh and my heart may fail, but God is the strength of my heart and my portion forever" (v. 26).

Thus, everything depends on where you start. If you begin by envying the prosperity of the wicked, the human mind can "interpret" the data so as to rule God out, to charge him with unfairness, to make piety and purity look silly. But if you begin with genuine delight in God, both in this world and in the world to come, you can put up with "flesh and heart failing," and be absolutely confident that, far from being the victim of injustice, you are in the best possible position: near to the good (v. 1) and sovereign (v. 28) God.

So the closing verses of the psalm set out the contrast in stark terms, and testify to the psalmist's renewed resolve: "Those who are far from you will perish; you destroy all who are unfaithful to you. But as for me, it is good to be near God. I have made the Sovereign LORD my refuge; I will tell of all your deeds" (vv. 27–28).

Amos 4

This is surely one of the most frightening passages in the Old Testament.

Here God addresses the women of Israel, but they are women who represent the sin of the entire nation. They are derisively described as "cows of Bashan," that is, cows from the best pastureland. We might today say, "you fat, grain-fed cows." They oppress the poor and crush the needy. Greedy to the core and abusive of their power, they order their husbands around like servants: "Bring us some drinks!" (v. 1). Even the plural "us" is a nice touch: they are talking as if they were royalty. But the Sovereign Lord swears by his holiness that they will be dragged away like squirming fish on a hook (v. 2). Their public piety will not save them then: "Go to Bethel and sin" (v. 4) is like saying, "Go to church and sin." Then, in bristling irony, the Sovereign Lord declares, "Bring your sacrifices every morning, your tithes every three years. Burn leavened bread as a thank offering and brag about your freewill offerings—boast about them, you Israelites, for this is what you love to do" (vv. 4–5). They are infinitely more interested in a reputation for godliness than in godliness itself.

And then God details the various judgments he has sent to the nation over the previous decades, all without significant result. "I gave you empty stomachs in every city and lack of bread in every town, yet you have not returned to me," he declares (v. 6). So God tries another tactic: "I also withheld rain from you when the harvest was still three months away. I sent rain on one town, but withheld it from another. One field had rain; another had none and dried up. People staggered from town to town for water but did not get enough to drink, yet you have not returned to me" (vv. 7–8). God goes on to list other judgments he has sent—plague, sword, locusts, mildew, decay—"yet you have not returned to me," declares the Lord.

Only the shattering climax is left: "'Therefore this is what I will do to you, Israel, and because I will do this to you, Israel, *prepare to meet your God.'* He who forms the mountains, who creates the wind, and who reveals his thoughts to mortals, who turns dawn to darkness, and treads on the heights of the earth—the LORD God Almighty is his name" (vv. 12–13, emphasis added). There follows the judgment itself: the prospect of massive deportation, the destruction of the nation, exile (5:1ff.). And all of this is cast as *meeting God*!

The truth of the matter is that meeting God is either transcendentally wonderful, or utterly horrific. If God meets sinners—sinners like you and me—in mere justice, in raw justice, the ultimate result is cataclysmic judgment; if God meets sinners in mercy and transforming power, the ultimate result is ecstasy.

That is why the final disclosure of God at the end of history is the ultimate watershed. That is a large part of what makes the book of Revelation so searching. Some cry, "Fall on us and hide us from the face of him who sits on the throne and from the wrath of the Lamb! For the great day of their wrath has come, and who can withstand it?" (Rev. 6:16–17), while others cry, "Hallelujah! Salvation and glory and power belong to our God, for true and just are his judgments. . . . Hallelujah! For our Lord God Almighty reigns. Let us rejoice and be glad and give him glory! For the wedding of the Lamb has come, and his bride has made herself ready" (Rev. 19:1–2, 6–7).

Matthew 11:20–24

This passage must be quoted in full along with one or two asides:

Then Jesus began to denounce the towns in which most of his miracles had been performed, because they did not repent. "Woe to you, Chorazin! Woe to you, Bethsaida! If the miracles that were performed in you had been performed in Tyre and Sidon [large, pagan cities just up the coast], they would have repented long ago in sackcloth and ashes. But I tell you, it will be more bearable for Tyre and Sidon on the day of judgment than for you. And you, Capernaum [another favored town in Galilee], will you be lifted up to the skies? No, you will go down to the depths. If the miracles that were performed in you had been performed in Sodom [proverbial for wickedness; see Gen. 18–19], it would have remained to this day. But I tell you that it will be more bearable for Sodom on the day of judgment than for you.

There are three important theological presuppositions bound up with this passage.

1. As there are degrees of felicity to be gained in heaven, so there are degrees of punishment to be shunned in hell. Otherwise it would be

meaningless to speak of what will be "more bearable" or "less bearable" on the day of judgment. In some parables, the rewards in heaven differ. For example, some are made rulers over more cities than others. The notion of diversity in positive rewards is bound up with the obligation to lay up treasure in heaven. But here it is the variation in punishment that is in view.

The same principle is taught elsewhere: "The servant who knows the master's will and does not get ready or does not do what the master wants will be beaten with many blows. But the one who does not know and does things deserving punishment will be beaten with few blows. From everyone who has been given much, much will be demanded; and from the one who has been entrusted with much, much more will be asked" (Luke 12:47–48). There are degrees of punishment to be shunned.

2. Both of these passages also presuppose that there are degrees of responsibility, largely based on what we have already been given. In other words, the degree of responsibility is in accord with the degree of privilege. If someone has enjoyed great access to God's gracious self-disclosure in Scripture, and supremely in Jesus, that person is in far more peril than the one who has never heard of him.

When Jesus applied this truth, it was most commonly directed against the Jews who sometimes thought that their heritage gave them an inside track to the blessings of God. But the same principle must be applied to the professing church: those who enjoy the heritage of open Bibles, ready access to literature, freedom of religion, a history of vital church life, are in far more peril than those who have experienced none of these blessings. I find it daunting that, in exactly the same way, "we who teach will be judged more strictly" (James 3:1).

3. For the comparisons in these verses to be realistic, Jesus presupposes that God not only knows all that has happened and all that is happening, but also what would have happened under different circumstances. Philosophers call this "middle knowledge," and many of them doubt that even God could have it. This text presupposes that he does: he knows what Sodom would have done under different circumstances, he knows what Tyre and Sidon would have done under different circumstances, and he takes this knowledge into account in the judgment of the last day.

Interestingly, this does not mean that Sodom, say, goes free. Even though Sodom would have repented if the miracles performed in Capernaum had been performed in Sodom, Sodom does not on that account stand acquitted. That would presuppose that God owes Sodom, and every other city, exactly the same privileges that Capernaum enjoyed. The truth is that God does not owe salvation to anyone; he does not owe "chances" and "opportunities" to anyone. But if he comes to us with free, unmerited favor, then either we appropriate it, or our situation is far worse than it was before he came to us. Sodom is still condemned; but on the day of judgment, it will be more bearable for Sodom than for cities which, though less renowned for blatant evil, enjoyed far more exposure to God's gracious self-disclosure.

This is simultaneously terrifying and enormously reassuring. It is terrifying if we stand with most of those to whom much is given (as is the case with most who will read this book). It urges us, by God's grace, to take up the opportunities and privileges that God gives us. But it is reassuring as well, for it ensures that God's justice on the last day will be perfect, and will be seen to be perfect. Every conceivable factor will be taken into account by omniscience.

That is why the prospect of the End, of the consummated kingdom, of the ultimate division between heaven and hell, are all enormously important aspects of all Christian thought about evil and suffering. We serve a just God, and at the end, not only will justice be done, but it will be seen to be done.

The view from the End will be very different from our present view. That is why we are called to live our lives now in faith and hope: faith in the God who already can see how things look from the end, firm hope in the God whose justice is unassailable and whose promises never fail.

Some Practical Implications

It is time to turn from these theological structures on which so much of the Bible turns, to some practical reflections on how we should live in their light—in particular, how we should think about evil and suffering in the light of these realities.

1. Christians ought to be developing a kind of homesickness for heaven. Some want to warn us against being so heavenly minded that we will be no earthly good. I suppose that is possible, but I haven't found anyone like that yet. Puffed up piety and sentimental religion can make one think much of heaven and love no one down here, but those who are genuinely heavenly minded have the highest incentive to serve well here: they are laying up treasure in heaven.

Preaching and teaching that do not constantly make heaven the Christian's hope and goal are not only unfaithful to the Scriptures, but rob believers of one of the most important perspectives for helping them to cope with pressures here and now. The drift in much popular American evangelicalism at the moment is toward evangelical pop psychology: sanctify the terminology and apply the benefits of pop theories on self-understanding. I would not say these developments are entirely without value. But if they displace a robust Christian faith that deals with guilt, suffering, values, faith, fidelity, hope, mercy, truth, righteousness, justice, forgiveness, and much more on biblical grounds, we have squandered our birthright for a mess of pottage.

Read these words from 1 Peter and ask yourself if they accurately reflect your own values. Does Peter summarize what you really think and feel, or are his sentiments essentially alien to you?

> Praise be to the God and Father of our Lord Jesus Christ! In his great mercy he has given us new birth into a living hope through the resurrection of Jesus Christ from the dead, and into an inheritance that can never perish, spoil or fade. This inheritance is kept in heaven for you, who through faith are shielded by God's power until the coming of the salvation that is ready to be revealed in the last time. In all this you greatly rejoice, though now for a little while you may have had to suffer grief in all kinds of trials. These have come so that your faith—of greater worth than gold, which perishes even though refined by fire—may be proved genuine and may result in praise, glory and honor when Jesus Christ is revealed. Though you have not seen him, you love him; and even though you do not see him now, you believe in him and are filled with an inexpressible and glorious joy, for you are receiving the end result of your faith, the salvation of your souls. (1 Pet. 1:3–9)

The same sort of perspective is summarized in 1 Peter 5:10: "And the God of all grace, who called you to his eternal glory in Christ, after you have suffered a little while, will himself restore you and make you strong, firm and steadfast."

It is not surprising, then, to find Paul saying that as far as he is concerned he would *prefer* to die and go to be with the Lord immediately. The principal reason why he hesitates to come out on that side absolutely is that he perceives he can still be of use to fellow Christians by saying: "I am torn between the two: I desire to depart and be with Christ, which is better by far; but it is more necessary for you that I remain in the body" (Phil. 1:23–24). I am not very prone to deep depressions. But when they come, I like to take time to meditate at length on, say, Revelation 4–5 and 21–22. To think about God and the salvation he has provided, to develop a certain longing for the new heaven and the new earth, to reestablish the Christian's goal, proves immensely restorative. Perhaps it is an index of our failure in this regard that modern Christian choruses and hymnody do not capture this theme. The following hymn, by James Montgomery (1771–1854), has some rather quaint lines in it, but it captures an entire way of looking at this life and the next that the modern generation of Christians, especially (but not exclusively) in the West, has largely abandoned:

For ever with the Lord!
Amen, so let it be!
Life from the dead is in that word,
'Tis immortality.
Here in the body pent,
Absent from Him I roam,
Yet nightly pitch my moving tent
A day's march nearer home.

My Father's house on high,
Home of my soul, how near
At times to faith's foreseeing eye
Thy golden gates appear!
Ah! then my spirit faints
To reach the land I love,
The bright inheritance of saints,
Jerusalem above.

For ever with the Lord!
Father, if 'tis Thy will,
The promise of that faithful word
E'en here to me fulfil.
Be Thou at my right hand,
Then I can never fail;
Uphold Thou me and I shall stand;
Fight and I must prevail.

So when my latest breath
Shall rend the veil in twain,
By death I shall escape from death
And life eternal gain.
That resurrection-word,
That shout of victory;
Once more, For ever with the Lord!
Amen! So let it be!

This is cast in the first person, but the same vision that supports believers who contemplate their own death is also of immense comfort to those who are bereaved—the point made at the end of the previous chapter.

2. The entailment of this confidence is the firm refusal to rely on other hopes. "Do not put your trust in princes, in human beings, who cannot save. When their spirit departs, they return to the ground; on that very day their plans come to nothing" (Ps. 146:3). Do not put your confidence in princes, politicians, social tinkerers, economists, academics, gurus,

legislators, administrators, preachers, psychologists—they all are mortal, they all are limited and fallible, and they all will die.

That is not to say that we cannot gain much help from the best of people in all of these categories. But in the final analysis, do not trust them, do not pin your hopes and expectations to them. Rather, "Blessed are those whose help is the God of Jacob, whose hope is in the LORD their God. He is the Maker of heaven and earth, the sea, and everything in them—he remains faithful forever" (Ps. 146:5–6). That is a moral decision; in the light of what the Bible says about God and this world, it is the only rational decision. It is a commitment to which we must return again and again.

3. For the believer, the time of death becomes far less daunting a factor when seen in the light of eternity. We have already seen that, granted we live under a sentence of death, the exact timing seems less foreboding a subject than it does for people who feel that threescore years and ten are their due. But now something more positive can be introduced. Although death remains an enemy, an outrage, a sign of judgment, a reminder of sin, and a formidable opponent, it is, from another perspective, the portal through which we pass to consummated life. We pass through death, and death dies. Christians whose hope is genuinely lodged in what it means to be "for ever with the Lord" cannot contemplate what the world would see as a premature death with the same indignation. Indeed, from one perspective, such death is a great blessing.

Isaiah certainly thought so. At the outbreak of judgment and violence, the death of the godly may be a sign that God is sparing them the temporal judgments he is about to inflict: "The righteous perish, and no one takes it to heart; the devout are taken away, and no one understands that the righteous are taken away to be spared from evil. Those who walk uprightly enter into peace; they find rest as they lie in death" (Isa. 57:1–2). Elsewhere, the removal by death of prophetic voices can be a sign of judgment on a nation.

I know these factors do not address every situation. I know that the pain of personal loss experienced by the bereaved is not reduced by assurance that the departed is better off. Nor does Isaiah's insight apply in every situation. My sole point is that, when the Christian contemplates a "premature death," his own, her own, or someone else's, the constraints of the Christian hope forbid us from thinking that something profoundly unfair has taken place. Death is coming; leave the timing to God.

4. Christians who have no answers to why this or that has happened can afford to take the long view. The God they know is a just God; he will ensure that justice is done, and seen to be done. That means they do not always have ready answers; they have, instead, a reasonable confidence

in One who does have the answers and the power to impose them. God will have the last word; we dare to wait for that.

Is this one of the reasons why the Book of Job has a "happy ending"?

Questions for Further Study

1. Summarize some biblical passages that present the kingdom of God as already present.
2. Summarize some biblical passages that present the kingdom of God as still to be consummated in the future.
3. What happens when one side of this balance (i.e., the balance presupposed by the combination of the first two questions) is emphasized at the expense of the other? Can you give examples, drawn either from the New Testament or from the history of the church? [*Hint:* Some scholars argue that the Corinthian church held to *over*realized eschatology, and that the Thessalonian church held to *over*futuristic eschatology. On what grounds would they think this?]
4. What practical help can Jesus' parable of the weeds offer as we look around at evil and suffering in our world?
5. The promise of justice ultimately done and seen to be done strikes many unbelievers as an excuse, a "cop-out"; for Christians, it is a "given." (a) How should this concept be tied to the Christian virtues of faith and hope? (b) How should believers respond to unbelievers on this issue?
6. Can you think of, and summarize, other biblical passages than those treated in this chapter, that encourage Christians to look at this life from the vantage of the End?
7. What can you do to develop your own "homesickness for heaven"? What bearing does such a stance have on your views of evil and suffering?

9

Job

Mystery and Faith

Struggle as we may with various facets of the problem of evil and suffering, there are times when particularly virulent evil or horribly inequitable suffering strikes us as staggeringly irrational, unfair. Quite frequently this impression is driven home when we cannot see how to escape the lack of proportion between the massive suffering and the relative inoffensiveness of the afflicted party.

I know a woman who served as a productive missionary for some years in a Latin American country. She returned home to marry a graduate of a Bible college, a man she had known for some years who promised to return to the mission field with her. She had not been married to him for more than a few hours before she suspected she had married a monster. Although couching himself in pious language, he turned out to be psychologically brutal. He was an insecure little runt who publicly maintained a veneer of religious respectability, but who in the intimacy of his own home could live with himself only by savagely demeaning everything his wife did, said, and stood for.

The mission board caught on pretty quickly, and refused to send them out. Years passed, and the abuse worsened. The woman tried talking to friends and counselors; some of them simply sided with her husband and told her to try harder. Eventually she turned to drink; a couple of years later, she was a confirmed alcoholic, herself brutal with her two children. She hated herself, she hated her husband, and she hated God. Why had she gone through so much? She was, after all, simply trying to serve the Lord—fallibly, no doubt, but sincerely.

Of course, it would have been theologically correct to tell her that, whatever her husband was or did, she was still responsible for her own conduct. But she knew that, and hated herself because she found she could not cope. And in any case, this sort of reproach did not answer her question; it merely compounded her sense of guilt.

The book of Job has been interpreted in several quite different ways. This short chapter is not the place to go into the variations. But virtually all sides agree that this book's special contribution to the canon, and to the topic of evil and suffering, is its treatment of what most of us would call irrational evil, incoherent suffering. Such evil and suffering do not easily fit into any glib "solutions." We may remember lessons learned elsewhere in the Bible, but when we try to apply them here there are too many loose ends. The physical suffering, as bad as it is, is compounded in Job's mind because it does not make any sense. Consequently, it threatens to destroy his understanding of God and the world, and is therefore not only massively painful in its own right, but disorienting and confusing.

Job's Sufferings and Initial Reactions (Job 1–3)

The prologue of the book, as the first two chapters are usually called, pictures a man called Job, living in the land of Uz (1:1), possibly ancient Edom. Three times he is called "blameless and upright, a man who fears God and shuns evil" (1:8; cf. 1:2; 2:3). He is the father of seven sons and three daughters, and enormously wealthy to boot. At a time when wealth was measured by livestock, he owned seven thousand sheep, three thousand camels, five hundred yoke of oxen, and five hundred donkeys: he was "the greatest man among all the people of the East" (1:3).

Not only so, he was unquestionably godly, even to the point of offering preemptive sacrifices on behalf of his children: "Perhaps my children have sinned and cursed God in their hearts," he reasoned (1:5). This, we are told, was no passing fancy, no faddish piety; this "was Job's regular custom" (1:5).

Behind the scenes, unknown to Job, Satan enters into a wager with God. God has presented Job as the prime example of a human being who truly loves God and his ways: "he is blameless and upright, a man who fears God and shuns evil" (1:8). Satan remains unconvinced. He charges that God has so protected Job, so made him prosper, that Job's "piety" is no more than knowing what side his bread is buttered on. Piety so surrounded by security can't prove much: "stretch out your hand and strike everything he has," Satan taunts God, "and he will surely curse you to your face" (1:11).

God takes up the wager, with only one restriction: Job himself is not to be harmed. Satisfied, Satan leaves and so operates behind the scenes that the Sabeans carry off the oxen and donkeys and murder the servants; a raging fire devours the sheep and their shepherds; the Chaldeans form raiding parties and carry off the camels, killing the herders; and a storm destroys the house where his children are having a party, killing all ten of them.

"At this, Job got up and tore his robe and shaved his head. Then he fell to the ground in worship and said: 'Naked I came from my mother's womb, and naked I will depart. The LORD gave and the LORD has taken away; may the name of the LORD be praised.' In all this, Job did not sin by charging God with wrongdoing" (1:20–22).

Satan is still not convinced. When the Lord points out that Job has still retained his integrity, Satan replies, "Skin for skin! . . . A man will give all he has for his own life. But now stretch out your hand and strike his flesh and bones, and he will surely curse you to your face" (2:4–5). God takes up this challenge as well, but lays down one restriction: Job's life must be spared.

Not knowing what has gone on in the courts of heaven, Job finds himself afflicted with painful sores from the crown of his head to the soles of his feet. In complete degradation, he sits in the ash pit and scratches his scabs with a piece of broken pottery. To make his misery infinitely worse, his wife, whose suffering must be not much less than Job's, throws in the towel: "Are you still maintaining your integrity? Curse God and die!" (2:9). But Job rebukes her, and reasons, "Shall we accept good from God, and not trouble?"

The writer concludes: "In all this, Job did not sin in what he said" (2:10).

The prologue concludes by introducing Job's three friends, Eliphaz, Bildad, and Zophar, who hear of his suffering and agree "to go and sympathize with him and comfort him" (2:11). In the custom of the day, they display their distress by crying loudly, tearing their robes, and sprinkling dust on their heads. And then they do the wisest thing they could have done, certainly much wiser than all the speeches they will shortly deliver: for seven days and seven nights, they keep silence, awed by the depths of Job's misery.

That is the substance of the prologue. But the picture of Job in these two chapters, it is sometimes argued, is so much at variance with the picture of Job in the bulk of the book that it must have come from a different author. Perhaps someone added the great speeches to a fairly simple morality story; or perhaps someone added the morality story to the great flights of oratory recorded in the speeches. But such theories solve nothing, for *someone* put together the speeches with the prologue and epilogue, and if that person did not detect an insuperable difficulty, then why should we think that an original writer would find an insuperable difficulty? Such source theories, even if right, do not solve the theological problem: the book as we have it stands or falls as a literary whole, for that is the only form in which it has come down to us.

A more subtle explanation of the prologue has been advanced by Athalya Brenner.[1] She argues that both the prologue and the epilogue (42:7–17) are written with self-conscious irony. Although formally they uphold the assumption that good men should be healthy and wealthy, that righteousness "pays" even in this world, and that the final proof is in the closing verses where Job turns out to be better off than he was before he began his ordeal, in fact the writer is so extravagant in his presentation that one has to believe he has his tongue firmly jammed in his cheek. The stylized numbers—seven sons, three daughters, seven thousand sheep, and so forth—plus the repeated emphasis on Job's goodness (1:1, 8; 2:3), even the preemptive sacrifices, all attest that Job is so extravagantly good as to be unbelievable. It is far easier, Brenner argues, to see the prologue and epilogue as exercises in irony. The author is quietly mocking the standard approaches to obedience and blessing, disobedience and punishment. It turns out, therefore, that the prologue and epilogue are not in any tension with the bulk of the book: the author raises questions about unjust suffering, and leaves plenty of room for mystery—whether in the speeches of Job and his friends, including God's response, or in the profoundly ironic prologue and epilogue.

I confess I am thoroughly unconvinced by this creative interpretation. For a start, it guts the book of Job, robbing it of any punch. Unless Job really is a very good man and singularly blessed in every realm, the problem of unjust suffering is not made to stand out very acutely. Why blessings are poured out on Job in the end, instead of ending the story at 42:6 with Job's repentance but with no restoration to health and prosperity, I shall discuss at the end of this chapter.

Above all, Brenner finds evidence for irony in various stylized forms of expression. But stylized forms of expression can function in other ways than to signal irony. There is a sense in which the entire book is stylized, whether the prologue and epilogue, which are written in prose,

1. "Job the Pious? The Characterization of Job in the Narrative Framework of the Book," *Journal for the Study of the Old Testament* 43 (1989): 37–52.

or the speeches, written in poetry. The material is presented as a drama; the stylizations are part of the technique to heighten the tension and to present the case in the strongest possible form.

Indeed, as we shall see, the main themes of the prologue and the epilogue, taken at face value, enhance the significance of the book. But before summarizing some of these themes, it is important to pause at chapter 3.

Chapter 3 is the record of Job's first "speech" (the term sounds terribly formal and pompous for what is, in fact, a lament; but I shall use "speech" to refer to all the lengthy interchanges that run to the end of chap. 41). It is something of a transition. Like the rest of the speeches, it is written in poetry. Nevertheless, Job does not reply to the charges of his friends, nor does he yet challenge God to explain himself. Chapter 3 is Job's lament: like Jeremiah (20:14–18), he wishes he had never been born. "May the day of my birth perish, and the night that said, 'A boy is conceived!' That day—may it turn to darkness; may God above not care about it; may no light shine on it" (3:3–4).

Job's lament turns to the unanswerable "whys," but still more as lament than as angry indignation: "Why is light given to those in misery, and life to the bitter of soul, to those who long for death that does not come . . . ?" (3:20–21). "Why is life given to a man whose way is hidden, whom God has hedged in?" (3:23). Then follows a somewhat astonishing admission: "What I feared has come upon me; what I dreaded has happened to me. I have no peace, no quietness; I have no rest, but only turmoil" (3:25–26).

The stage is thus set for the interchanges between Job and his three friends. But before surveying them, it will prove useful to summarize some of the points the book has made so far.

1. The book of Job frankly insists that suffering falls within the sweep of God's sovereignty. The reader understands, as Job does not, that Job's afflictions owe everything to the exchange between God and Satan. Satan himself recognizes his limitations: he has to secure permission to afflict Job. He charges God with "putting a hedge" around Job to protect him. Only when God grants permission can Satan lash out at Job's family and livelihood. Even then he must secure separate permission to strike Job's body.

Intuitively, Job recognizes that nothing of the sort could have happened to him without God's sanction. He feels trapped, "hedged in"; but he sees that it is *God* who has hedged him in (3:23). All the while he has enjoyed a hedge around him, protecting him; now that it is gone, he feels hedged in. Even so, he does not rush to the conclusion that an enemy has done this outside God's sanction. Job asks, rhetorically, "Shall we accept good from God, and not trouble?" (2:10).

In short, all forms of dualism are radically rejected. Job will not resort to easy comfort about this not really being the will of God: it must be the work of Satan. Of course, it *was* the work of Satan. But in God's universe, even Satan's work cannot step outside the outermost boundaries of God's sovereignty. While that is what raises the problem, it is also what promises hope.

2. The emphasis on Job's goodness is meant to highlight the fact that there is such a thing as innocent suffering. This means more than that not all suffering is directly related to a specific sin; it means that some suffering in this world is not directly related to any sin. Undoubtedly one can posit indirect connections by appealing to other Scriptures about the fall and the universality of sin. But they do not rob the book of Job of the point being strongly emphasized: the link between suffering and retribution found in, say, Deuteronomy, Proverbs, and Romans, is never so mathematically rigid, so symmetrically precise, as to rule out the kind of suffering this book considers.

Intuitively, we know it is so. When a father rapes his six-year-old daughter, in what conceivable sense is the daughter "responsible"? Of course, her suffering is the result of sin—someone else's sin. But that is exactly what makes her the innocent victim. Doubtless she is not innocent on any absolute scale. Six-year-old girls cannot possibly be innocent on any absolute scale: they take after their parents. But what sin has the girl committed that makes her incestuous rape an appropriate "retribution"?

The losses Job faced were, on the natural plane, the result of a mixture of human malice (the Sabeans, the Chaldeans) and of natural disasters (the fire, the wind). But behind them stood Satan; and behind Satan stood God himself. In a theistic universe, it could scarcely be otherwise, if God is the God described in the Bible. Undoubtedly there were public renegades and socially revolting sinners who, we might have thought, deserved the reverses Job suffered. But they happened to Job, whom God himself puts forward as "blameless and upright, a man who fears God and shuns evil." Although the Bible insists that all sinners will (eventually) suffer, it does not insist that each instance of suffering is retribution for sin. Doubtless if this were not a fallen world, there would be no suffering; but just because it is a fallen world, it does not follow that there is no innocent suffering.

The book of Job will not let us off the hook: there is such a thing as innocent suffering.

3. The degree to which we struggle with this question is likely to be related to the extent of our own sufferings. That Job can say, "What I feared has come upon me; what I dreaded has happened to me" (3:25) is not a sign that he did not *really* trust God, and therefore he got what

he deserved: that would subvert the purpose of the entire book—in the third chapter, at that! The purpose of these words, rather, is to show that Job had already thought about these matters. He was no amateur in the things of God. He had thought enough about them to know that, from his own observations, from his own knowledge of God, he could not consider himself exempt from the possibility of disastrous loss. Such loss was what he feared. To that extent, he was prepared for it; probably that prepared mind was also one of the reasons why his initial responses are so entirely noble.

But thinking through the theology of suffering, and resolving in advance how you will respond, however praiseworthy the exercise, cannot completely prepare you for the shock of suffering itself. It is like jumping into a bitterly cold lake: you can brace yourself for the experience all day, but when you actually jump in the shock to your system will still snatch your breath away.

4. God does not blame us if in our suffering we frankly vent our despair and confess our loss of hope, our sense of futility, our lamentations about life itself. One cannot read chapter 3 without recalling that God will later excoriate the miserable comforters, but insist that Job himself said right things (42:7).

Of course, it is possible in grief and misery to say the wrong things, to say blasphemous things. Job's wife is not praised for her counsel: "Curse God and die!" (2:9). But within certain boundaries, yet to be explored, it is far better to be frank about our grief, candid in our despair, honest with our questions, than to suppress them and wear a public front of puffy piety. God knows our thoughts in any case. Whatever "resolution" the book of Job provides turns on Job's questions and God's responses. Without the questions, there would have been no responses.

5. Already the theme of mystery has intruded. Neither at the beginning of the affliction nor at the end does God tell Job about Satan's challenge and his own response. Indeed, had he done so, the purpose of the affliction would have been subverted. God's intent (the readers know) is to show that a human being can love God, fear God, and pursue righteousness without receiving any prompt reward. This pursuit of God is therefore independent of material comfort; it may be in defiance of material comfort. Satan's thesis, that all religious interest is ultimately grounded in self-interest, or worse, in mercenary commitment, is thus shown to be false. But Job himself is not permitted to see this dimension to his suffering. As far as he is concerned, he faces inscrutable mystery.

6. That is why Job's initial lament, and his later questions, must be placed within the right framework. At no point does Job abandon faith in God; at no point does he follow his wife's advice to curse God. It is

precisely because he knows God to be there, and to be loving and just, that he has such a hard time understanding such injustice. Job wrestles with God, he is indignant with God, he challenges God to come before him and provide some answers; but all his struggles are the struggles of a believer. That is why Job can be praised, by God himself, for saying the right things: at least he spoke within the right framework. His miserable friends did not. We shall have occasion to return to this point in the next section, to learn what it tells us today.

Job's Plaintive Outrage and His Miserable Comforters (Job 4–31)

Job's lament is all the encouragement his three friends need to break their silence. The way the drama is set out, each of them—Eliphaz, Bildad, and Zophar—have a go at Job, trying to correct his theology and lead him to repentance. After each speaks, Job himself replies. Then the entire cycle is repeated, and starts to be repeated yet again. The third cycle sputters out with a short contribution from Bildad (25:1–6); Zophar never does contribute to the third round. By this time, Job is really indignant, and makes a lengthy speech (chaps. 26–31) that silences his interlocutors without convincing them.

Job and his friends represent deeply entrenched and opposed positions on the questions surrounding Job's sufferings. To simplify a bit, we may summarize their positions.

1. *Job's friends offer glib answers and a condemning spirit.* The heart of their theological position is summed up by Eliphaz's question: "Consider now: Who, being innocent, has ever perished? Where were the upright ever destroyed? As I have observed, those who plow evil and those who sow trouble reap it" (4:7–8).

2. *Job responds with self-justification and hard questions.* He is guilty of nothing that can justify such suffering. The readers know this to be true: Job is suffering because God is demonstrating his servant's spiritual integrity to Satan, not because Job is being punished.

But to feel the weight of their arguments, we need to follow the line of some of their speeches. Eliphaz begins with a sly swipe at Job's distress. After all, Job has offered advice and help to many others who have suffered. "But now trouble comes to you, and you are discouraged; it strikes you, and you are dismayed" (4:5). The charge is more than mere inconsistency, as the next verse shows: there is an ironic suggestion that Job is guilty of rank hypocrisy. "Should not your piety be your confidence and your blameless ways your hope?" (4:6). By itself, the question could be taken as a form of encouragement, a gentle compliment. But the next verses, already cited, show it is all a trap: "Who, being innocent, has ever perished?" And so the question itself becomes rather nasty sarcasm.

Reason alone is not enough for Eliphaz. He claims he learned the truths he enunciates in a vision of the night. The form that appeared to him asked, "Can a mortal be more righteous than God? Can human beings be more pure than their Maker?" (4:17). In itself, of course, the question points to something important: we need to exercise humility when we approach God on these difficult questions. But Eliphaz applies it more strongly. Fools and reprobates are destroyed by God: he is so holy that he devours them while they scramble around in futility. "But if I were you," suffering as you are, Job, "I would appeal to God; I would lay my cause before him" (5:8). I would recognize him as the One who is also capable of restoring his people. I would shut my mouth, confess my sin, and plead for his deliverance. "Blessed are those whom God corrects; so do not despise the discipline of the Almighty. For he wounds, but he also binds up; he injures, but his hands also heal. From six calamities he will rescue you; in seven no harm will touch you" (5:17–19). In other words, Job, if you confess your sin, and plead God's goodness, you will find yourself restored to your former comforts. "We have examined this, and it is true," Eliphaz rather grandly proclaims. "So hear it and apply it to yourself" (5:27).

But Job will not be put off so easily. For a start, he resents his friends' lack of compassion, their winking condescension. "Anyone who withholds kindness from a friend forsakes the fear of the Almighty. But my brothers are as undependable as intermittent streams, as the streams that overflow" (6:14–15). Job can see through his friends' unexpressed fears: if the universe is not as ordered as they would like to think it is, then *they themselves cannot count on security:* "Now you too have proved to be of no help; you see something dreadful and are afraid" (6:21).

His plea is emotional, and pitiable: "But now be so kind as to look at me. Would I lie to your face [i.e., by hiding sins]? Relent, do not be unjust; reconsider, for my integrity is at stake" (6:28–29).

Job reviews his sufferings again. All he wants is to die before he is tempted to deny the words of the Holy One (6:10). Eventually he turns to God and begs for pity: "Remember, O God, that my life is but a breath; my eyes will never see happiness again" (7:7). But he is not willing to concede that what he is suffering is only fair: "I will not keep silent; I will speak out in the anguish of my spirit, I will complain in the bitterness of my soul" (7:11). He begs God to back off, to let him die; his days have no meaning. Why pick on me? he asks, in effect. Why pick on any man in this way (7:17–19)?

Job does not claim sinless perfection. He simply argues that any conceivable sin he may have committed does not justify being made a target of the Almighty. "If I have sinned, what have I done to you, you who watch over us all? Why have you made me your target? Have I become a burden to you?" (7:20).

All this is too much for Bildad. He cannot rise to the sly poetry of Eliphaz, nor claim any midnight vision in which to ground the authority of his opinion. He simply reiterates, forcefully, the traditional answers. "How long will you say such things?" he asks Job. "Your words are a blustering wind. Does God pervert justice?" (8:2–3).

That is the nub of the problem. Job is so sure he has suffered undeservedly that he is only a whisker from charging God with injustice. It must be, rather, that God is just, and his justice prevails. If you suffer, it is because you deserve it; on the other hand, Bildad assures Job, "if you are pure and upright, even now he will rouse himself on your behalf and restore you to your prosperous state" (8:6). Any fool can see the implication: that God has not restored Job to his rightful place proves that Job must be impure, unrighteous. The only alternative is that God is unjust; and that is unthinkable.

With Bildad's fundamental assumption—that God is just—Job has no quarrel. "Indeed, I know that this is true" (9:2), he protests; he has never denied it. "But how can mere mortals prove their innocence before God?" In its context, this question does not ask how a mortal can be pure or holy before God, but how a mortal can be *vindicated* before God. Take it as a given that God is just, Job says. But my problem is that in this case I too am just; I am suffering unfairly. But how can I prove it to God? How can I be vindicated before him? "Though they wished to dispute with him, they could not answer him one time out of a thousand. His wisdom is profound, his power is vast. Who has resisted him and come out unscathed?" (9:3–4).

Job's problem is not that God is simply too distant, but that Job could not win—even though he is quite certain he is suffering innocently. (And again, his readers know he is right on the latter score!) Job himself surveys some of the evidence that attests God's greatness and concludes: "How then can I dispute with him? How can I find words to argue with him? Though I were innocent, I could not answer him; I could only plead with my Judge for mercy" (9:14–15). Indeed, all the references to God's power can be read another way, Job argues. "Even if I summoned him and he responded, I do not believe he would give me a hearing. He would crush me with a storm and multiply my wounds for no reason. He would not let me catch my breath but would overwhelm me with misery. If it is a matter of strength, he is mighty! And if it is a matter of justice, who can challenge him?" (9:16–19). The evidence of Job's misery suggests that God is sovereign, all right—and cruel. God is so sovereign that even Job's speech would be constrained in any trial: "Even if I were innocent, my mouth would condemn me; if I were blameless, it would pronounce me guilty" (9:20).

Job is not denying that God is sovereign; far from it. "When a land falls into the hands of the wicked," Job argues, it is God himself who "blindfolds its judges. If it is not he, then who is it?" (9:24). Not for Job some glib theodicy about God simply letting nature take its course, about God not being strong enough or farseeing enough or powerful enough to bring about the good. God is so sovereign that he brings about the bad as well as the good. And that is just the problem: if I also believe that God is just, how can I answer him? "It is all the same; that is why I say, 'He destroys both the blameless and the wicked'" (9:22).

So Job returns some of the vitriol to his friends. No matter how pure he is, his friends would find him impure: their position demands it. "Even if I washed myself with soap and my hands with cleansing powder, you would plunge me into a slime pit so that even my clothes would detest me" (9:30–31).

Again Job turns from his friends to address God, speaking out in the bitterness of his soul (10:1). "Does it please you to oppress me, to spurn the work of your hands, while you smile on the plans of the wicked?" (10:3), he asks. "Are your days like those of a mortal or your years like those of a human being, that you must search out my faults and probe after my sin—though you know that I am not guilty and that no one can rescue me from your hand?" (10:5–7). The truth of the matter, Job insists, is that God gave him life, showed him kindness, and providentially watched over him (10:12), only to set him up for this tragedy. Why bring Job to birth in the first place if God knew he was to end up this way? "Why then did you bring me out of the womb? I wish I had died before any eye saw me" (10:18).

Zophar weighs in. He paints a picture of God in grandiose and transcendent terms. Job's talk, in his view, is appalling. How dare any mortal tell God, "My beliefs are flawless and I am pure in your sight" (11:4)? Job has been begging God to speak, to provide an explanation. "Oh, how I wish that God would speak," Zophar agrees, "that he would open his lips against you" (11:5). God is so holy and transcendent, and Job so flawed and sinful, that Job's suffering is in fact much less than the measure of his guilt. Job's sin is so great God has forgotten some of it. Can't Job concede that this unfathomably great God cannot be duped or tricked? "Surely he recognizes deceivers; and when he sees evil, does he not take note?" (11:11).

Job replies with scorn: "Doubtless you are the people, and wisdom will die with you!" (12:2). He sees through them: "Those who are at ease have contempt for misfortune as the fate of those whose feet are slipping" (12:5). "If only you would be altogether silent! For you, that would be wisdom" (13:5). If they are going to rabbit on with such rubbish, they should return to the only wisdom they have displayed so far, the wisdom of the first seven days: they should shut up.

Job reiterates several points. None can escape this God; there is plenty of evidence for suffering that has nothing to do with punishment ("Mortals, born of woman, are of few days and full of trouble," 14:1); Job himself is innocent, and is certain that in a fair trial he would be vindicated (13:18).

The second cycle of speeches begins, and then the third. There is not space here to survey them, nor to detail Job's responses to his "miserable comforters" (16:2). But several things must be said in summary.

1. Job's friends have a tight theology with no loose ends. Suffering is understood exclusively in terms of punishment or chastening. There is no category for innocent suffering: in their understanding, such a suggestion besmirches the integrity of the Almighty.

2. Although they are quick to defend God and say many wonderful things about him, their arguments are cast in tones so condescending to Job that one begins to lose patience with them. There is very little hint of compassion, empathy, or honest grief. The defense of God can be unbearably hard.

3. Job's arguments must not be confused with the atheism of Bertrand Russell, the challenge of David Hume, the theological double-talk of Don Cupitt, or the poetic defiance: "I am the master of my fate! I am the captain of my soul!" Job's speeches are the anguish of a man who knows God, who wants to know him better, who never once doubts the existence of God, who remains convinced, at bottom, of the justice of God—but who cannot make sense of these entrenched beliefs in the light of his own experience.

That is why, in the midst of his confusion and self-justification, Job utters some remarkably assured statements of faith. He is so sure of his case that he wishes he could find someone to arbitrate between himself and God (9:33–35). Of course, this is God's universe, so he can't; but the Christian cannot read these words without thinking of the mediatorial role of Jesus. Nor does Job become apostate: "Though he slay me, yet will I hope in him; I will surely defend my ways to his face. Indeed, this will turn out for my deliverance, for no godless person would dare come before him!" (13:15–16). He is so sure of ultimate vindication that he can say, "But [God] knows the way that I take; when he has tested me, I will come forth as gold" (23:10). However the difficult verses in 19:25–27 be translated,[2] the least they affirm is that Job is absolutely confident in his final vindication—by God himself.

2. For adequate discussion of the difficulties, see John E. Hartley, *The Book of Job*, NICOT (Grand Rapids: Eerdmans, 1988), 292–97.

4. The final lengthy speech of Job (26:1–31:40) reiterates many of the themes already developed, but it reaches a new intensity of bitterness. Now Job is not satisfied with hints: he openly charges God with injustice, and he almost savagely defends his integrity: "As surely as God lives, who has denied me justice, the Almighty, who has made my life bitter, as long as I have life within me, the breath of God in my nostrils, my lips will not say anything wicked, and my tongue will not utter lies. I will never admit you are in the right; till I die, I will not deny my integrity. I will maintain my innocence and never let go of it; my conscience will not reproach me as long as I live" (27:2–6). Chapters 29–31 are a moving recital of all the godly things that made up Job's life in the days before he was afflicted. They bear the most careful reading: would to God I could claim half so much. Job has been honest, generous, disciplined; he rescued the poor, helped the blind, comforted those who mourned; he made a covenant with his eyes "not to look lustfully at a virgin" (31:1); he was host to countless strangers; he made sure he never rejoiced over the misfortune of another; he never trusted in his own wealth. He frankly feared God (31:23). And he is utterly determined to maintain that his own integrity totally precludes the possibility that his sufferings constitute punishment for sin. As far as he is concerned, confession of sin that he has not committed, just to satisfy his friends and perhaps win some sort of reprieve, would itself be sinful. His integrity is too important to him for that.

5. Job is therefore not looking for a merely intellectual answer, a merely theological argument. He wants personal vindication by God himself. He wants God to appear and give an account of what He is doing. The drama does not concern an agnostic professor of philosophy; it concerns a man who knows God, who loves and fears God, and whose utter assurance of his own integrity drives him to long for a personal encounter with God that will not merely provide "answers" but will also vindicate the sufferer.

6. It is important to glance ahead a little. The "three men stopped answering Job, because he was righteous in his own eyes" (32:1). They were at an impasse: they could make sense of his suffering only by insisting on his guilt, and he kept insisting on his innocence. But God, after disclosing himself to Job, says to Eliphaz, "I am angry with you and your two friends, because you have not spoken of me what is right, as my servant Job has" (42:7). Indeed, Job must offer sacrifice and pray for them.

This is remarkable. The three miserable comforters thought they were defending God, and he charges them with saying the wrong things about him. Job defends his own integrity so virulently that he steps over the line now and then and actually charges God with injustice, yet God insists that his servant Job has spoken what is right. Of course, this does not mean that Job's speeches have been entirely without fault. As we shall see, God charges Job with darkening his counsel "with words without knowledge" (38:2). In the last section of this chapter I shall explore more fully in which ways Job is right and his three friends are wrong. But under any reading of God's vindication of Job's discourses, room is made for innocent suffering; a simple theory of retributive justice—punishment proportionate to sin—is inadequate to explain some of the hard cases.

Job and Elihu (Job 32–37)

Chapters 32–37 are among the most interesting, and the most difficult, in the book. They start off by raising our expectations. Elihu, not mentioned until this point, has kept his peace throughout the debate, because the other participants are older than he: custom demanded that age take precedence. But now they fall silent, and Elihu, whose wrath has been stoked by the debate, declares himself angry with both Job and his three friends. He is angry with the three friends, "because they had found no way to refute Job, and yet had condemned him" (32:3), and he is angry with Job "for justifying himself rather than God" (32:2). And so his lengthy contribution begins.

The remarkable thing about Elihu's speech is that at the end of the book it is neither praised nor condemned. Some think it adds little, that it simply reiterates the sentiments of the three miserable comforters (e.g., 34:11), and therefore that he *ought* to be condemned if they are. Some conclude that these chapters must therefore have been added by a later editor.

But a more sympathetic reading of Elihu teases out his contribution, and shows how this young man avoids the opposing pitfalls into which both Job and his comforters have fallen. Perhaps one of the reasons why Elihu does not get a very sympathetic reading in some circles is that he is patently an arrogant and pretentious young man. Probably he is a great wise man in the making, but still far too full of himself and too certain of his opinions. Nevertheless, his main themes prepare the way for the central thrusts of the answer that God himself ultimately gives. If he is not praised, it is because his contribution is eclipsed by what God himself says; if he is not criticized, it is because he says nothing amiss.

We may summarize his argument this way:

1. Elihu begins with a rather lengthy apology for speaking to his seniors (32:6–22). Among the factors that compel him to speak is his conviction (as he says to Job's three friends) that "not one of you has

proved Job wrong; none of you has answered his arguments" (32:12). This does not mean he thinks Job is entirely right, as we shall see; but Elihu has carefully distanced himself from the theology of the "miserable comforters."

2. When Elihu turns to Job, he first rebukes him for impugning God's justice (33:8ff.). Job may be innocent (Elihu will come to that in due course), but that does not give him the right to charge God with injustice. There is a sense in which Job himself has been snookered by a simplistic doctrine of mathematically precise retribution. The major difference between Job and his three friends is not their underlying views of retribution, but their views of Job's guilt or innocence. Because Job is convinced he is innocent, he is prepared to skirt the view that God himself is guilty. Elihu will not have it: "But I tell you, in this you are not right" (33:12).

The first reason why Job is not right is that "God is greater than any mortal" (33:12). By this Elihu does not mean to say that greatness provides an excuse for wrongdoing, but that God may well have some purposes and perspectives in mind of which Job knows nothing. However much Job insists he is innocent, he must therefore put a guard on his tongue and refrain from making God guilty.

3. The second thing Elihu says to Job is that God speaks more often and in more ways than Job acknowledges. "Why do you complain to him that he responds to no one's words?" (33:13). The truth of the matter, Elihu insists, is that "God does speak—now one way, now another—though no one perceives it" (33:14). He speaks in revelation: in dreams and visions (33:15–18). *But God may also speak in the language of pain* (33:19ff.). This is an advance on the argument between Job and his friends. Here is a chastening use of suffering that may be independent of some particular sin. Its purpose may be preventative: it can stop a person from slithering down the slope to destruction.

4. In chapter 34, Elihu is so concerned to defend the justice of God that his rhetoric becomes a little overheated. On the positive side, Elihu is determined to stop Job from charging God with injustice. The proper response to suffering is to accept it: God cannot possibly do wrong. By speaking the way he has, Job has added rebellion to his sin (34:37); "scornfully he claps his hands among us and multiplies his words against God."

If Elihu is at times dangerously close to siding with the three miserable comforters, it is here. Certainly he has not empathetically entered into Job's suffering, or tried to fathom the anguish that leads Job to defend his integrity in such extravagant terms. But Elihu is right to defend the justice of God, and he has advanced the discussion by suggesting that Job's greatest sin may not be something he said or did *before* the suffering started, but the rebellion he is displaying *in* the suffering. Even so, that does not explain the genesis of the suffering. It may, however, prepare Job to be a little more attentive to listen to God when God finally does speak.

In chapter 35, Elihu expressly disavows that Job is innocent. But unlike Eliphaz (22:5–9), he does not compose a list of sins Job must have committed, but challenges Job's fundamental presumption. To take but one example: Job assumes that when people are oppressed they cry to God for help, and charges that God does not answer. Not so, insists Elihu: one is far more likely to find people crying out "under a load of oppression" and vaguely pleading "for relief from the arm of the powerful" (35:9), *but still not praying*. They want relief, but do not turn to God and pray. They cry for freedom, "[but] no one says, 'Where is God my Maker . . . ?'" (35:10). God does not listen to such empty pleas (35:13). What makes Job think, then, that God will answer him when the assumption underlying his entire approach to God is that God owes him an answer, and may well be guilty of injustice (35:14–16)?

5. In the last two chapters devoted to Elihu (chaps. 36–37), several themes come together, and Elihu begins to appear in more compassionate guise. The burden of the passage is this: whatever else may be said about the problem of evil and suffering, the justice of God must be the "given": "I will ascribe justice to my Maker," Elihu pledges (36:3). But God is not malicious. He does care for his people. Therefore the proper response to suffering we cannot fathom is faith and perseverance; the response to avoid is bitterness (for it is the godless who harbor resentment, 36:13). Job is in danger here: "Beware of turning to evil, which you seem to prefer to affliction" (36:21)—that is, Job must not turn to evil as a way of alleviating his suffering. Be patient, Elihu is saying; "those who suffer [God] delivers in [literally through] their suffering; he speaks to them in their affliction. He is wooing you from the jaws of distress to a spacious place free from restriction, to the comfort of your table laden with choice food" (36:15–16). Be patient; it is better to be a chastened saint than a carefree sinner.

Job and God (Job 38:1–42:6)

Finally God himself speaks, answering Job out of the storm (chaps. 38–41). "Who is this that obscures my plans with words without knowledge? Prepare to defend yourself; I will question you, and you shall answer me" (38:2–3). There follows question after question, each designed to remind Job of the kinds of things he cannot do, and that only God can. "Where were you when I laid the earth's foundation? Tell me, if you understand" (38:4). "Have you ever given orders to the morning, or shown the dawn its place . . . ?" (38:12). "Have you entered the store-houses of the snow or seen the storehouses of the hail, which I reserve for times of trouble, for days of war and battle?" (38:22–23). "Can you bind the chains of the Pleiades? Can you loosen Orion's belt? Can you bring forth the constellations in their seasons or lead out the Bear with its cubs?" (38:31–32). "Do you hunt the prey for the lioness and satisfy the hunger of the lions when they crouch in their dens or lie in wait in a thicket? Who provides food for the raven when its young cry out to God and wander about for lack of food?" (38:39–41). God then goes on to describe some of the more spectacular features of the mountain goat, the wild donkey, the ox, the ostrich, the horse, the hawk, the eagle. "Will the one who contends with the Almighty correct him? Let him who ac-cuses God answer him!" (40:2).

Job had wanted an interview with the Almighty. He had, as it were, sworn an affidavit demanding that the Almighty appear and put his indictment in writing (31:35). But God's defense wasn't quite what Job had in mind. At the first pause, Job answers, "I am unworthy—how can I reply to you? I put my hand over my mouth. I spoke once, but I have no answer—twice, but I will say no more" (40:4–5).

But God hasn't finished yet. "Prepare to defend yourself; I will question you, and you shall answer me" (40:7). Then come the most blistering questions: "Would you discredit my justice? Would you condemn me to justify yourself? Do you have an arm like God's, and can your voice thunder like his? Then adorn yourself with glory and splendor, and clothe yourself in honor and majesty. Unleash the fury of your wrath, look at all who are proud and bring them low, look at all who are proud and humble them, crush the wicked where they stand. Bury them all in the dust together; shroud their faces in the grave. Then I myself will admit to you that your own right hand can save you" (40:8–14).

It is important to recognize that God does not here charge Job with sins that have brought on his suffering. He does not respond to the "whys" of Job's suffering, nor does he challenge Job's defense of his own integrity. The reason he calls Job on the carpet is not because of Job's justification of himself, but because of Job's willingness to condemn God in order to justify himself. In other words, God does not here "answer" Job's questions about the problem of evil and suffering, *but he makes it unambiguously clear what answers are not acceptable in God's universe.*

The rest of chapter 40 and all of chapter 41 find God asking more rhetorical questions. Can Job capture and subdue the behemoth (40:15ff.) and the leviathan (41:1ff.)? These two beasts may be the hippopota-mus and the crocodile, respectively, but they probably also represent primordial cosmic powers that sometimes break out against God. The argument, then, is that if Job is to charge God with injustice, he must do so from the secure stance of his own superior justice; and if he cannot subdue these beasts, let alone the cosmic forces they represent, he does not enjoy such a stance, and is therefore displaying extraordinary arrogance to call God's justice into question.

Job's response must be quoted in full (42:2–6), along with two or three explanatory asides: "I know that you can do all things," Job tells God, "no purpose of yours can be thwarted. You asked, 'Who is this that obscures my plans without knowledge?' [38:2]. Surely I spoke of things I did not understand, things too wonderful for me to know. You said, 'Listen now, and I will speak; I will question you, and you shall answer me' [38:3; 40:7]. My ears had heard of you but now my eyes have seen you [i.e., Job has come to have a far clearer understanding of God than he had before]. Therefore I despise myself and repent in dust and ashes."

What shall we make of this exchange between God and Job?

Many doubtful interpretations have been put forward by various writers. Because God refers to so many natural phenomena, one writer argues that a major purpose of God's speech is to tell Job that the beauty of the world must become for him an anodyne to human suffering, a kind of aesthetic aspirin. When one basks in the world's beauty, one's problems become petty, "because they dissolve within the larger plan" of the harmony of the universe.[3] But to someone suffering intensely, the beauty of the world can just as easily become a brutal contrast that actually intensifies the suffering. Worse, it does not dissolve pain; rather, it is in danger of "dissolving" the sufferer in some kind of pantheistic sense of the fitness of things. This is surely a massive misunderstanding of God's response. Not once does God minimize the reality of Job's suffering.

Others, such as George Bernard Shaw, simply mock God's answer. Job wants an answer as to why he is suffering, and the best that God can do is brag about making snowflakes and crocodiles. A contemporary author like Elie Wiesel, writing in the aftermath of the Holocaust, holds that Job should have pressed God further. Doubtless Job needed to repent of his attitude, but he still should have pressed God for an answer: Why do the righteous suffer?

Both of these approaches misunderstand the book rather badly. They have this in common: they assume that everything that takes place in God's universe *ought* to be explained to us. They assume that God owes us an explanation, that there cannot possibly be any good reason for

3. So Robert Gordis, *The Book of God and Man: A Study of Job* (Chicago: University of Chicago Press, 1965), 133, 304.

God not to tell us everything we want to know immediately. They assume that God Almighty should be more interested in giving us explanations than in being worshiped and trusted.

The burden of God's response to Job is twofold. The first emphasis we have already noted: Job has "obscured God's plans" by trying to justify himself at the expense of condemning God; and Job is in no position to do that. "God's speeches show Job that his lowly station point was not the appropriate place from which to judge whether cosmic orders were sufficiently askew to justify the declaration 'let there be darkness.'"[4] The second emphasis is implicit: if there are so many things that Job does not understand, why should he so petulantly and persistently demand that he understand his own suffering? *There are some things you will not understand, for you are not God.*

That is why Job's answer is so appropriate. He does not say, "Ah, at last I understand!" but rather, "I repent." He does not repent of sins that have allegedly brought on the suffering; he repents of his arrogance in impugning God's justice, he repents of the attitude whereby he simply demands an answer, as if such were owed him. He repents of not having known God better: "My ears had heard of you but now my eyes have seen you. Therefore I . . . repent" (42:5–6).

To those who do not know God, to those who insist on being God, this outcome will never suffice. Those who do know God come in time to recognize that it is better to know God and to trust God than to claim the rights of God.

Job teaches us that, at least in this world, there will always remain some mysteries to suffering. He also teaches us to exercise faith—not blind, thoughtless submission to an impersonal status quo, but faith in the God who has graciously revealed himself to us.

Job's Happy Ending (Job 42:7–16)

These verses may be divided into two parts. The first, which we have already glanced at, reports God's wrath with Eliphaz and his two friends for not speaking of God what was right, as Job did (42:7–8). They are required to offer sacrifice to God, and Job, whom they have despised and abused, must pray for them, for God will accept his prayers for them (and, by implication, not their own!).

In the second part (vv. 10–17), after Job prays for his friends, the Lord makes him prosperous again. His siblings and acquaintances gather

4. Stuart Lasine, "Bird's-eye and Worm's-eye Views of Justice in the Book of Job," *Journal for the Study of the Old Testament* 42 (1988): 344.

around him and provide gifts, presumably to help him start up again. He sires another family, seven more sons and three more daughters, and gains herds twice the size of what he had before. No women were more beautiful than his daughters, and Job left them an inheritance along with their brothers—further evidence of Job's compassionate and enlightened treatment of those traditionally squeezed to the periphery of life (cf. chap. 31). He lived to a ripe old age, seeing his children and their children to the fourth generation. Eventually he died, "old and full of years"—an epitaph reserved for the choicest or most favored of God's servants (Abraham [Gen. 25:8], Isaac [Gen. 35:29], David [1 Chron. 29:28], and Jehoiada the priest [2 Chron. 24:15]).

If some critics are displeased with God's answer to Job out of the storm, even more are incensed by this "happy ending." The story, they argue, should have ended with Job's repentance. Whether he was restored is irrelevant; in any case it is untrue to the experience of many, who suffer at length without reprieve. To end the story this way makes the doctrine of retribution basically right after all. The conclusion is therefore anticlimactic at best, contradictory at worst.

This is, I think, a shallow reading of the text. Perhaps the following reflections will help unpack the purpose of this conclusion a little:

1. We must beware of our own biases. One of the reasons why many people are dissatisfied with this ending is because in the contemporary literary world ambiguity in moral questions is universally revered, while moral certainty is almost as universally despised. The modern mood enjoys novels and plays where the rights and wrongs get confused, where every decision is a mixture of right and wrong, truth and error, where heroes and antiheroes reverse their roles.

Why this infatuation with ambiguity? It is regarded as more mature. Clear-cut answers are written off as immature. The pluralism of our age delights in moral ambiguity—but only as long as it costs nothing. Devotion to contemporary moral ambiguity is extraordinarily self-centered. It demands freedom from God so that it can do whatever it wants. But when the suffering starts, the same self-centered focus on *my* world and *my* interests, rather ironically, wants God to provide answers of sparkling clarity.

2. Throughout his excruciating suffering, Job has demonstrated that he serves the Lord out of a pure heart. True, he has said some stupid things and has been rebuked; but at no point does he simply curse God and turn his back on him. Even his demand that God present himself before Job and give an answer is the cry of a believer seeking to find out what on earth God is doing. Even while sitting in the ash pit, Job trusts God enough to express extraordinary confidence in him, and for no ulterior motive.

In that sense, God has won his wager with the devil. Job may utter words that darken God's counsel, but he does not lose his integrity or abandon his God. Is it therefore surprising that there should be full reconciliation between God and Job? And if the wager has been won, is there any reason for Job's afflictions to continue?

3. No matter how happy the ending, nothing can remove the suffering itself. The losses Job faced would always be with him. A happy ending is better than a miserable one, but it does not transform the suffering he endured into something less than suffering. A survivor of the Holocaust has not suffered less because he ultimately settles into a comfortable life in Los Angeles.

4. The book of Job has no interest in praising mystery without restraint. All biblical writers insist that to fear the Lord ultimately leads to abundant life. If this were not so, to fear the Lord would be stupid and masochistic. The book does not disown all forms of retribution; rather, it disowns simplistic, mathematically precise, and instant applications of the doctrine of retribution. It categorically rejects any formula that affirms that the righteous always prosper and the wicked are always destroyed. There may be other reasons for suffering; rewards (of blessing or of destruction) may be long delayed; knowledge of God is its own reward.

Job still does not have all the answers; he still knows nothing about the wager between God and Satan. He must simply trust God that something far greater was at stake than his own personal happiness. But he has stopped hinting that God is unjust; he has come to know God better; and he enjoys the Lord's favor in rich abundance once again.

5. The blessings that Job experiences at the end are not cast as rewards that he has earned by his faithfulness under suffering. The epilogue simply describes the blessings as the Lord's free gift. The Lord is not nasty or capricious. He may for various reasons withdraw his favor, but his love endures forever.

In that sense, the epilogue is the Old Testament equivalent to the New Testament anticipation of a new heaven and a new earth. God is just, and will be seen to be just. This does *not* smuggle mathematical retribution in through the back door. Rather, it is to return, in another form, to the conclusion of chapter 8 of this book.

6. Although I have repeatedly spoken of God entering into a wager with Satan, or winning his wager with Satan, I have done so to try to capture the scene in the first chapter. But there is a danger in such language: it may sound as if God is capricious. He plays with the lives of his creatures so that he can win a bet.

Clearly that is not true. The challenge to Satan is not a game; nor is the outcome, in God's mind, obscure. Nothing in the book tells us *why*

God did this. The solemnity and majesty of God's response to Job not only mask God's purposes in mystery, but presuppose they are serious and deep, not flighty or frivolous.

Nevertheless, the wager with Satan is in certain ways congruent with other biblical themes. God's concern for the salvation of men and women is part of a larger, cosmic struggle between God and Satan, in which the outcome is certain while the struggle is horrible. This is one way of placing the human dimensions of redemption and judgment in a much larger framework than what we usually perceive.

7. We are perhaps better situated now to understand precisely why God says that his servant Job spoke of him "what was right," while the three miserable comforters did not. True, Job is rebuked for darkening the Lord's counsel: he became guilty of an arrogance that dared to demand that God give an account of his actions. But Job has been genuinely groping for the truth, and has not allowed glib answers to deter him. He denies neither God's sovereignty nor (at least in most of his statements!) God's justice. Above all, so far as the wager between God and Satan is concerned, Job passes with flying colors: he never turns his back on God.

Contrast the three friends. Although they are trying to defend God, their reductionistic theology ends up offering Job a temptation: to confess sins that weren't there in order to try to retrieve his prosperity. If Job had succumbed, it would have meant that Job cared more for prosperity than for his integrity or for the Lord himself; and the Lord would have lost his wager. Their counsel, if followed, would have actually led Job *away* from the Lord; Job would have been reduced to being yet one more person interested in seeking God for merely personal gain.

This is, at the end of the day, the ultimate test of our knowledge of God. Is it robust enough that, when faced with excruciating adversity, it may prompt us to lash out with hard questions, but will never permit us to turn away from God?

But perhaps it is better to put the matter the other way round: the God who put Job through this wringer is also the God of whom it is said that, with respect to his own people, "he will not let [them] be tempted beyond what [they] can bear. But when [they] are tempted, he will also provide a way out so that [they] can endure it" (1 Cor. 10:13). God could not trust me with as much suffering as Job endured; I could not take it. But we must not think that there was any doubt in God's mind as to whether he would win his wager with Satan over Job!

When we suffer, there will sometimes be mystery. Will there also be faith?

Questions for Further Study

1. Summarize the main lessons to be learned from the book of Job.
2. Could God say of you that you seek him without regard for prompt, personal gain?
3. Do you ever talk to God the way Job did? Why, or why not?
4. What does Elihu contribute to the argument of the book?
5. What lessons are to be drawn from God's speech?
6. Why does Job prosper at the end? What bearing does this have on Christians today?
7. What can you do to increase your own knowledge of and confidence in God, the better to cope when suffering or trials come your way?

10

The Suffering God

When we suffer, there will sometimes be mystery. Will there also be faith?

The last sentence of the previous chapter provides a suitable entry point into this chapter. For in Christian thought, faith is never naive or sentimental gullibility. To be useful, faith depends on the reliability, the faithfulness, of its object. Faith that depends on a God who is a cruel tyrant or a cheap trickster will be bitterly disappointed in the end. For faith to be praiseworthy, it must repose in a faithful God.

To provide a list of reasons as to why we Christians hold that God is worthy of all the faith that rests on him would turn this book into something it is not designed to be. But when Christians think seriously about evil and suffering, one of the paramount reasons we are so sure that God is to be trusted is because he sent his Son to suffer cruelly on our behalf. Jesus Christ, the Son who is to be worshiped as God, God's own agent in creation (John 1:2–3), suffered an excruciatingly odious and ignominious death. The God on whom we rely knows what suffering is all about, not merely in the way that God knows everything, but by experience.

This theme is so vast, and in various circles has become so popular, that it cries out for detailed discussion. But in this short chapter I make no pretense of offering a balanced treatment of what was accomplished on the cross.[1] My concerns are narrower and more selective: I shall focus on four simple truths about the cross, all related to the theme of evil and suffering.

The Cross Is the Triumph of Justice and Love

When we are convinced that we are suffering unjustly, we may cry out for justice. We want God to be just and exonerate us immediately; we want God to be fair and mete out suffering immediately to those who deserve it.

The trouble with such justice and fairness, however, is that, if it were truly just and truly fair and as prompt as we demand, we would soon be begging for mercy, for love, for forgiveness—for anything but justice. For very often what I really mean when I ask for justice is implicitly circumscribed by three assumptions, assumptions not always recognized: (1) I want this justice to be dispensed immediately; (2) I want justice in this instance, but not necessarily in every instance; and (3) I presuppose that in this instance I have grasped the situation correctly.

We need to examine these three assumptions. First, the Bible assures us that God is a just God, and that justice will be done in the end, and will be seen to be done. But when we urgently plead for justice, we usually mean something more than that. We mean we want vindication *now*! Second, to ask for such instantaneous justice in *every* instance is inconceivable: it would too often find me on the wrong side, too often find me implicitly inviting my own condemnation. But justice instantaneously applied only when it favors me is not justice at all. Selective justice that favors one individual above another is simply another name for corruption. And no one wants a corrupt God. And third, when I plead so passionately for justice, it is usually because I think I understand the situation pretty well. I wouldn't be quite so crass as actually to say I need to explain it to God, but that is pretty close to the way I act.

Someone might object that since the psalmist frequently appeals for justice, for vindication, it cannot be wrong to do so. And I agree, so long as those three hidden assumptions are not surreptitiously operating together. For instance, if the psalmist, or any believer since then for that matter, appeals to God for justice, not simply in this instance, but because God is a just God, the appeal is somewhat transformed. If such a believer also recognizes that the Lord's timing is perfect, that unless

---

1. For a more comprehensive treatment, see Leon Morris, *The Apostolic Preaching of the Cross* (London: Tyndale, 1965); John R. W. Stott, *The Cross of Christ* (Leicester: Inter-Varsity, 1986); J. I. Packer, "What Did the Cross Achieve? The Logic of Penal Substitution," *Tyndale Bulletin* 25 (1974): 3–45.

the Lord extends his mercy we will all be consumed (after all, the psalmist asks for mercy more often than he asks for vindication), and that sometimes our cries for justice cannot be more than vague but intense appeals for help, precisely because we do not understand what is going on very well, then the nasty, hidden assumptions that frequently mar our cries for justice have largely been done away with.

Suppose, for argument's sake, that God gave instant gratification for every good deed, every kind thought, every true word; and an instant jolt of pain for every malicious deed, every dirty thought, and every false word. Suppose the pleasure and pain were in strict proportion to the measure of goodness or badness God saw in us. What kind of world would result?

Many writers have asked this sort of question. They conclude that such a system would turn us into automata. We would not join in worship because of the intrinsic worth of God, but because it gave us selfish pleasure. We would not refrain from lying because it is wrong and abominated by the God we love, but because we wanted to avoid the next nasty jolt. We would not love our neighbor because our hearts had been transformed by the love of God, but because we preferred personal pleasure to personal pain.

I think that if God were to institute such a world order, things would be far worse yet. God does not look only on our external acts. He looks on our heart. Such a system of enforced and ruthlessly "just" discipline would not change our hearts. We would be smouldering with resentment. Our obedience would be external and apathetic; our hearts and devotion would not be won over. The jolts might initially gain protestations of repentance, but they would not command our allegiance. And since God examines the heart, he would be constantly administering the jolts. The world would become a searing pain; the world would become hell. Do you really want nothing but totally effective, instantaneous justice? Then go to hell.

There is another factor we must frankly face. When we ask for justice, we presuppose some sort of standard of justice. If the standards are God's standards, he has made them clear enough: the wages of sin is death (Rom. 6:23). We have returned to hell by another route.

We must be grateful that God is a God of justice. If God were not just, if there were no assurance that justice would be served in the end, then the entire moral order would collapse (as it has in atheistic humanism). But we must be equally grateful that God is not only a God of justice. He is a God of love, of mercy, of compassion, of forgiveness.

Nowhere is this more effectively demonstrated than in the cross. At one level, this was the most unjust act, the least fair act, in all of history. He who was sinless became our sin offering; he who had never rebelled against his heavenly Father was brutally executed by rebels; he who had never known what it was *not* to love God with heart and soul and mind and strength was abandoned by God, prompting him to cry out, "My God! My God! Why have you forsaken me?" And it was this act, this most "unfair" act, that satisfied divine justice, and brought sinful rebels like me to experience God's forgiveness, to taste the promise of an eternity of undeserved bliss.

In thinking about these things, there is an important and common error to be avoided. We must avoid the view that God the Father is characterized exclusively by justice and wrath, while his Son Jesus Christ is characterized exclusively by mercy and grace. In this view, the Son by his death somehow won over the Father, who would otherwise have simply wiped us out.

This will not do. The Father and Son are both described in Scripture as being, on the one hand, holy and therefore wrathful in the face of sin, and, on the other hand, full of compassion. It was because the Father *loved* the world that he sent his Son (John 3:16). It is therefore God himself who demonstrates his love for us in this fact: while we were still sinners, Christ died for us (Rom. 5:8).

This does not mean that there is no sense in which Jesus' death on the cross propitiates God, that is, makes God propitious, favorable toward us. But when Christians talk about the doctrine of propitiation, they do not mean to suggest (if they are at all knowledgeable) that Christ is the subject of propitiation and the Father is the object: the Son (subject) propitiates the Father (object). True, the Son is himself the "propitiation" for our sins (1 John 2:2; TNIV "atoning sacrifice"), since it is he who died, not the Father. But God is both the subject and the object of this propitiation. He is the subject, in that out of love he sends his Son to die and thus provides the sacrifice; he is the object, in that it is his own justice that is satisfied when his Son dies in place of sinners who deserve to come under the sentence of his justice. In this nuanced sense, one may speak of the Son propitiating the Father, but never in such a way that the Father and the Son have fundamentally different attitudes toward sinners and their sin.

As Paul says, it was God himself who presented his Son "as a sacrifice of atonement" (Rom. 3:25), or, better, as a propitiation, in his blood (that is, in his death on the cross). Then comes the most startling part. We might have expected Paul to say that God did this to demonstrate his love for fallen sinners. Instead, he says that God "did this to demonstrate his *justice*, because in his forbearance he had left the sins committed beforehand unpunished—he did it to demonstrate his *justice* at the present time, so as to be just and the one who justifies those who have faith in Jesus" (Rom. 3:25–26, emphasis added). In other words, God had not finally dealt with the sins of earlier generations, let alone with sins then being committed and still to be committed. But by sending his Son to the cross, he dealt with them, and thus demonstrated his justice. His justice demanded that sin be punished. How then could he let sinners go free, acquitted, uncondemned, declared just ("justified") when in fact they were guilty? He sent his Son to die in their place. This bloody sacrifice, designed and purposed by God himself, enabled him simultaneously to ιοrgive sinners and to retain the standards of his own justice. "*God* was reconciling the world to himself in Christ, not counting people's sins against them" (2 Cor. 5:19, emphasis added). His Son died where sinners should have died. Thus God shows himself "to be just and the one who justifies those who have faith in Jesus."

The cross, then, is the place where God's justice and love meet. God retains the integrity of his justice; God pours out the fullness of his love. In the cross, God shows himself to be just and the one who justifies sinners whose faith rests in his Son. The death of God's own Son is the only adequate gauge of what God thinks of my sin; the death of God's own Son is the only basis on which I may be forgiven that sin. The cross is the triumph of justice and love.

You might think we have strayed a long way from the problem of evil and suffering. What I have tried to show, however, is that when we utter anguished cries for "justice," simple justice, we do well to think through what we are saying. There is no doubt a place for asking God to display his justice in a particular case. But such requests must not presuppose that justice is the only thing we need, or that we are more just than God, or that we can afford to tell God that he is not just enough. Justice alone will destroy us all. Only the triumph of justice *and* love will meet our needs; and this triumph is so integrally linked to the very heart of the gospel, the cross of God's dear Son, our Savior, Jesus Christ, that we dare not, as Christians, take our eyes off this perspective.

The Cross Reveals the Kind of God We Trust

It is not only the cross that reveals what God is like, of course. But any Christian reading of the whole Bible gathers up the diverse strands and finds them focused in the cross and resurrection of Jesus.

To gain insight here, it may be worthwhile taking a small excursus into theological realms not normally traversed by Christians today. Probably a majority of theologians hold to the doctrine of the impassibility of God. This means, in its weaker form, that God cannot suffer; in its stronger form, that God cannot be acted upon at all. In the stronger form, three aspects of divine passibility were frequently denied to God in the past:

"(1) external passibility or the capacity to be acted upon from without, (2) internal passibility or the capacity for changing the emotions from within, and (3) sensational passibility or the liability to feelings of pleasure and pain caused by the action of another being."[2]

It is not hard to see how this view developed. Job himself rightly declares, "I know that you can do all things; no purpose of yours can be thwarted" (Job 42:2). Does not God himself insist, "I the Lord do not change" (Mal. 3:6)? Surely God acts, he is not acted upon, for he "works out everything in conformity with the purpose of his will" (Eph. 1:11). God "does not change like shifting shadows" (James 1:17).

If then someone were to ask these theologians, "That's all very well, but what about the many passages that speak of God loving, or becoming very angry when he sees something?" they too would have a lot of texts on their side. Long before the cross, we hear God's passion, tenderness, anger, and yearning in passages like these: "'Is not Ephraim my dear son, the child in whom I delight? Though I often speak against him, I still remember him. Therefore my heart yearns for him; I have great compassion for him,' declares the Lord" (Jer. 31:20). "How can I give you up, Ephraim? How can I hand you over, Israel? . . . My heart is changed within me; all my compassion is aroused. I will not carry out my fierce anger, nor will I turn and devastate Ephraim again. For I am God, and not a human being" (Hos. 11:8–9). "Woe to you, destroyer, you who have not been destroyed! Woe to you, betrayer, you who have not been betrayed!" (Isa. 33:1). "My people, what have I done to you? How have I burdened you? Answer me" (Mic. 6:3). "For God so loved the world . . ." (John 3:16). The pattern does not vary much when we turn to Jesus. "He looked around at them in anger . . . deeply distressed" (Mark 3:5). "As he approached Jerusalem and saw the city, he wept over it and said, 'If you, even you, had only known on this day what would bring you peace—but now it is hidden from your eyes'" (Luke 19:41–42).

What, then, do those who defend the impassibility of God say about these passages? In fact, there are different approaches to impassibility. Those who adhere to the tightest definitions reply with three points.

First, they insist that these expressions are anthropomorphisms, that is, figures of speech that talk about God as if he were a human being. For example, when the Bible says that God lays bare his arm, it does not mean that God has a literal, physical arm. The expression is an anthropomorphism. It means something like "God rolled up his sleeves and set to work," that is, God displayed his power in some way.

2. See F. L. Cross and E. A. Livingstone, eds., *The Oxford Dictionary of the Christian Church* (London: Oxford University Press, 1974), 694.

Second, they argue that since God created everything, he stands outside time. Therefore he must be above time. Since all our notions of change are bound up with changes across time, we must assume that God, in his own timeless eternity, is himself impassible. The reason the Bible speaks to us as if he were passible is that it is trying to reveal what God is like to us who are locked in time, and it must therefore use our categories.

Third, as far as the emotions of Jesus are concerned, these theologians regularly assign them to the *human* nature of Jesus, but deny that they pertain to his *divine* nature.

With all respect to the many fine theologians who uphold this line of reasoning, I sharply disagree. The God who is left seems too much like Buddha (though of course these theologians intend no such similarity): impassibility is seeping over into impassiveness. The crucial question for this book can be simply put: Does God suffer? And if he does not, why does the Bible spend so much time depicting him as if he does? It simply will not do to hide behind anthropomorphisms. Other ancient writers—Plato, for instance—found it possible to talk about an impassible god. If they could, and if that was what the biblical writers also meant to convey, why did they not simply come out and say so?

Moreover, it will not do to hide behind the relationship between time and eternity, for the very good reason that we know almost nothing about it. We scarcely know what time is; we certainly do not know what the relationship between time and eternity is. Is it so very obvious that there is no sequence in eternity? Granted that sequence, if there is such, must look very different to an eternal being than to us, does it follow that there is *no* such notion? Does it appear to God as if Christ is eternally coming, eternally dying, eternally rising, eternally returning? Moreover, if the sufferings of Jesus Christ are somehow restricted to his human nature, are we not in danger of constructing (dare I say it?) almost a schizophrenic Christ? I know that one form of conservative theology likes to go through the Gospels and assign this little bit to Jesus' human nature and that little bit to Jesus' divine nature, but I am persuaded that a much more profound christological integration is possible.

The methodological problem with the argument for divine impassibility is that it selects certain texts of Scripture, namely those that insist on God's sovereignty and changelessness, constructs a theological grid on the basis of those selected texts, and then uses this grid to filter out all other texts, in particular those that speak of God's emotions. These latter texts, nicely filtered out, are then labeled "anthropomorphisms" and are written off. But if they are anthropomorphisms, why were they selected? They are figures of speech, but figures of speech that refer to *something*. To what? Why were they selected? Granted that neither

God's emotions nor his sovereignty looks exactly like what we mean by emotions and sovereignty, nevertheless the biblical writers chose terms to make us think of God as not only absolutely sovereign, but also as a personal, emotional, responding, interacting God.

In contemporary theological literature, there is something of a backlash. In recent years quite a number of theologians around the world have written of God as a suffering God.[3] These works are quite different from one another, except that they all reject any notion of divine impassibility. Unfortunately, almost without exception, they commit the opposite error. They begin with all the texts that depict God as a suffering God, create a theological grid on this basis, and filter out the texts that point in another direction. The result is a picture of God who is vulnerable, halting, suffering, sympathetic, ever-changing, in process of growth. But the cost is great. At least those who defend divine impassibility had a category for explaining the texts that were difficult to them: they labeled them "anthropomorphic." But these new theologians have no such excuse. They simply ignore them, or so subordinate them to the "suffering" passages that the texts are no longer allowed to mean what they say. Alternatively, they assign the passages that speak of God's transcendence and sovereignty to some other layer of "biblical tradition," but have such a loose view of biblical authority that they feel they can pick and choose among the "biblical traditions." The biblical traditions are not to be taken together, they argue; indeed, they cannot be reconciled. The Bible is less like an entire meal, where the polite thing is to eat the whole, than a smorgasbord, where the idea is to choose what seems congenial. What seems congenial, in this violent yet proud twentieth century, is a suffering but decidedly finite God. Indeed, one of the reasons why some conservative theologians are reaffirming the impassibility of God is in order to challenge the selectivity and reductionism of the newer breed. They feel that at least some of the more recent contributions have unnecessarily sold out to modern skepticism. Perhaps so, but the conservatives themselves have sometimes been too unaware of how far they have "sold out" to Greek philosophical traditions.[4]

It would take us too far afield to engage either of these positions at length. In the next chapter, I shall try to put together a model for dealing with

3. See esp. Warren McWilliams, *The Passion of God: Divine Suffering in Contemporary Protestant Theology* (Macon: Mercer University Press, 1985); Douglas John Hall, *God and Human Suffering: An Exercise in the Theology of the Cross* (Minneapolis: Augsburg, 1986).

4. The best recent treatment of impassibility is doubtless that of Thomas Weinandy, *Does God Suffer?* (Edinburgh: T & T Clark, 2000). See also the important earlier work of Richard E. Creel, *Divine Impassibility: An Essay in Philosophical Theology* (Cambridge: Cambridge University Press, 1986).

the biblical polarities. My sole point at the moment is simple. The biblical evidence, in both Testaments, pictures God as a being who can suffer. Doubtless God's suffering is not exactly like ours; doubtless metaphors litter the descriptions. But they are not metaphors that refer to nothing, that are suggestive of nothing. They are metaphors that refer to God and are suggestive of his profound emotional life and his distinctly personal relationships with his people. If the term "impassible" is to be preserved—and I think it can be—then one must use it to affirm that God is never controlled or overturned by his emotions. We human beings speak of "falling in love" and "exploding in anger" or simply "losing it." God never "loses it." What he does—whether in righteous wrath or in tender love—he does out of the constancy of all his perfections. In that sense, I think, we may usefully speak of God being "impassible." But never should we succumb to the view that God is exclusively cerebral, utterly without emotions.

Here, then, the cross is climactic. God's plan of redemption cost the Father his Son; it cost the Son his life. And the Son learned suffering *in human terms*: "Since the children [i.e., human beings] have flesh and blood, he too shared in their humanity so that by his death he might break the power of him who holds the power of death—that is, the devil—and free those who all their lives were held in slavery by their fear of death" (Heb. 2:14–15).

The cross, then, reveals the kind of God we trust. And that brings us to the next point.

The Cross Both Destroys and Establishes the Credibility of God

Today the cross adorns our church buildings, graces our bishops, turns up on our lapels, and hangs from gold chains around our necks.

In the first century, it was not so. The cross was obscene. To wear a piece of jewelry fashioned to look like a cross would have been grotesque, an odious bit of macabre humor considerably more shocking than, say, wearing a bit of jewelry fashioned like the mushroom cloud of an atomic bomb.

We have already noted that no Roman citizen could be crucified without the emperor's consent. Crucifixion was reserved for the scum of society: for slaves, traitors, barbarians. Quite apart from the hideous and public nature of the death, there was a public odium to crucifixion that sent a shudder of revulsion down the spine whenever the subject was brought up.

Small wonder, then, that Paul can write that "the message of the cross is foolishness to those who are perishing" (1 Cor. 1:18). In particular, the Jews of Paul's day tended to think of God invading history in a powerful display of signs that would authenticate his claims and restore Israel to international prominence. They "demand signs," Paul writes (1:22). The Gentiles ("Greeks," in Paul's terminology) "look for wisdom"—self-contained philosophies that were essentially centered on one guru or another, holistic theories that allegedly integrated all human perceptions of the universe.

And what, Paul asks, do we offer? We preach Messiah crucified: a contradiction in terms to most people. To the Jews, this was a stumbling block: the Messiah was to be victorious, not a crucified, ignominiously shamed criminal. To the Greeks, this was foolishness: how can one build a decent philosophy on the back of a barbarian Jew publicly executed for treason in the most despicable way possible?

But to us Christians, "to us who are being saved" (1:18), the message of the cross is nothing less than the power of God and the wisdom of God. It is powerful where Jews see only weakness; it is wise where Greeks see only foolishness.

Thus the cross destroys the credibility of God among those whose god is not the God of the Bible. But it establishes the credibility of God among those who are being saved.

We must be careful here. Some modern writers extrapolate from the sufferings of Christ on the cross to the assumption that Christ actually shares personally in all suffering in the world. The cross thus becomes a kind of immanentist identification of God with all human suffering. But that is not the way it is treated in the New Testament. In many respects it is unique: it is Christ's suffering on our behalf, once and for all, to reconcile his people to God. If that unique and redemptive suffering is not appropriated by faith, all the pictures of divine empathy reduce to so much mawkish sentimentality. Many people rather like a sentimental God; he is so easily domesticated. But as we have seen, the cross does not demonstrate God's impotent sentiment; it establishes his justice and his love.

Sometimes the New Testament does indeed portray Jesus as sharing in the continuing sufferings of his church. When Paul was persecuting the church, the risen Lord challenged him with the question, "Saul, Saul, why do you persecute *me*?" (Acts 9:4, emphasis added). But typically, this is not only an identification of Jesus with his church and not with the world at large, but more precisely with those sufferings of the church that have to do with their pilgrim passage through an alien world. To extend this without qualification to all suffering everywhere, without even the effort to tie together some of the other biblical emphases on suffering, is reductionism that radically deforms God.

For Christians who see in the cross the most sublime expression both of God's justice and his love, the cross is immensely reassuring. It was a sacrifice offered once for all time (Heb. 10:12); Christ, having died once, dies no more, and in that sense no longer participates in the sufferings of the cross. But that does not negate the fact that he knows what suffering is like. "For we do not have a high priest who is unable to sympathize with our weaknesses, but we have one who has been tempted in every way, just as we are—yet he did not sin" (Heb. 4:15). Above all, the fact that Jesus is no longer suffering crucifixion cannot mask the love that brought him to the cross on our behalf.

And that is enough. How many men and women have been won to Christ because by God's grace they came to see that Jesus died on the cross for them? How many countless millions have first truly grasped what the love of God means because they have glimpsed the cross? "This is love: not that we loved God, but that he loved us and sent his Son as an atoning sacrifice [literally propitiation] for our sins" (1 John 4:10). Our hymns have made the point again and again, as this well-known example from Isaac Watts (1674–1748):

> Alas! and did my Saviour bleed?
> And did my Sovereign die?
> Would He devote that sacred head
> For such a worm as I?
>
> Was it for sins that I had done
> He groaned upon the tree?
> Amazing pity! Grace unknown!
> And love beyond degree!
>
> Well might the sun in darkness hide,
> And shut his glories in,
> When Christ, the mighty Maker, died
> For man the creature's sin.
>
> Thus might I hide my blushing face,
> While His dear cross appears,
> Dissolve my heart in thankfulness,
> And melt mine eyes to tears.
>
> But drops of grief can ne'er repay
> The debt of love I owe;
> Here, Lord, I give myself away:
> 'Tis all that I can do.

Frequently it is when we are crushed and devastated that the cross speaks most powerfully to us. The wounds of Christ then become Christ's credentials. The world mocks, but we are assured of God's love by Christ's wounds. Edward Shillito understood this. Writing in the wake of the First World War, when an entire generation of young men was mown down by machine guns and artillery in the endless trench warfare that marked that conflict, Shillito composed the poem "Jesus of the Scars":

> If we have never sought, we seek Thee now;
>> Thine eyes burn through the dark, our only stars;
> We must have sight of thorn-pricks on Thy brow;
>> We must have Thee, O Jesus of the Scars.
>
> The heavens frighten us; they are too calm;
>> In all the universe we have no place.
> Our wounds are hurting us; where is the balm?
>> Lord Jesus, by Thy Scars, we claim Thy grace.
>
> If, when the doors are shut, Thou drawest near,
>> Only reveal those hands, that side of Thine;
> We know to-day what wounds are, have no fear,
>> Show us Thy Scars, we know the countersign.
>
> The other gods were strong; but Thou wast weak;
>> They rode, but Thou didst stumble to a throne;
> But to our wounds only God's wounds can speak,
>> And not a god has wounds, but Thou alone.[5]

In the darkest night of the soul, Christians have something to hang onto that Job never knew. We know Christ crucified. Christians have learned that when there seems to be no other evidence of God's love, they cannot escape the cross. "He who did not spare his own Son, but gave him up for us all—how will he not also, along with him, graciously give us all things?" (Rom. 8:32).

The Cross Sets Forth Jesus as the Example

In chapter 5, I tried to show that part of what it means to be a Christian is to suffer for Christ's sake. *Every* Christian must "take up his cross" and follow Jesus. Now I want to reflect on the fact that our model in this regard is Jesus himself, and in particular his death on the cross.

5. The poem is found in Shillito's *Jesus of the Scars, and Other Poems*, but I have not been able to obtain a copy. The poem is reprinted in William Temple, *Readings in St. John's Gospel* (London: Macmillan, 1939–40; New York: St. Martin's, 1968), 366. I am grateful to Sir Norman Anderson for drawing it to my attention.

Some people see in the cross nothing more than a fine example of sacrificial love. They cannot find there anything of atonement, of triumph over the powers of darkness, of the satisfaction of God's justice, of bearing away the sins of others. They see only an example of self-sacrificing love, an example to be emulated.

James Denney gave one of the most trenchant responses to that emphasis almost a century ago. What would we think, he asks, of someone who ran down the Brighton pier at full tilt, loudly proclaiming his love for the world, and who jumped off the end of the pier and drowned? Surely we would not praise his love; surely we would pity his dementia. For one cannot meaningfully speak of self-sacrificing love unless there is a purpose to the self-sacrifice. This pathetic person's "self-sacrifice" is a tragic waste to be pitied, not a noble example to be emulated.

In exactly the same way, to speak grandly of the example of Jesus' love, or even of his identification with human suffering, is entirely meaningless unless there is some end in view. We must never lose sight of the fact that that end is our salvation—our pardon, our reconciliation to God, our restoration to a proper relationship with both God and other human beings, and ultimately our transformation when Jesus comes again. That is what gives meaning to Jesus' self-sacrifice. His was not the death of the demented, the deluded, or the disillusioned; his was the death of the ransom (Mark 10:45), a sacrifice voluntarily laid down at his Father's command (John 10:18) in order that we might be forgiven.

But having rightly emphasized these points, some of us have become unnecessarily skittish about the idea of Jesus' death on the cross as an example to be emulated. It is we who should be most loudly proclaiming the exemplary nature of Jesus' death, for we hold most strongly that it was a purposeful, meaningful sacrifice.

This is precisely the connection that the New Testament writers repeatedly draw. For instance, in John 12:23, Jesus responds to the request of some Gentiles who are seeking an interview with him. Apparently this is the "trigger" by which he discerns that the "hour" of his death, burial, resurrection, and exaltation is at hand, for he says, "The hour has come for the Son of Man to be glorified." The next verse is most naturally read in light of Jesus' impending death: "Very truly I tell you, unless a kernel of wheat falls to the ground and dies, it remains only a single seed. But if it dies, it produces many seeds" (v. 24). As an analogy of Christ's death, it is reasonably self-explanatory and rather moving. But immediately Jesus goes on to say, "Those who love their life will lose it, while those who hate their life in this world will keep it for eternal life. Whoever serves me must follow me" (vv. 25–26a). Thus, if the image of the seed dying to bring forth many seeds is peculiarly applicable to the death of Jesus Christ, in a slightly different way it is properly applicable to Jesus' followers. The thought rapidly moves from Jesus' uniquely fruitful death (the death of one seed producing many seeds) to the mandated death of Jesus' followers as the necessary condition of their own life.

It could not be otherwise. To love one's life in any absolute sense is to disavow God's right of sovereignty, and therefore a brazen elevation of self to the level of idol. Those who love their own life in that way lose it, that is, they cause their own perdition. Those who hate their own life (the love/hate contrast reflects a Semitic idiom articulating fundamental preference; it is not advocating absolute self-loathing) "will keep it for eternal life" (cf. Mark 8:35, which also follows a passion prediction).

Probably no passage makes this connection between the unique features of Jesus' death and the exemplary nature of Jesus' death clearer than 1 Peter 2:20–24. Peter has been telling his readers that there is no credit to them if they suffer punishment for doing wrong.

> But if you suffer for doing good and you endure it, this is commendable before God. *To this you were called, because Christ suffered for you, leaving you an example, that you should follow in his steps.* "He committed no sin, and no deceit was found in his mouth" [Isa. 53:9]. When they hurled their insults at him, he did not retaliate; when he suffered, he made no threats. Instead, he entrusted himself to him who judges justly. "He himself bore our sins" in his body on the cross, so that we might die to sins and live for righteousness; "by his wounds you have been healed." (emphasis added)

Here, there is no diminution of the uniquely redemptive features of Jesus' death: he "himself bore our sins in his body on the cross." Even so, he died leaving us an example, that we should walk in his steps.

There is a structural parallel to be found in the pages of the New Testament. Repeatedly we are told that Christ first suffered, and then entered into his glory (e.g., Luke 24:26; 1 Pet. 1:11). This sequence accomplished our salvation, but it also established a pattern for us (Rom. 6:2–7; 1 Pet. 2:24).

But if the cross thus sets forth Jesus as the example, the conclusion is inevitable: we, too, in our small ways, should expect to suffer unfairly, as he did. Peter insists that such unjust suffering is among the tasks to which we as Christians have been called.

The applications are countless. For instance, among the things that Jesus unfairly suffered were treason by one of his closest followers and abandonment by the rest. Similarly, from what we can read in his correspondence, Paul agonizes far more over the difficult things he has had to suffer at the hands of his own converts in Corinth than over the beatings and privations he has endured at the hands of outsiders. Thus, pastors and other Christian leaders must not be surprised by the extraordinary emotional pressures that may befall them, imposed by thoughtless or even renegade church members. These will rarely be fair; they can be soul-destroying. But from a biblical perspective, they are scarcely surprising. To expect them is to rob them of part of their power; to endure them with grace and fortitude is nothing other than following the example of Jesus.

To focus on the cross of Christ not only grounds our faith on the God who is loving and faithful, but also gives us an example in his sacrificial and redemptive love that we can never outstrip.

When we suffer, there will sometimes be mystery. Will there also be faith?

Yes, if our attention is focused more on the cross, and on the God of the cross, than on the suffering itself.

Questions for Further Study

1. List some reasons why Christians find God trustworthy. What part does the cross play?
2. How does the cross establish God's justice?
3. How does the cross reveal the kind of God we trust?
4. Are propitiation and impassibility, as outlined in this chapter, taught in the Bible? Support your answer.
5. How does the cross support God's credibility? What part did it play in your conversion? What part should it play in your thinking when you go through suffering?
6. What bearing does the example of Jesus' suffering have in your life? What bearing should it have?

Part 3

Glimpses of the Whole Puzzle

Evil and Suffering in the World of a Good and Sovereign God

II

The Mystery of Providence

A little girl was asked why the sun rises. She replied (with the condescending scorn that only a little girl who is sure of herself can muster),
"Because it is morning, of course!"

At one level, that answer is adequate; at many other levels, it is not.
Even the idea of the sun *rising* will not fly in many courses on astronomy.
Of course, at one level the notion of the sun rising is still adequate: just
look at any newspaper, calmly announcing the time of the "sunrise" as if
Copernicus and Galileo never existed. In all fairness, the average reader
who wants to know what time the sun "rises" does not really need a great
deal of information about the earth's rotation, the relationship between
time and the speed of light, and curved space.

Similarly in almost every area of thought. Certain answers and perspectives are perfectly adequate for some purposes, hopelessly inadequate
for others. Some Christians witness a terrible tragedy, and immediately
remember that this is a fallen world, or that Jesus told the parable of the
weeds and said, "An enemy has done this." Their immediate response is
right, so far as it goes. For many purposes they need probe no farther.

But exposure to a cynical expert in, say, ethics or epistemology, may
force the believer to think through possible responses at a much deeper
level. Severe suffering may have the same effect, with much more urgency and poignancy than a merely intellectual problem is likely to have.
We have returned to the subjective nature of the "epistemic dilemma" I
outlined in the first chapter of this book.

177

Although in the course of this book we have reflected on many biblical themes and perspectives that bear on the problem of evil and suffering, we have not yet squared away on the central issue. If God is sovereign, all-knowing, and good, then whence evil? How are we to think of evil without impugning either the integrity of God, or his capacity to change things?

> Believers are trapped in a dilemma. If they seek an explanation for the apparent incompatibility of God and evil, then it seems that they are trying to take heaven by storm. Yet if they rest their case in mystery, they run the risk of naive credulity, or even of believing self-contradictory nonsense. There really is no escape from this predicament, so we must be content with trying to "muddle through," as the British so aptly put it. There are no final answers, but surely some answers are better than others. So we seek the best answers we can find, all the while acknowledging the circumambient mystery.

So writes Richard Vieth,[1] and he is right.

There is no harm in trying to resolve the mystery. As Vieth says, some answers are better than others. But all the purported resolutions of which I am aware turn out on close inspection to involve the sacrifice of one or more clearly articulated biblical truths. The name of the game is reductionism. The place to begin is in attempting to locate just where the mystery lies. If this is not properly done, inevitably the rest of the discussion will be skewed. But if certain biblical "givens" can be tied down, then among believers any discussion that happily sacrifices those "givens" (wittingly or otherwise) will not prove very attractive.

The issues to be dealt with in this chapter are sufficiently difficult and contentious that Christians often disagree over them. You must make up your own mind. My only suggestion is that as you make up your mind, you try to distinguish the biblical "givens" from the arguments often used to filter them.

I am deeply persuaded that, even though the kind of approach to suffering taken in this chapter and the next may not be the sort of thing you feel you need right now, it is nevertheless the sort of thing that many more Christians ought to absorb *before* the evil day strikes.

It may be helpful if I provide a brief "map" of where we are heading in this chapter and the next. In chapter 11, I try to locate the mystery, largely inductively, by considering a substantial number of biblical passages. Then I outline a few approaches to the mystery of providence that are inadequate, and provide some reasons why there is a mystery for

1. Richard F. Vieth, *Holy Power, Human Pain* (Bloomington: Meyer-Stone, 1988), 55.

us to confront, and why it is a mystery and not a contradiction or sheer nonsense. In chapter 12, I work out some of the practical implications of the mystery of providence, and how it should operate in our lives, especially when we face evil and suffering.

But it may be convenient to begin by introducing a word.

Compatibilism Defined

The Bible as a whole, and sometimes in specific texts, presupposes or teaches that both of the following propositions are true:

1. God is absolutely sovereign, but his sovereignty never functions in such a way that human responsibility is curtailed, minimized, or mitigated.
2. Human beings are morally responsible creatures—they significantly choose, rebel, obey, believe, defy, make decisions, and so forth, and they are rightly held accountable for such actions; but this characteristic never functions so as to make God absolutely contingent.

In what follows, I shall argue that the Bible upholds the truth of both of these propositions simultaneously. The view that both of these propositions are true I shall call *compatibilism*. We could call this view anything we like, but for various historical reasons this seems like a good term to use. All I mean by it is that, so far as the Bible is concerned, the two propositions are taught and are mutually compatible.

I hasten to insist that this is not the imposition of a certain philosophical grid onto the biblical texts. That both of these propositions are true is based on an inductive reading of countless texts in the Bible itself, as we shall see. If in this chapter I have begun with compatibilism and not with the inductive study itself, that is because I have begun by giving you the first preliminary conclusion of the inductive study, before summarizing the evidence that supports it. The larger study on which this part of the chapter is based began with inductive study, and introduced the term "compatibilism" only when enough evidence had been compiled to warrant it.[2]

I hold, then, that according to the Bible both of these propositions are true, that is, that the Bible everywhere teaches or presupposes compatibilism. So now we must turn to a summary of the biblical evidence.

2. See D. A. Carson, *Divine Sovereignty and Human Responsibility: Biblical Perspectives in Tension* (London: Marshall, Morgan and Scott; Atlanta: John Knox, 1981).

Compatibilism Assumed or Taught in Scripture

The Sweep of the Evidence

We may begin with the first part of the first proposition: God is absolutely sovereign. The evidence is so sustained that a very large book would be required to expound all the relevant texts. "Why do the nations say, 'Where is their God?' Our God is in heaven; he does whatever pleases him" (Ps. 115:2–3). "The LORD does whatever pleases him, in the heavens and on the earth, in the seas and all their depths" (Ps. 135:6). Indeed, he is the one who "works out everything in conformity with the purpose of his will" (Eph. 1:11). He not only assigns times and places (Acts 17:26), but so reigns that even the most mundane natural processes are ascribed to his activity. If the birds feed, it is because the Father feeds them (Matt. 6:26); if wild flowers bedeck the meadow, it is because God clothes the grass (Matt. 6:30). The writer of Ecclesiastes knows of the water cycle, but biblical authors prefer to speak of God sending the rain than to say, "It is raining." God is the One who opens and shuts, who kills and brings to life, who raises up and puts down kings. He calls the stars by name, and keeps track of the number of hairs on each head (a rapidly descending count in some cases).

God's sovereignty is so broadly inclusive that, from a biblical point of view, it is not surprising to find, say unintentional manslaughter (Exod. 21:13) and family misfortune (Ruth 1:13, 20) both related to the will of God. Nor is the human will exempt from his sway: "In their hearts human beings plan their course, but the LORD establishes their steps" (Prov. 16:9). "LORD, I know that people's lives are not their own; it is not for them to direct their steps" (Jer. 10:23). It was God himself who turned the hearts of the Egyptians "to hate his people, to conspire against his servants" (Ps. 105:25).

So certain is Amos of the Lord's sovereignty even in the military crushing of a city that he can mock the stupidity of those who fail to acknowledge it and learn from it (Amos 3:6). "I am the LORD, and there is no other. I form the light and create darkness, I bring prosperity and create disaster; I, the LORD, do all these things" (Isa. 45:6–7). Doubtless God "does not willingly bring affliction or grief to any human being" (Lam. 3:33); but even so, "Who can speak and have it happen if the Lord has not decreed it? Is it not from the mouth of the Most High that both calamities and good things come?" (Lam. 3:37–38). God hardens whomever he pleases (Rom. 9:18). Shimei is wicked to curse the Lord's anointed, but David rightly understands that behind Shimei is the God who commanded him so to speak (2 Sam. 16:10). God himself authorizes the spirit of deception who seduces Ahab's prophets (1 Kings 22:21ff.); God himself stands behind the refusal of the sons of Eli to bow to discipline, "for it was the LORD's will to put them to death" (1 Sam. 2:25); God himself sends certain wicked people a powerful delusion so that they will believe the lie (2 Thess. 2:11); God himself, in his wrath, incites David to number the people (2 Sam. 24:1).

Now the most remarkable feature of these passages—and there are scores and scores more just like them—is that at no point is the human agent exonerated of responsibility just because God is in some way behind this or that act. We shall look at several passages more closely in a moment, but it is worth verifying the point in some of the passages just cited. God in his wrath incites David to take a census, but David is held fully accountable for his act. Eli's sons are wicked; those who are strongly deluded can also be described as those who refuse "to love the truth and so be saved." At no point whatsoever does the remarkable emphasis on the absoluteness of God's sovereignty mitigate the responsibility of human beings who, like everything else in the universe, fall under God's sway.

The second proposition could be demonstrated with equal detail. "Now fear the LORD and serve him with all faithfulness. . . . But if serving the LORD seems undesirable to you, then choose for yourselves this day whom you will serve. . . . But as for me and my household, we will serve the LORD" (Josh. 24:14–15). This is one of only countless passages where human beings are commanded to obey, or where they are entreated to do something, or told to choose or take firm resolution. The Ten Commandments have bite precisely because they can be obeyed or disobeyed. The gospel call itself lays down profound responsibility: "If you declare with your mouth, 'Jesus is Lord,' and believe in your heart that God raised him from the dead, you will be saved. . . . As Scripture says, 'Anyone who believes in him will never be put to shame'" (Rom. 10:9, 11). Human beings are tested by God, who wants to find out what is in their hearts (Gen. 22:12; Exod. 16:4; 2 Chron. 32:31). Human responsibility may even arise out of God's initiative in election (Exod. 19:4–6; Deut. 4:5–8; 6:6ff.; Hosea 13:4; Mic. 3:1–12). God utters moving pleas for human repentance, and finds no pleasure in the death of the wicked (Isa. 30:18; 65:2; Lam. 3:31–36; Ezek. 18:30–32; 33:11; Hosea 11:7ff.).

Yet nowhere does such material ever function to make God absolutely contingent, that is, absolutely dependent for his being or choices on the moves taken by human beings.

We must tread carefully here. I am not saying that there is *no* sense in which the Scriptures picture God as contingent. He talks with people, he responds to them; he can even be said (in almost forty cases) to "repent" of his decisions (KJV), that is, to change his mind or to relent in his declared purposes. I shall return to such passages a little farther on. But in no case is human responsibility permitted to function in such a way that God becomes *absolutely* contingent: that is, God is absolutely stymied, thwarted, frustrated, blocked, quite unable to proceed with what he himself had absolutely determined to do. There is nothing in the Bible quite like those modern writings that argue, for instance, that because men and women make moral choices, therefore God *must* be limited in power or knowledge (whether *self*-limited or limited in his very being). If there were such absolute constraints upon God, of course, then the first proposition could not possibly be true. But the remarkable thing about the Bible is that it adopts compatibilism: that is, it assumes or teaches that *both* propositions are true.

There is one more biblical emphasis that must be enunciated before we go on to look at a number of specific passages. It is to be distinguished from the two propositions that constitute compatibilism, but it is profoundly related to the theme of this book. It is this: Despite everything it says about the limitless reaches of God's sovereignty, the Bible insists again and again on God's unblemished goodness. God is *never* presented as an accomplice of evil, or as secretly malicious, or as standing behind evil in exactly the same way that he stands behind good. How to hold all this together we shall struggle with in due course; but the fact itself cannot reasonably be doubted. "He is the Rock, his works are perfect, and all his ways are just. A faithful God who does no wrong, upright and just is he" (Deut. 32:4). "God is light; in him there is no darkness at all" (1 John 1:5). It is precisely because Habakkuk can say to God, "Your eyes are too pure to look on evil; you cannot tolerate wrongdoing" (Hab. 1:13), that he has a difficult time understanding how God can sanction the terrible devastations of the Chaldeans upon his own covenant community. Note, then, that the goodness of God is the assumption, the nonnegotiable. Heaven swells with the chorus, "Great and marvelous are your deeds, Lord God Almighty. Just and true are your ways, King of the nations. Who will not fear you, Lord, and bring glory to your name? For you alone are holy" (Rev. 15:3–4).

In the selection of passages that follow, no attempt is made to offer a detailed exposition. Rather, my aim is to show how biblical compatibilism can be assumed or taught within concrete texts. One does not have to trace out the sweeping themes that I have just outlined; one can find the tension between the two propositions within the same contexts. The examples that follow are only a small but representative number of the many that could have been adduced.

Genesis 50:19–20

After Jacob's death, his sons approach Joseph out of fear that he may have been awaiting their father's death before exacting revenge. They had, after all, sold him into slavery. As the first minister of Egypt, he held them entirely in his power. What would he do?

Joseph allays their fears, and insists he does not want to put himself in the place of God. Then he looks back at that brutal incident when he was so badly treated, and comments, "You intended to harm me, but God intended it for good to accomplish what is now being done, the saving of many lives."

The parallelism is remarkable. Joseph does not say that his brothers maliciously sold him into slavery, and that God turned it around, after the fact, to make the story have a happy ending. How could that have been the case, if God's *intent* was to bring forth the good of saving many lives? Nor does Joseph suggest that God planned to bring him down to Egypt with first-class treatment all the way, but unfortunately the brothers mucked up his plan somewhat, resulting in the slight hiatus of Joseph spending a decade and a half as a slave or in prison. The story does not read that way. The brothers took certain evil initiatives, and there is no prior mention of Joseph's travel arrangements.

As Joseph explains, God was working sovereignly in the event of his being sold into Egypt, but the brothers' guilt is not thereby assuaged (they intended to harm Joseph); the brothers were responsible for their action, but God was not thereby reduced to a merely contingent role; and while the brothers were evil, God himself had only good intentions.

Leviticus 20:7–8

"Consecrate yourselves and be holy, because I am the LORD your God. Keep my decrees and follow them. I am the LORD, who makes you holy." This is only one of many passages where the command and responsibility to perform in a certain way or to be a certain thing are paired with the assurance that it is God who does the work in people. It must be remembered that in Hebrew "to consecrate," "holy," "to make holy [or to sanctify]" all have the same root (cf. Lev. 22:31–32).

1 Kings 8:46ff.

At the dedication of the temple, Solomon not only can ask that God will respond to his people in a certain way when they repent of their sin and turn again to him, but he can also say, "May he turn our hearts to him, to walk in obedience to him and to keep the commands, decrees and laws he gave our ancestors" (v. 58).

1 Kings 11:11–13, 29–39; 12:1–15 [cf. 2 Kings 10:15; 11:4]

The writer tells us that God became angry with Solomon for his flagrant idolatry, not least because the Lord had graciously revealed himself to the king twice. In consequence God tells him, "I will most certainly tear the kingdom away from you and give it to one of your subordinates. Nevertheless, for the sake of David your father, I will not do it during your lifetime. I will tear it out of the hand of your son. Yet I will not tear the whole kingdom from him, but will give him one tribe for the sake of David my servant and for the sake of Jerusalem, which I have chosen" (11:11–13). About the same time, the prophet Ahijah from Shiloh tells a man called Jeroboam that God will give him ten tribes to rule (11:29ff.).

When the story actually plays out, however, Solomon's son Rehoboam is found responding to the people's request for a lighter levy of tax and labor. He consults his advisors. The older, wiser heads unite in advising him to follow the wishes of the people; the young turks tell him to respond harshly and make repression sting the more. Rehoboam foolishly follows the counsel of the latter group. "So the king did not listen to the people, for this turn of events was from the LORD, to fulfill the word the LORD had spoken to Jeroboam son of Nebat through Ahijah the Shilonite" (12:15). The result is predictable: there is a rebellion, and the kingdom is split.

A secular observer would have seen nothing of the Lord's dealings in these events. Such an observer might bemoan the folly of Rehoboam, and lament the breakup of so splendid a kingdom. And indeed there was folly; a great kingdom was broken up. But even so, the same event that was Rehoboam's folly was the Lord's wise dealing. God's sovereign action did not mitigate Rehoboam's insensitive stupidity; Rehoboam's stupidity did not bring about events that were either unforeseen or unplanned by God himself.

Isaiah 10:5ff.

Here God addresses the mighty Assyrian nation. "Woe to the Assyrian, the rod of my anger, in whose hand is the club of my wrath!" (v. 5). In other words, God has been using the Assyrians as his instrument of wrath, his own chastening hand, his "rod" and his "club" against his own covenant people. "I send him against a godless nation [God is referring to the Jews], I dispatch him against a people who anger me, to seize loot and snatch plunder, and to trample them down like mud in the streets" (v. 6).

But if God is using the Assyrians in this way, why is he now pronouncing a "woe" on them? He goes on to explain. Although God is using the Assyrians as his own weapon, "this is not what he [the Assyrian] intends, this is not what he has in mind; his purpose is to destroy, to put an end to many nations" (v. 7). In the verses that follow, the Assyrians make many boasts: even their commanders are like the kings of other nations. Look at the lengthy list of cities that have been destroyed! The Assyrian boasts, "Shall I not deal with Jerusalem and her images as I dealt with Samaria and her idols?" (v. 11).

The prophet Isaiah comments, "When the Lord has finished all his work [!] against Mount Zion and Jerusalem, he will say, 'I will punish the king of Assyria for the willful pride of his heart and the haughty look in his eyes'" (v. 12). And *why* will God do this? Because the Assyrian says, "By the strength of my hand I have done this, and by my wisdom, because I have understanding. I removed the boundaries of nations, I plundered their treasures; like a mighty one I subdued their kings" (v. 13). In other words, what God is holding Assyria responsible for, and the reason why he is pronouncing his "woe" upon the nation, is *not* because they punished the Lord's covenant people, but because they thought in their arrogance that they were doing it by their own strength. This is nothing less than an act of rebellion against God himself, the worst sort of proud self-love. "Does the ax raise itself above the one who swings it, or the saw boast against the one who uses it?" (v. 15). "Therefore, the Lord, the LORD Almighty, will send a wasting disease upon his sturdy warriors; under his pomp a fire will be kindled like a blazing flame. The Light of Israel will become a fire, their Holy One a flame . . ." (vv. 16–17).

This one passage—and there are dozens like it in the prophets— demonstrates beyond reasonable doubt that Isaiah, at least, was a compatibilist.

John 6:37–40

"All whom the Father gives me will come to me, and whoever comes to me I will never drive away" (v. 37). This verse has often been taken as a fine example of the tension between God's sovereignty and human responsibility. God's sovereignty is understood to operate in the first part of the verse: by God's choice, certain people are given by the Father to the Son, and they are the ones who come to Jesus. Human responsibility is then understood to operate in the second part of the verse: it remains true that whoever comes to Jesus he will certainly receive.

Doubtless both points are true, and can be sustained from other passages. But it is doubtful if the second one is taught in this verse. The clause "I will never drive away" does not mean "I will welcome in, I will happily receive," or the like, but "I will certainly keep in, I will certainly preserve." The flow of the thought, then, is this: All those whom the Father gives to Jesus will come to him, and whoever thus comes to him, Jesus will never drive away—or, to put it positively, these people he undertakes to preserve, to keep in.

There are several ways of demonstrating that this is what the text means, but perhaps the most convincing is what follows next in the text. Whoever comes to me, Jesus promises, I will never drive away; "*For* I have come down from heaven not to do my will but to do the will of him who sent me" (v. 38, emphasis added). And what is that will? "And this is the will of him who sent me, that I shall lose none of all those he has given me, but raise them up at the last day" (v. 39). In other words, in its context verse 37 affirms both God's election and his preservation, through the Son, of all those he gives to Jesus.

But that does not mean it is not possible to describe the same sort of thing by placing a little more emphasis on the individual convert: "For my Father's will is *that everyone who looks to the Son and believes in him* shall have eternal life, and I will raise them up at the last day" (v. 40, emphasis added).

Once again, this is but one passage among scores of similar examples in the New Testament. The book of Acts, for instance, can report Peter's evangelistic pleading, "Save yourselves from this corrupt generation" (2:40), and describe the response of the crowd: "Those who accepted his message were baptized" (2:41). Yet elsewhere, at another evangelistic meeting, without any blush of embarrassment Luke describes the conversions this way: "When the Gentiles heard this, they were glad and honored the word of the Lord; and all who were appointed for eternal life believed" (13:48). Compatibilism is simply assumed.

Acts 18:9–10

When Paul arrives in Corinth, apparently he is tired and somewhat discouraged. The opening stages of his first efforts at evangelism in Europe have included a severe beating and imprisonment at Philippi, being run in Athens. True, he has seen considerable fruit. Even so, the emotional drain has been enormous. Corinth presents another challenge: it was known throughout the empire as a notoriously immoral city.

In this context, then, God graciously speaks to Paul in a night vision, and reassures him: "Do not be afraid; keep on speaking, do not be silent.

For I am with you, and no one is going to attack and harm you, because I have many people in this city."

Clearly, certain responsibilities are laid on Paul. God uses means in evangelism, and in this instance Paul figures centrally in those means. Nevertheless the encouragement that God showers on Paul depends on the doctrine of election. The "many people" that God "has" in Corinth are the people whom he regards as his own *even before they are converted*. Thus election in this passage functions as *an incentive* to evangelism.

Philippians 2:12–13

"Therefore, my dear friends, as you have always obeyed—not only in my presence, but now much more in my absence—continue to work out your salvation with fear and trembling, for it is God who works in you to will and to act in order to fulfill his good purpose."

This passage is extremely important, as much for what it does not say as for what it does. It does not say that God has done his bit in your salvation, and now it is up to you. Still less does it suggest that because God is working in you "to will and to act in order to fulfill his good purpose" you should therefore be entirely passive and simply let him take over. Nor is it (as not a few commentators wrongly suggest) that God has done the work of justification in you, and now you must continue with your own sanctification.

Paul describes what the Philippians must do as obeying what he has to say, and as working out (not working *for*!) their own salvation. The assumption is that choice and effort are required. The "working out" of their salvation includes honestly pursuing the same attitude as that of Christ (2:5), learning to do everything the gospel demands without complaining or arguing (2:14), and much more. But at the same time, they must learn that it is God himself who is at work in them "*to will and to act* in order to fulfill his good purpose." God's sovereignty extends over both their willing and their actions.

Indeed, far from being embarrassed by this candid compatibilism, Paul sees in God's sovereignty an incentive to encourage the Philippians on their way. "Work out your own salvation," he tells them, "*for* it is God who works in you." God's sway in their lives is, for Paul, not a *dis*incentive to action, but an *incentive*: get in step with what God is doing.

Acts 4:23–31

After Peter and John have been released from prison, following their interrogation after the miraculous healing of the cripple who had lain for years at the temple gate called Beautiful (Acts 3:1ff.), they return "to their own people" (v. 23)—to Christians—and report the details of what had occurred. The response of the church is to pray. The prayer begins by acknowledging God's sovereignty over the heaven and earth that he himself created. They then recall Psalm 2:1–2, words that God himself spoke "by the Holy Spirit through the mouth of your servant, our father David" (v. 25): "Why do the nations conspire and the peoples plot in vain? The kings of the earth rise up and the rulers band together against the LORD and against his anointed" (vv. 25–26). Naturally enough, the Christians cannot help but see the fulfillment of this Scripture in the events surrounding Jesus' death. But it is the way they phrase themselves that is so important: "Indeed Herod and Pontius Pilate met together with the Gentiles and the people of Israel in this city to conspire against your holy servant Jesus, whom you anointed. They did what your power and will had decided beforehand should happen" (vv. 27–28). They then proceed with their petition.

There is lots of guilt to go around: Herod, the Roman governor Pontius Pilate, the people of Israel—all were involved in a conspiracy. The word is a strong one, and in light of the psalm just quoted leaves no doubt that the Christians held them all to be profoundly guilty before God. Yet at the same time, the Christians could confess to God that the conspirators "did what your power and will had decided beforehand should happen."

It only takes a moment's reflection to show that, if the Christian gospel is true, this tension could not have been otherwise. If the initiative had been entirely with the conspirators, and God simply came in at the last minute to wrest triumph from the jaws of impending defeat, then the cross was not his plan, his purpose, the very reason why he had sent his Son into the world—and that is unthinkable. If on the other hand God was so orchestrating events that all the human agents were nonresponsible puppets, then it is foolishness to talk of conspiracy, or even of sin—in which case there is no sin for Christ to remove by his death, so why should he have to die? God was sovereignly at work in the death of Jesus; human beings were evil in putting Jesus to death, even as they accomplished the Father's will; and God himself was entirely good.

Christians who may deny compatibilism on front after front become compatibilists (knowingly or otherwise) when they think about the cross. There is no alternative, except to deny the faith. And if we are prepared to be compatibilists when we think about the cross—that is, to accept both of the propositions I set out at the head of this chapter as true, as they are applied to the cross—it is only a very small step to understanding that compatibilism is taught or presupposed everywhere in the Bible.

Compatibilism Explored

Granted that the Bible everywhere teaches or assumes that compatibilism as defined in this chapter is true, we have still not come any closer to thinking through *how* it is true. Perhaps the following reflections will help to clarify the issue, or at least to specify a little more closely where the mystery lies—which is, after all, what I set out to find at the beginning of this chapter!

1. Most people who call themselves compatibilists are not so brash as to claim that they can tell you exactly how the two propositions I set forth in the last section fit together. All they claim is that, if terms are defined carefully enough, it is possible to show that there is no necessary contradiction between them. In other words, it is possible to outline some of the "unknowns" that are involved, and show that these "unknowns" allow for both propositions to be true. But precisely because there are large "unknowns" at stake, we cannot show *how* the two propositions cohere.[3]

I think this analysis is correct. But what it means is that I am still going to be left with mysteries when I am finished. All that I hope to achieve is to locate those mysteries more precisely, and to show that they are big enough to allow me to claim that when the Bible assumes compatibilism it is not adopting nonsensical positions.

2. If compatibilism is true and if God is good—all of which the Bible affirms—then it must be the case that God stands behind good and evil in somewhat different ways; that is, he stands behind good and evil *asymmetrically*. To put it bluntly, God stands behind evil in such a way that not even evil takes place outside the bounds of his sovereignty, yet the evil is not morally chargeable to him: it is always chargeable to secondary agents, to secondary causes. On the other hand, God stands behind good in such a way that it not only takes place within the bounds of his sovereignty, but it is always chargeable to him, and only derivatively to secondary agents.

In other words, if I sin, I cannot possibly do so outside the bounds of God's sovereignty (or the many texts already cited have no meaning), but I alone am responsible for that sin—or perhaps I and those who tempted me, led me astray, and the like. God is not to be blamed. But if I do good, it is God working in me both to will and to act according to his good pleasure. God's grace has been manifest in my case, and he is to be praised.

If this sounds just a bit too convenient for God, my initial response (though there is more to be said) is that according to the Bible this is the only God there is. There is no other.

3. See R. Young, *Freedom, Responsibility, and God* (London: Macmillan, 1975).

3. Both propositions make much of human moral responsibility. But so far I have not tried to tie human moral responsibility to the notion of freedom. That is because the notion of freedom, in any biblical perspective, is exceedingly difficult to nail down.

I hasten to say that it is not only in Christian thought that the notion of freedom is more difficult than at first meets the eye. Among atheists, for instance, a debate is currently taking place as to what is meant by "human freedom." Are human beings so tied to the banging around of subatomic particles, whose collisions and their effects are tied to immutable natural laws, that "freedom" is nothing more than illusion? Or are there necessarily uncertainties in these statistical collisions that allow human beings to have some kind of interactive influence on what takes place in their own universe? I mention these disputes among atheist scholars, not because they are exactly like those in Christian circles, but because far too many writers enter into discussion on these matters as if "freedom" itself is easy to understand, or entirely self-evident.

If compatibilism is true—and I cannot see how the biblical evidence supporting it can be evaded—then any Christian definition of freedom must lie within two constraints.

First, human freedom cannot involve absolute power to contrary; that is, it cannot include such liberal power that God himself becomes contingent. That would deny the second of the two propositions that constitute compatibilism. That is why some of the best treatments of the will have argued that freedom (sometimes called "free agency") should be related not to absolute power to contrary, but to voluntarism: that is, we do what we want to do, and that is why we are held accountable for what we do.

For instance, no matter how God operates behind the scenes in the crucifixion of his Son, Herod, Pontius Pilate, and the others did what they chose to do; they did what they wanted to do. That is why they are rightly held responsible. But that is quite different from saying that they had absolute power to contrary in the event, for then God himself would have been contingent, and then the cross becomes an afterthought in the mind of God. It certainly becomes impossible to say that the human participants did what God ordained would happen! The human participants were thus *not* absolutely free; for if they were, God could have ordained that the events of the crucifixion take place, and then the human beings involved could have decided otherwise. But God did not ordain that they do something as if they were mere puppets, or, still worse, against their will. *They did what they wanted to do,* and that is why they are rightly held accountable.

Second, human freedom since the fall cannot be discussed without reference to the fall. Jesus insists that everyone who sins is a slave to sin (John 8:34). Even when doing our best, we hear a little whisper over our shoulder telling us how good we look while we are doing it. We devote ourselves to God for an hour of prayer, and spend part of the time wondering if people realize how pious we are. We give ourselves sacrificially to some good cause, then spoil it by being condescending or unforgiving to those who have not similarly given themselves. We live for a few moments or a few hours with God genuinely at the center of our affections, our desires, our goals, and then get sidetracked by personal ambition, lust, or greed. Our wills, then, are not truly free; they are enslaved by sin.

Within this framework, real freedom is freedom to obey God without restraint or reserve. It is not absolute power to contrary; it is wanting to please God at every moment.

Nowhere is this clearer than in the Christology of John's Gospel.[4] There Jesus is repeatedly shown to be the one who fulfills what has been written of him and who aligns himself with the Father's plan, but who does this in self-conscious obedience to his Father. The cross is inevitable: Jesus is the lamb of God, the predicted "hour" must arrive, the passion is foreseen in Scripture; yet on the other hand, no one simply takes Jesus' life from him: he voluntarily lays it down of his own will (10:18). In Jesus the divine determining and the perfection of human obedience come together in one person, since his very food is to do the will of him who sent him (4:34), and he always does what pleases the Father (8:29). Here we see "free will" operating at its best!

4. The real nub of the tension lies in the kind of God who presents himself to us in the Bible. This is best seen by reflecting a little more on the nature of human responsibility.

For the Christian, virtually all of what we are held responsible for, all that we obey or disobey, all that we choose or disavow, is foundationally defined by what God has commanded or forbidden. But the notion of God commanding or forbidding depends on understanding that God is personal. Christians are not saying that there is an impersonal "it" tied up with the creation, and we must get ourselves in line with the way the creation operates if we are to function smoothly within creation. Christians are saying that there is a personal "he" out there, a heavenly Father, separate from the creation. What makes sin heinous is that it is defiance of what he prescribes or forbids. Our moral responsibility is tied to our accountability to *him*.

The trouble comes from the fact that all that we customarily mean by personhood or personal or personality is time-bound and finite. I speak to my wife, she speaks to me: that involves sequence, time. I tell

---

4. Carson, *Divine Sovereignty*, 146–60.

my son to get dressed for school, he obeys or disobeys, as the case may be. My daughter asks my wife a question; my wife answers. She asks me for chocolate; I say yes or no. We love each other; we resent each other; we forgive each other. These are functions that are characteristic of what it means to be a person. And all of our (admittedly earthly) models entail finitude.

But when I say that God is personal, I must also say that he is transcendent—above space and time, and utterly sovereign. When God asks a question, does he not, on the Bible's showing, also know the answer? When he pleads, or forgives, or forbids, or exhorts, I dare not forget that he cannot be personal in exactly the same way that finite human beings are personal; for God's transcendence and sovereignty establish one of the poles in compatibilism. That he is a person is the presupposition behind my moral accountability; but that does not permit me to think of him as finite, for I know he is not.

The problem of compatibilism, then, is tied to the fact that the God who discloses himself in the Bible and supremely in the person of his Son is himself both transcendent and personal, and not less than both. We have pursued the lines of thought that suggest themselves from the Bible's straightforward adoption of compatibilism, and find they lead to the nature of God.

It should now be a little clearer why, in chapter 10 of this book, I was unwilling to endorse the doctrine of the so-called impassibility of God—at least as it is usually taught. That doctrine is too tied to just one side of the biblical evidence. But that does not mean that the other side—that stresses God's suffering, his love, his responding—is any more reliable if it is abstracted from the complementary pole of God's transcendence. We must zealously hold, as well as we are able, to the fullest biblical picture of the nature of God, lest we create a mere subset of God, an idol that suits us but that does not really exist.

5. It appears, then, that the problems involved in holding to the truth of both of the propositions that constitute compatibilism are profoundly tied to the very nature of God himself. Ironically, this provides us with a way forward. We are reasonably well placed to isolate some of the things we do *not* know about God; that is, we see that the Bible describes God as both transcendent and personal, and in part we justify this strange pairing because we can identify some of the things we do not know about him. But some of these things that we do not know about God turn out to be facets of ignorance that make it reasonable to hold that both the propositions of compatibilism are also true, even though we do not see *how* they can be true.

Examples may help. The God of the Bible created all things; he lives above or outside time and space as we know them. He is transcendent. But that means I do not really understand his relationship to time and space. I see that he has revealed himself to human beings *in* time and space, but I don't have a clue how he manages it, or how it looks to him. I cannot be certain, for instance, whether he experiences sequence. If he does, it cannot be exactly the way I do, for my notion of sequence is bound by the categories of space and time. Yet that he is *not* bound by space and time does not entail the conclusion that he does not experience sequence in any sense. Certainly he has chosen to reveal himself to us in the space/time categories we more or less understand. Clearly this has enormous relevance to *fore*ordination, *pre*destination, to affirmations that the conspirators at Jesus' crucifixion did what God decreed beforehand that they would do, to the notions of prophecy and fulfillment. But if he had been willing to sacrifice the biblical emphasis on the personhood of God, on the personal, speaking, interacting, responding nature of God, he could have conveyed the impression of transcendence without overlaying it with this emphasis on God the person. The problem of compatibilism reduces to a number of things we do not know about the very nature of God.

I see that he presents himself as personal, but I have no idea how a personal God can also be transcendent.

I see that the Bible ascribes everything to him in one way or another, that his sovereignty leaves nothing out. I see that the biblical descriptions of his causation of evil deeds insist that he is good, and that secondary agents are evil. I do not know how he uses secondary agents in this way. Transparently, how he does this is related to who he is, to his "domain" outside or above space and time, to the nature of his sovereignty and his choices as a person; but I still do not see *how* he does it.

So I am driven to see not only that compatibilism is itself taught in the Bible, but that it is tied to the very nature of God; and on the other hand, I am driven to see that my ignorance about many aspects of God's nature is precisely the same ignorance that instructs me not to follow the whims of many contemporary philosophers and deny that compatibilism is possible.

The mystery of providence is in the first instance not located in debates about decrees, free will, the place of Satan, and the like. It is located in the doctrine of God.

Compatibilism Defended

There are many Christians who deny the account of compatibilism just given. Before trying to use what we have gleaned in this chapter to address the problem of evil and suffering, I should say a few words about the objections that are most commonly raised. I shall restrict myself to objections raised by those who have a high view of Scripture but who nevertheless reject the account of providence I have lightly sketched in this chapter. Three are worth noting.

The Ruthless Definition

Here objections are made possible because those who object make use of a priori definitions that force the evidence into an artificial mold. By "a priori definition" I mean a definition of a crucial term that is based not on an evenhanded and inductive study of the biblical evidence, but on some prior assumption, usually a philosophical bias.

Doubtless the most frequent abuse in this regard concerns the expression "free will." Everyone who holds that human beings are not just puppets who cannot be held responsible for what they say, do, think, and are holds to some definition of free will. But many people simply assume that free will must entail absolute power to contrary.[5] And that brings free will into irreconcilable conflict with the biblical evidence that denies God ever becomes absolutely contingent. For instance, when the Basingers posed the question of the book they edited, they put the matter this way: "To what extent does human freedom pose limitations on God's sovereign control over earthly affairs?"[6] That, of course, begs the question. They have assumed that any definition of human freedom *must* "pose limitations [*sic*: I think they mean "*impose* limitations"] on God's sovereign control." And they have done this without reflecting on whether such an assumed definition of freedom is either warranted or forbidden by the biblical texts themselves.

The result is that theologians and thinkers in this camp take all kinds of creative steps that cannot be squared with the biblical evidence. Bruce Reichenbach cannot believe that Ephesians 1:11 means what it says, so he reinterprets it to mean nothing more than that "everything God does he does in conformity with his purposes."[7] That is such a truism it is scarcely worth saying; in any case, it is not what the text of Scripture says. In the same volume, one author adopts this definition of free will and limits God's power but not his knowledge: God knows what free moral agents will do in advance but does not in any way determine it. Another

5. To cite but one example of hundreds, see Michael L. Peterson, *Evil and the Christian God* (Grand Rapids: Baker, 1982), who argues that it is logically impossible for an omnipotent God to control a free being. But it is logically impossible only if the definition of freedom already embraces absolute power to contrary. The definition of freedom has ensured his conclusion, without any attempt to see if such a definition is either required or permitted by Scripture.

6. Basinger and Basinger, *Predestination and Free Will*, 10.

7. Ibid., 52.

author, who lapses into regrettable sarcasm, limits God's knowledge: the nature of free decisions is such that not even omniscience could know the outcome. But neither of these authors works through any of the relevant biblical material that flatly eliminates their a priori definitions.

Quite apart from the failure of these writers to engage the biblical texts, they have not addressed the most common of objections.[8] For instance, if "free will" necessarily entails absolute power to contrary, will we enjoy such "free will" in heaven? Most Christians agree that in heaven there will no longer be any danger of apostasy: we will be kept from sinning. But if God can keep us from sinning there, does this mean that "free will" is sacrificed? Are human beings in glory deprived of this sublime capacity that (allegedly) makes them moral creatures? Is it not better to question whether the a priori definition is right?

Or consider the term "foreknowledge." Certainly the Bible gives numerous instances of God knowing certain things in advance. In an earlier chapter we even charted evidence of God knowing things that would have occurred under different circumstances (so-called middle knowledge). But when Paul says, "For those God foreknew he also predestined to be conformed to the likeness of his Son . . ." (Rom. 8:29), is that the kind of "foreknowledge" Paul has in mind? Countless philosopher-theologians simply assume it is, and in consequence insist that predestination is nothing more than God choosing to do what he foresees the human being will choose to do.

This way of wording things, of course, makes the human being the pivotal "decider"; God's decision is not predestination in any meaningful sense, but a kind of ratification-in-advance. Moreover, too little attention is paid to the fact that this text does not speak of God foreknowing that such and such will take place, but that God foreknows *the person*. Many have shown that in Semitic thought "to know" a person can have overtones of intimacy: if a husband "knows" his wife, for instance, he has sexual intercourse with her. For God to "foreknow" certain people, especially in the context of Romans 8:28–30, means (as most serious commentators point out) that God has a personal relationship with the individual in advance. Those whom God foreknows in this sense, he predestines "to be conformed to the likeness of his Son." Besides, it is a strange method that takes a doubtful definition of one occurrence of "foreknowledge" and pits it against the many references in which it is clearly stated that God has *chosen* his people (e.g., Deut. 4:37–39; 7:6–9; Ps. 4:3; Matt. 24:22, 31; Luke 18:7; John 15:16; Acts 13:48; Gal. 4:27, 31;

8. E.g., Roger Nicole, "Some Comments on Hebrews 6:4–6 and the Doctrine of the Perseverance of God with the Saints," in *Current Issues in Biblical and Patristic Interpretation*, ed. Gerald Hawthorne (Grand Rapids: Eerdmans, 1975), 357.

Eph. 1:4–6; 2 Tim. 2:10; 1 Pet. 1:2). Those who opt for this route have "made sense" of a mystery that should not be explained away, and have done so in defiance of the biblical evidence.[9]

In short, the ruthless definition must not be permitted to disallow the clear teaching of biblical texts.

The Triumph of Mutual Annihilation

This technique is also fairly common. It is found, for instance, in the more responsible essays in the two books edited by Clark Pinnock on this subject, namely, *Grace Unlimited* and *The Grace of God and the Will of Man.* I am thinking of the essays of I. Howard Marshall, Grant R. Osborne, and others.

Osborne's approach is revealing, because he thoughtfully lets his readers in on his mental processes. He can weigh up a number of texts that emphasize the sovereignty of God, for instance, and be quite careful not to permit his exposition of them to curtail what they actually say. Then he turns to those texts that emphasize human responsibility, human choices, human failures, or the like, and tries hard not to milk them for more than they are worth. The doubtful step comes when he sets the conclusions of the one set of texts against the conclusions of the other set of texts. Some kind of mutual annihilation takes place (as when a quark smashes into an antiquark). The result is that neither set of texts means quite what we thought they meant after all—though in Osborne's hands it is the set of texts on divine sovereignty that suffers the most.

But if the inductive study of the passages I have surveyed in this chapter is correct, not to mention many more passages like them, this is precisely what must *not* be done. It is another way of pitting human responsibility or human will or human freedom *against* God's sovereign activity, as if they were mutually limiting, as if they *must* be mutually limiting. But that assumption is what Scripture expressly disavows: namely, that the biblical writers are compatibilists.

The Early Creation of Grids

All of us, of course, create grids or models of what we have understood from the text, and these grids or models help us to interpret other material

9. The point is implicitly conceded by Paul K. Jewett, *Election and Predestination* (Grand Rapids: Eerdmans, 1985), 77, when he asks whether the approach of Arminius (using "foreknowledge" to explain "predestination") is justified. Jewett comments: "I would suggest that it is. We may or may not agree that his doctrine is biblical, that his exegesis is sound, but we can hardly doubt that it makes sense in its own right, that it resolves the problem." Exactly. And that is the problem.

we find in the texts. But these grids must not be built too early in the inductive process, and they must remain open to correction from the text itself. If the grid is built too early or is too rigid, then instead of being a helpful guide to the text and a useful organizer of fresh material, it becomes a way of filtering out of the text whatever cannot slip through the grid.

For example, consider the thirty-five or so passages that speak of God "repenting" of something or other (to use the language of the KJV). It can easily be shown that much of this repenting is not quite like human repenting. Human beings repent of moral evil; God never does, since he performs no evil of which to repent. That is why most modern translations use words such as "regret," "relent," "grieve over," "retract," or the like.

Still, the passages are intriguing. God can "relent" over a step he has already taken (Gen. 6:6–7; 1 Sam. 15:11, 35). He may "relent" over what he has said he would do or even started doing (Pss. 90:13; 106:44–45; Jer. 18:7–10; 26:3, 13, 19; Joel 2:13–14; Jon. 3:9–10; 4:3), perhaps in response to the prayer of an intercessor (Exod. 32:12–14; Amos 7:3–6). On the other hand, there are certain matters and occasions over which he will not "relent" (Num. 23:19; 1 Sam. 15:29; Ps. 110:4; Jer. 4:28; 15:6; Ezek. 24:14; Zech. 8:14). In one remarkable passage, God *does* "relent" because he is *not* a human being (Hosea 11:8–9): God is so compassionate that his heart "is changed within [him]," and he does not carry out the fierce anger and devastation he had planned for Ephraim.

These passages are not all of a piece. God's "relenting" and not sending a promised judgment turns on a repeated and sometimes articulated pattern: if a people to whom judgment is promised turn from their sin, the Lord will not carry out the judgment (e.g., Ezek. 33). If God "relents" or "grieves over" the choice of Saul as king (1 Sam. 15:11, 35), it is *after* we have been told that God has already sought out another man, a man after his own heart (1 Sam. 13:14).

Nevertheless these passages are part of the web of the biblical narrative. They are part of the picture of God as a personal God who interacts with his people. But it is precisely for that reason that one must be very cautious about extrapolating such texts to the point where they are in danger of denying complementary truths about God the transcendent Sovereign. For instance, in a generally fine article on the "repentance" of God, Terence Fretheim crosses over this forbidden line when he draws this conclusion: "To confess that God is a God who repents says something about a God who is ready to reverse himself. . . . It says that God's own history (what has been said and done in the past) may not be fully adequate for dealing with a changed present."[10] This assumes

---

10. Terence E. Fretheim, "The Repentance of God: A Key to Evaluating Old Testament God-Talk," *Horizons in Biblical Theology* 10 (1988): 60.

that God has a "history" in the same way that we do; it assumes a God locked into space and time categories. Above all, it fails to wrestle with the problem as to how this set of texts should be linked with those that stress God's immutability, boundless wisdom, omniscience, and power.

For another example, consider the verse, "He is patient with you, not wanting anyone to perish, but everyone to come to repentance" (2 Pet. 3:9). There are only four principal things it could mean: (1) God wants everyone to come to repentance, and so therefore everyone will finally be saved, since no one can thwart his will; (2) God wants everyone to come to repentance, but for whatever reason he cannot bring this to pass, since some will not be saved; (3) the "everyone" whom God wants to be saved is established by the context to be the elect only; or (4) the text establishes God's saving stance toward the entire world: he is the God who wants everyone without exception to be saved. But since this is not the only way the Bible speaks of God's "wants" or his "will," one must not appeal to the text to say anything for or against some particular view of election or free will.

A universalist might well adopt the first position. Appealing to this text and one or two others like it, the universalist then creates a grid, and any text that speaks of some *not* being saved (and there are hundreds) has to be explained away. Someone else might appeal to the text assuming the second interpretation is correct. In this view God has done everything he can, and now any individual's salvation depends entirely and exclusively on the "free will" (understood to entail absolute power to contrary, as already defined) of that individual. The grid is constructed, and all that the Bible has to say about election is simply filtered through that grid. The result is never any real choice on the part of God, but at most a kind of ratification-in-advance. And so we could work our way through the third and fourth options.

In fact, biblical theologians have long noted that when the Bible says God wills something or wants something, the language is used in different ways. God sometimes wills something in a sense no different from decree, from efficient accomplishment. The texts previously cited provide many examples: what God wills in heaven and on earth takes place, and he works everything in conformity with the purpose of his will. On the other hand, the Bible can speak of what God wills in terms of his desires. God's will is that we Christians should be holy (1 Thess. 4:3), but it does not take many powers of observation to note that this cannot be a reference to God's efficient or decretal will. Still other passages speak of God's permission, as, for instance, when God grants Satan permission to afflict Job. Similarly, God gives sinners over to their evil ways (Rom. 1:24, 26, 28); in this sense God does not willingly afflict his people (Lam. 3:33): that is, he permits it, but it is not his desire. Because he is slow to anger and rich in mercy, only reluctantly does he afflict his people.

We must be extremely careful how we handle this diversity of uses when we come, say to 2 Peter 3:9. At the risk of simplification, it appears that when the Bible speaks of God's will in an efficient or decretal fashion, that use of language belongs to the assumption that God is transcendent and sovereign; when the Bible speaks of God's will as his desire, quite possibly unfulfilled desire, that use of language belongs to the assumption that God is a person who interacts with other persons. To appeal to such usage to deny that God is sovereign is as irresponsible as it is to appeal to the first usage to deny that God is personal.

Similarly, when the Bible speaks of God's permission of evil, there is still no escape from his sovereignty. A sovereign and omniscient God who knows that, if he permits such and such an evil to occur it will surely occur, and then goes ahead and grants the permission, is surely decreeing the evil. But the language of permission is retained because it is part of the biblical pattern of insisting that God stands behind good and evil asymmetrically (in the sense already defined). He can never be credited with evil; he is always to be credited with the good. He permits evil to occur; the biblical writers would not similarly say that he simply permits good to occur! So even though permission in the hands of a transcendent and omniscient God can scarcely be different from decree, the use of such language is part and parcel of the insistence that God is not merely transcendent, but that he is also personal and entirely good. That God's permission of evil does not in any way allow evil to escape the outermost bounds of God's sovereignty is presupposed when we are told, for instance, that the Lord persuades the false prophet what to say (Ezek. 14:9), or that his wrath incites David to sin by taking a census (2 Sam. 24:1). When the Chronicler describes the same incident and ascribes the effective temptation to Satan (1 Chron. 21:1), this is not in contradiction of the passage in 2 Samuel (for the biblical writers, including the Chronicler, are far too committed to compatibilism to allow such a view), but in complementary explanation. One can say that God sends the strong delusion, or one can say that Satan is the great deceiver: it depends on whether the sovereign transcendence of God is in view, or his use of secondary agents.

Some theologians are shocked by and express bitter reproach against other theologians who speak of God "causing" evil in any sense. At one level, they are to be applauded: everywhere the Bible maintains the unfailing goodness of God. On the other hand, if you again scan the texts cited in this chapter, it must be admitted that the biblical writers are rather bolder in their use of language than the timid theologians!

Little is gained by being more "pious" in our use of language than the Bible is, and much may be lost. By being too protective of God, we are in fact building a grid out of only a subset of the biblical materials, and filtering out some of what is revealed in the Bible about the God who has so graciously disclosed himself. The result, rather sadly, is a god who is either less than sovereign or less than personal, either incompetent and frustrated or impassive and stoical. But the God and Father of our Lord Jesus Christ is utterly transcendent and passionately personal. These are among the "givens" of Scripture, and we sacrifice them to our peril.

Some Concluding Reflections

1. One of the common ingredients in most of the attempts to overthrow compatibilism is the sacrifice of mystery. The problem looks neater when, say, God is not behind evil in any sense. But quite apart from the fact that the biblical texts will not allow so easy an escape, the result is a totally nonmysterious God. And somehow the god of this picture is domesticated, completely unpuzzling.

After reading some neat theodicies that stress, say, that all suffering is the direct result of sin, or that free will understood as absolute power to contrary nicely exculpates God, I wonder if their authors think Job or Habakkuk were twits. Surely they should have seen that there is no mystery to be explained, and simply gone home and enjoyed a good night's sleep.

It is better to let the biblical texts speak in all their power. Many things can then be said about the God who has graciously disclosed himself, but all of them leave God untamed.

2. It is *essential*—I cannot say this strongly enough—it is *utterly essential* to doctrinal and spiritual well-being to maintain the diverse polarities in the nature of God simultaneously. For instance, if you work through the biblical passages that bluntly insist God in some sense stands behind evil, and do not simultaneously call to mind the countless passages that insist he is unfailingly good, then in a period of suffering you may be tempted to think of God as a vicious, sovereign thug. If you focus on all the passages that stress God's sovereign sway over everything, and do not simultaneously call to mind his exhortations to pray, to intercede, to repent, to examine yourself, you may turn into a Christian fatalist, and mistake your thoughtless stoicism for stalwart faith. The same lesson can be configured in many more ways: provide your own examples of distortion.

Perhaps I can make the point another way. In an earlier book I discussed the tension between divine sovereignty and human responsibility at some length.[11] One writer who has taken me to task on some points, William Lane Craig, follows the line of my exposition in some places, and then inserts statements like this: "Carson admits that the Scriptures do sometimes distinguish between what God does . . . and what humans do. . . . Carson also concedes that there is in the Scriptures a sort of asymmetry in the way in which our deeds are ascribed ultimately to God."[12] The truth of the matter is that I neither "admit" nor "concede" anything of the sort: I *insist* on them. Craig's work has considerable value; but he has wrongly tried to make me out to emphasize only one side of the tension, so that I can be shown to be forced into "concessions" and "admissions." That way I can serve as a foil for Craig's own philosophical agenda! But my point, in both that earlier book and this chapter, is that the fullness and balance of the biblical tension that surrounds the doctrine of God must be vigorously maintained.

3. The mystery of providence defies our attempt to tame it by reason. I do not mean it is illogical;[13] I mean that we do not know enough to be able to unpack it and domesticate it. Perhaps we may gauge how

---

11. Carson, *Divine Sovereignty*.

12. William Lane Craig, *The Only Wise God: The Compatibility of Divine Foreknowledge and Human Freedom* (Grand Rapids: Baker, 1987), 47.

13. Owing to the popularity of the little book by J. I. Packer, *Evangelism and the Sovereignty of God*, it has become common to designate the two truths, that God is utterly sovereign and human beings are morally responsible, as an antinomy. But there is some confusion over the term, and a comment may help.

According to the *Oxford English Dictionary*, an antinomy is: (1) "a contradiction in a law, or between two equally binding laws"; (2) "a contradictory law, statute, or principle; an authoritative contradiction"—and here an illustration is drawn from Jeremy Taylor, who in 1649 wrote that certain signs of grace "are direct antinomies to the lusts of the flesh"; (3) "a contradiction between conclusions which seem equally logical, reasonable, or necessary; a paradox; intellectual contrariness"—and this last meaning OED attributes to Kant.

Packer means none of these things. He certainly does not see in these truths a genuine contradiction (meanings 1 and 3), nor does he see in them the kind of opposition one finds between signs of grace and lusts of the flesh. He means something like "an *apparent* contradiction that is not in fact real."

Although OED does not offer that as one of its definitions, the term has come to have that meaning in some branches of philosophy (whence, probably, Packer borrowed it). In *The Critique of Pure Reason*, Kant was occupied in exposing the fallacies that arise when one applies space and time and some other categories to things that are not experienced. He argued that if these categories are *not* appealed to, we necessarily find four antinomies (which we need not detail here). Superficially, Kant thus uses the term in the OED sense of real contradictions: the antinomies arise only when the categories of space and time are adopted. But precisely because he says these categories should *not* be adopted, the antinomies turn out *not* to be real contradictions, but only apparent ones. This generates the implicit meaning of "antinomy" that Packer utilizes.

My sole point in this note is to insist that when antinomy be applied to these truths, we understand that we are dealing with mystery, not contradiction.

content we are to live with our limitations by assessing whether we are comfortable in joining the biblical writers in utterances that mock our frankly idolatrous devotion to our own capacity to understand. Are we embarrassed, for instance, by the prophetic rebuke to the clay that wants to tell the potter how to set about his work (Isa. 29:16; 45:9)? Is our conception of God big enough to allow us to read "The Lord works out everything to its proper end—even the wicked for a day of disaster" (Prov. 16:4) without secretly wishing the text could be excised from the Bible?

We voice our "Amen!" to many truths written by Paul. Can we voice our "Amen!" to this? "One of you will say to me: 'Then why does God still blame us? For who is able to resist his will?' But who are you, a mere human being, to talk back to God?" (Rom. 9:19–20). This side of glory, at least, there is no other answer. Paul is prepared not only to live with it, but to tease out its implications: "'Shall what is formed say to the one who formed it, "Why did you make me like this?" [Isa. 29:16; 45:9].' Does not the potter have the right to make out of the same lump of clay some pottery for noble purposes and some for disposal of refuse? What if God, although choosing to show his wrath and make his power known, bore with great patience the objects of his wrath—prepared for destruction? What if he did this to make the riches of his glory known to the objects of his mercy, whom he prepared in advance for glory . . . ?" (Rom. 9:21–23).

Of course, this would be intolerable, if it were all that Paul says about God, all that the Bible says about God. But Paul still assumes that the "objects of his wrath" are guilty, that God is holy, that God loves us, that God has disclosed himself to us, and so forth. He can let each relevant truth spring forth in power. And if that means he does not know, cannot now know, just how God operates in this fallen and broken world, or even why God sanctioned the fall in the first place, he refuses to domesticate God to get out of the dilemma. He is prepared to sound not a little like God addressing Job: "But who are you, a mere human being, to talk back to God?"

4. But how should the mystery of providence function in my life as a believer? Do I simply throw up my hands, acknowledge God's mysterious providence, and stagger on, struggling under the bondage of evil or suffering?

That is the topic for the next chapter.

Questions for Further Study

1. What is meant by saying that the biblical writers assume or teach compatibilism?

2. How should one arrive at a definition of free will? What definition would you offer? Why?

3. Choose two or more of the specific texts where God's sovereignty and human responsibility are in close proximity, and memorize them. Then explain them to someone else.

4. What is meant by saying that God stands behind good and evil asymmetrically? Why is this important?

5. What are some things we do not know about God?

6. Find a number of biblical passages that reflect the different ways the Bible speaks of God's "will" or "desire" or the like.

7. Why is it "essential to doctrinal and spiritual well-being" to maintain the diverse polarities in the nature of God simultaneously?

8. In anticipation of the next chapter, how do you think the mystery of providence should function in your life?

12

The Comfort of Providence

Learning to Trust

To say that something is mysterious is not to say that nothing can be said of it.

Christians learn to accept two or three profound mysteries: the nature of the Trinity, for instance, or the way the human and the divine unite in Jesus Christ. Much has been said about these subjects, some of it wise and insightful. Not a little of what has been said seeks to demonstrate that we are not dealing with contradictions but with mysteries. Other works attempt to trace the connections between one aspect or another of these mysteries, and the entire structure of Christian doctrine.

So it is—or should be—with the mystery of providence, part and parcel of the larger tension between God's sovereignty and human responsibility. In practice, however, the implications of this tension bear so immediately on the way we live, pray, conceive of evangelism, think about suffering, and much more, that we may be somewhat stymied in our Christian growth before we learn to handle the tension responsibly. For example, everyone knows of Christians who come into some deepened awareness of the sovereignty of God, and who in consequence find the urgency of their prayer life wilting. It is not enough to say this shouldn't be; we need to find out why this happens, and take steps to prevent it.

The aim of this chapter, then, is to think through the way compatibilism (as defined in the previous chapter)—the tension between God's sovereignty and human responsibility—ought to function in the life of the believer, especially with reference to the problem of evil and suffering. But before turning to evil and suffering, it may help us get our bearings if we reflect a little on how this tension properly functions in other areas of Christian life and thought.

Compatibilism Applied: Living Responsibly under God's Sovereignty

I shall begin by stating the principle, and then apply it to two or three areas.

When seeking to apply to any part of life and thought the biblically based tension between God's sovereignty and human responsibility, or between God's sovereign transcendence and his personhood, the most useful constraint is the close observation of how each component in the tension functions in Scripture. Success in this endeavor is wonderfully liberating; failure always corrodes the beauty of the biblical balance, and generates enervating fanaticism or catastrophic fatalism.

Examples make plain the operation of this principle more quickly and clearly than abstract discussion.

Prayer

It is very easy to show how the tension between divine sovereignty and human responsibility can tie people up in knots when it is applied to prayer.

For example, Clark Pinnock, who holds that human "free will" includes absolute power to contrary (discussed in the previous chapter) and insists that God's omniscience cannot include knowledge of our future free decisions (or else, he says, they would not be truly "free"), writes, "If you believe that prayer changes things, my whole position is established."[1] But if God is so impotent that he cannot save my unconverted cousin (for that would infringe upon my cousin's free will), then why bother praying for this at all?

On the other hand, J. I. Packer argues that our habit of praying that God would save this person or that proves that when we are on our knees we really do think that it is God alone who has the power to bring about salvation.[2] That is doubtless true, but opponents may be pardoned for

1. Clark Pinnock, in *Predestination and Free Will: Four Views of Divine Sovereignty*, ed. David Basinger and Randall Basinger (Downers Grove: InterVarsity, 1986), 152.
2. J. I. Packer, *Evangelism and the Sovereignty of God* (Downers Grove: InterVarsity, 1967), 15–16.

asking why it is necessary to pray at all, since God's election has already established who will and who will not be saved, and all the praying in the world is not going to change God's sovereign decree.

If there are some Christians who think that intercessory prayer is likely to be successful in proportion to its length, fervency, intensity, volume, and high-mindedness, that individual conversions or even wide-scale revival can be had for the asking, and that the key to successful praying is badgering God into doing what he otherwise would not be willing to do, there are other Christians who have so elevated God's sovereignty at the expense of his personality that they cannot quite see what the point of prolonged intercessory prayer is at all. They know, of course, they should engage in prayer: that point is too unmistakable in the Bible to be missed. But after they have said, "Your will be done on earth, as it is in heaven," there does not seem to be much point in intercession about details—not, at least, in intercession directed to a sovereign God. They find it easier to make sense of Jesus' injunction not to let our prayers rabbit on and on under the assumption we will be heard because of our many words (Matt. 6:7), than to imitate Jesus' example in praying right through the night (Luke 6:12).

It is important to see what is happening in both cases. In both instances Christians are drawing inferences about prayer that the Bible does not draw. To put the matter another way, they are permitting one aspect or the other of the tension between divine sovereignty and human responsibility to function in ways that never occur in Scripture. In particular, they are allowing inferences drawn from one leg of the tension to destroy the other leg of the tension. One side argues that prayer brings results, it "changes things," and therefore the future cannot be entirely mapped out under God's omniscience and sovereignty. God himself cannot be sovereign. The other side argues that since everything is under God's sovereign sway, and the future is already known to him, therefore our prayers must never be more than an acknowledgment that his will is best. They cannot achieve anything, or make any real difference; God's will must be done in the very nature of who God is, and our prayers simply bring our wills into line with his. And thus God becomes less than personal: he no longer responds to and answers prayer.

If we grant that the tension between God's sovereign transcendence and his personhood, outlined in the previous chapter, is of the very essence of God's gracious self-disclosure to us in Scripture, then both of these approaches to prayer cannot possibly be right. Methodologically, they err the same way: they permit inferences drawn from one pole of the biblical presentation of God to marginalize or eliminate the other pole.

What we must ask, then, is what inferences the biblical writers themselves draw from each pole. How do the poles in the tension between

God the transcendent and God the person function in the prayers of the characters in Scripture? When believers have answered that question, they should firmly resolve to make the poles of the tension function in their own prayers in the same way—and in no other. In other words, compatibilism must be applied in our prayers in the same way it is applied in the prayers of Scripture.

It would take up too much space to provide a comprehensive catalogue of such applications: this is not, after all, a book on prayer. But a few examples will illustrate the point.

In his prayer recorded in John 17, Jesus begins with the words, "Father, the hour has come." In John's Gospel, the "hour" is above all the Father's appointed time for Jesus' death, burial, resurrection, and exaltation—in short, for his glorification. With the cross now immediately impending, Jesus sees that the "hour" for his glorification has arrived. So he prays, "Glorify your Son. . . ."

It is the connection between the two clauses that is important for our purpose. The "hour" marks God's own time for the death/exaltation of his Son. That is God's sovereign plan. But Jesus does not therefore conclude there is no point praying. Rather, he prays *in line with* God's sovereign plan. The logic is: "The sovereignly determined time for the glorification of the Son is here, so glorify your Son."

This is not anomalous. To pray in Jesus' name is to pray (among other things) in accord with all that Jesus' name represents; it is to pray in accord with Jesus' will. When the persecuted church cries, "Even so, come, Lord Jesus!" it is not talking Jesus into something he does not plan to do.

When the church prays after the first whiff of persecution (Acts 4:23ff.), the believers address God as "Sovereign Lord," but that does not inject fatalism into their requests. They might have said (had they followed some contemporary models): "Sovereign Lord, if we are to be persecuted, so be it. Your will be done. Amen!" Instead, they see their persecution as of a piece with the opposition and suffering their Master endured—suffering which was predicted by Scripture and brought about through evil men by the hand of a sovereign God working out his plan of redemption. And then they pray, "Now, Lord, consider their threats and enable your servants to speak your word with great boldness. Stretch out your hand to heal and perform miraculous signs and wonders through the name of your holy servant Jesus." In this they assume that the God whom they address is a prayer-hearing, responding God. The implicit ground of their petition is the scriptural presentation of God as so sovereign that he laughs at the machinations of the nations and the "peoples" who "plot in vain."

One of the most remarkable prayers in Scripture is the intercession of Moses after the idolatry of the golden calf. When the Lord threatens to wipe out the nation and replace it with a nation made up of Moses' descendants, the language God uses is very strong: "I have seen these people . . . and they are a stiff-necked people. Now leave me alone so that my anger may burn against them and that I may destroy them. Then I will make you into a great nation" (Exod. 32:9–10).

But Moses will not "leave the Lord alone." Why should the Lord abandon the people whom he brought out of Egypt? After going to all that work, shall he now simply write them off (32:12)? Does God want to become the laughingstock of the pagan nations? "Why should the Egyptians say, 'It was with evil intent that he brought them out, to kill them in the mountains and to wipe them off the face of the earth'?" (32:12). "Turn from your fierce anger," Moses pleads. "Relent and do not bring disaster on your people" (32:12). Then Moses appeals to the faithfulness of God, the immutability of his own declared purposes: "Remember your servants Abraham, Isaac and Israel, to whom you swore by your own self: 'I will make your descendants as numerous as the stars in the sky and I will give your descendants all this land I promised them, and it will be their inheritance forever'" (32:13). In other words, God is never less than personal, and never less than sovereign. Both poles of the biblical presentation of God are appealed to by Moses—never to reduce the one by the other, but only in mutual reinforcement.

And the outcome? "Then the LORD relented and did not bring on his people the disaster he had threatened" (32:14).

Perhaps we gain another insight when we compare two or three other Old Testament passages with a similar theme. In Amos 7, the prophet repeatedly intercedes on behalf of Israel when the Lord threatens various judgments: "I cried out, 'Sovereign LORD, forgive! How can Jacob survive? He is so small!' (v. 2). Repeatedly we read, "So the LORD relented" (vv. 3, 6). By contrast, the false prophets of Israel are denounced in these terms: "You have not gone up to the breaches in the wall to repair it for the house of Israel so that it will stand firm in the battle on the day of the LORD" (Ezek. 13:5). That is a metaphorical way of saying that they have not interceded with God on behalf of the nation: that is the way the wall is maintained (both here and in Ezek. 22). That would have been God's way; but instead, the false prophets have prophesied false visions and uttered lying divinations. So judgment threatens: "I looked for someone among them who would build up the wall *and stand before me in the gap on behalf of the land so I would not have to destroy it,* but I found no one. So I will pour out my wrath on them and consume them with my fiery anger, bringing down on their own heads all they have done, declares the Sovereign LORD" (Ezek. 22:30–31, emphasis added).

This is remarkable. God seeks out believers who will pray in this intercessory way. He *expects* to be pleaded with along these lines. It is true (though inadequate) to say that he sees prayer as a means to the end, the preservation of the people. Certainly in the light of his own covenant promises and the larger presentation of his sovereignty in the pages of the Old Testament, it is hard to believe that he would become hopelessly frustrated if he could not "find" someone to stand in the gap, for where God determines to save his people he is always able to ensure that deliverance will come "from another place" than the one people expect (Esther 4:14).

For that matter, judging by the still larger categories of God's ultimacy behind all good acts, of his Spirit working in the hearts of men and women, of his sway in all matters small and great, the responsibility of his people to pray rests heavily upon them, while if his people do in fact pray it is already a mark of his grace. For the prayer itself does not escape God's sovereignty; yet it is not meaningless recital since it is addressed to a personal God. And thus if God does not "find" someone to intercede before him "in the gap," it would be true to say, simultaneously, that it is because those who should have been praying have failed to do so and will be held morally accountable for their failure, and that God himself has withheld his gracious work in their lives because he is determined to bring down the judgment he has long threatened.

Thus both God's sovereignty and God's personhood, rightly applied, become an incentive to pray.

Evangelism

To many modern minds, the free offer of the gospel entails the view that men and women are so free that God himself becomes contingent, and therefore that what the Bible says about election must be denied or explained away by appealing to an exegetically doubtful understanding of "foreknowledge" (discussed in the previous chapter). To others, once they believe that the Bible insists on God's sovereign election of some men and women to eternal life, some of the fire goes out of their enthusiasm for evangelism. If people are going to close with God, they will close with God regardless of what I do: though few would be so crass as to put it that way, one comes away with a vague feeling that there is no point getting too upset over the lost. Where these attitudes are displayed, of course, they reinforce all the biases of the zealous evangelists on the other side: See, they say, as soon as you start believing in the absoluteness of God's election, you cut the heart out of evangelism.

The problem, again, is that biblical truths are not being permitted to function in biblical ways. Inferences are being drawn from things truly taught in the Bible that are being used to disallow what the Bible clearly says elsewhere. The solution, again, is to insist that biblical doctrines function in our lives and thinking the way they do in the Bible.

It is not possible in this short chapter to do more than offer a few samples of the kind of usage to which election and free invitations to trust Christ are put in the Scriptures. We have already seen that in Acts 18:9–10 election functions as an incentive to evangelism, not as a disincentive. The idea is that if God has "his people" out there, then the appropriate thing for Christians to do is to get involved in evangelism, precisely because that is working with God and not against him. Moreover, if God has his people out there, Paul is assured of results—not because he is such a gifted evangelist, but because God's people will in due course come to him. I know more than one missionary working quietly in exceedingly difficult situations who press on with their hard and, from a merely human standpoint, thoroughly unrewarding work, because they are convinced that God has his people, who will come to him in God's own good time.

Historically, there is no necessary connection between a firm belief in what the Bible transparently says about election and some sort of cooling of evangelistic ardor. One need only think of George Whitefield and Howell Harris, or of most of the early British missionaries, or of many of the Southern Baptist leaders in the last century.

Another function of election is the abatement of human pride. This is true in many passages. At the end of John 6, for instance, when many are deserting him, Jesus asks the Twelve if they will also drift away. Simon Peter replies with a trace of bravado: "Lord, to whom shall we go? You have the words of eternal life. We have come to believe and to know that you are the Holy One of God" (6:68–69). Confronted by a claim like that, Jesus chooses this opportunity to make a counterclaim by his gentle rhetorical question: "Have I not chosen you, the Twelve? And [not "Yet," as in the TNIV] one of you is a devil!" (6:70). Thus Jesus informs Peter that the initiative rested with Jesus himself, and that in any case Peter should not speak for all of the Twelve: one would prove to be the betrayer. Even this was not outside Jesus' knowledge or control: he himself *chose* the Twelve, yet he knew that one of them would betray him. Some election may be to less than eternal life!

In Romans 9, election is again tied to the freedom of grace: "I will have mercy on whom I have mercy, and I will have compassion on whom I have compassion" (v. 15). But this does not mean that saving faith is simply imposed, that the prospective "convert" is dragged, kicking and screaming, to confess faith that is not really personal faith. "For it is with *your heart* that you believe and are justified, and it is with *your mouth* that you profess your faith and are saved" (Rom. 10:10, emphasis added). Our hymns sometimes keep this tension together better than our prose:

> I sought the Lord, and afterward I knew
> He moved my heart to seek him, seeking me;
> It was not I that found, O Savior true;
> No, I was found by Thee.
>
> Thou didst reach forth Thy hand and mine enfold;
> I walked and sank not on the storm-vexed sea;
> 'Twas not so much that I on Thee took hold
> As Thou, dear Lord, on me.
>
> I find, I walk, I love, but O the whole
> Of love is but my answer, Lord to Thee!
> For Thou wert long beforehand with my soul;
> Always Thou lovedst me.

In some instances the emphasis on obedient hearing is used to locate blame and responsibility. Paul insists that "faith comes from hearing the message, and the message is heard through the word about Christ" (Rom. 10:17). But this does not function in his thought as a mitigation of divine election. It functions, rather, to focus blame on the nation of Israel for hearing yet not believing (10:18ff.).

The challenge "And how can they hear without someone preaching to them? And how can anyone preach unless they are sent?" (10:14–15) not only justifies Paul's ministry but probably also prepares his readers, in the context of this epistle, to provide some help for the apostle in his projected evangelistic expedition to Spain (15:24ff.).

Much more could be said, but the point is simple enough: we will not be so likely to destroy the mysteries that are part of the warp and woof of Scripture, of Scripture's disclosure about the nature of God, if we take care to allow the poles of these mysteries to function *only* in the way they do in Scripture.

Other Examples

In chapter 11, I briefly sketched other examples without exploring them. Nor can I take the space to explore them here, but it might be worth mentioning them.

In John's Gospel, Jesus is simultaneously the one whose ministry and death/exaltation are determined by his Father's will (whether expressed in Scripture or in Jesus' inner awareness), and the one who voluntarily obeys his Father. His obedience therefore provides us with a model of how we *ought* to respond to the claims of God's sovereignty. Indeed, the Son's dependence and obedience are so perfect that it is precisely in such dependence upon and obedience to his Father that the Father's will is communicated and his sovereignty extended (5:19ff.).

Above all, it is the cross of Jesus Christ where all the elements of these mysteries coalesce. The cross was nothing less than God's sovereign plan, and his sovereign sway extended not only to many details "modeled" in advance in Old Testament prophecy, but to the wicked machinations of the human agents who arranged for Jesus to be executed. Yet Jesus went to the cross voluntarily: he *chose* to obey the Father. He prayed, "Not my will, but yours be done!"—a prayer which needed praying, even though at one level it is scarcely conceivable that God's redemptive will on the cross could *not* have been accomplished. Here is the outbreak of the most odious evil, and here is the ultimate manifestation of God's love. Here is vile, brutal injustice, and here the justice of God is manifested as he justifies sinners. Here the Son learns the climactic lesson in obedience, and here is the hour of the power of darkness.

In each case, we have learned to live with irony and paradox, because we have come to see that, for the cross to make any sense at all, we simply *must* affirm that God was sovereign, that human beings were rebellious and morally responsible, that God's love and justice were displayed, and that Christ died voluntarily. If we forsake any one of these truths, the significance of the cross is destroyed and we are lost.

Learning to Trust

So also we must learn to handle the "given" of compatibilism: God is sovereign, and we are responsible, and these two truths are so construed in Scripture that neither is allowed to relativize the other. To the "givens" of compatibilism we add the "given" that God loves us, and is unfailingly good. And yet evil and suffering exist. The fall occurred. How shall we hold these pieces together?

What we must *not* do is to draw inferences from part of the evidence that contradicts other parts of the evidence. The presence of evil does not function in the Bible so as to deny the goodness of God. The absoluteness of God's sovereign sway never operates so that his ultimacy behind good and evil is entirely symmetrical. Nor does the presence of evil function in such a way as to deny God's sovereignty, or his personal attachment to his covenant people.

After we have accepted that the "givens" are nonnegotiable and done our best to see just where the mystery lies—at heart, it is bound up with the very nature of God—we must ensure that biblical truths function in our lives in much the same way that they function in Scripture. That way we will avoid implicitly denying one truth when we affirm another; we will grow in stability; above all, we will better know the God who has in his grace disclosed himself to rebels like us, taken up our guilt, participated in human suffering, and sovereignly ensured that we will not be tempted above what we are able to bear. In knowing him better we will learn to trust him; and in trusting him we will find rest.

In what follows, then, I offer a mixture of principles and vignettes that articulate or suggest the way God's sovereignty functions in the minds of biblical writers when they observe evil or suffering taking place under its aegis. In a sense, most of the book you are reading has been dealing with this topic. To avoid repeating myself, I shall focus on a few of the many passages and emphases still but little explored.

1. God's sovereignty functions to assure us that things are not getting out of control. Coupled with his love, God's sovereignty assures the Christian that "in all things God works *for the good* of those who love him, who have been called according to his purpose" (Rom. 8:28, emphasis added).

This is particularly important where suffering is compounded by sheer uncertainty. A young mother who learns that her mate has disappeared on a military front, with nothing heard from him in the ensuing weeks, will suffer not only the loss, the fear, the loneliness, but also agonizing uncertainty. If someone were to come up to her at that point and glibly quote Romans 8:28 to her, it might well be unbearably insensitive, even cruel—not because the text is not true, but because the quick quotation could easily be viewed by her as a formulaic sop thoughtlessly uttered by someone who did not understand the depth of the hurt. Such pastoral questions I shall briefly address in the next chapter. Yet the fact remains that this young woman needs to discover and rest in Romans 8:28 for herself. Her uncertainties will not thereby disappear, but they will be reduced to proper proportions: they will be brought under the hand of the God she knows. She may not know the future, but she knows the God who controls the future.

To our limited perspectives, there are plenty of accidents that determine so many tragedies. To the eyes of faith, there are, finally, no accidents, only incidents; and in these, Paul assures us, God is working *for our good*. To walk into the unknown with a God of unqualified power and unfailing goodness is safer than a known way.

2. We repeatedly learn from Scripture that the scale of time during which God works out his purposes for us is far greater than our incessant focus on the present. Toddlers pester their parents with their urgent cries of "Now!" From God's perspective, we adults cannot appear greatly different.

Naomi and her husband abandon their homeland because of the curse of drought. The years pass, and Naomi loses her husband, then both sons—this is in an age and culture when men provided the support and ballast of life, when a single woman was in a precarious position. Small wonder that when she returns to her homeland, accompanied by only one of her daughters-in-law, she complains, "Don't call me Naomi [Pleasant]. . . . Call me Mara [Bitter], because the Almighty has made my life very bitter. I went away full, but the LORD has brought me back empty. Why call me Naomi? The LORD has afflicted me; the Almighty has brought misfortune upon me" (Ruth 1:20–21).

When things begin to look up because of the personal interest Boaz shows in Ruth, Naomi exclaims, "The LORD bless him! . . . He has not stopped showing his kindness to the living and the dead.[3] . . . That man is our close relative; he is one of our family guardians" (Ruth 2:20). When Boaz and Ruth are united in marriage, it is the Lord who enables her to conceive and bring forth a son. The women say to Naomi: "Praise be to the LORD, who this day has not left you without a family guardian. May he become famous throughout Israel! He will renew your life and sustain you in your old age. For your daughter-in-law, who loves you and is better to you than seven sons, has given him birth" (Ruth 4:14–15).

This is all very interesting: a love story with a happy ending, in which God is seen to be operating behind the scenes. But the writer sees more than that, more than Naomi herself could have known. He comments, "And they named him [the child] Obed. He was the father of Jesse, the father of David" (Ruth 4:17). The writer then ends with the genealogy spelled out.

Naomi never knew she would be an ancestor of Jesus the Messiah. She could not possibly have enjoyed any prospect of being written up in the canon of Scripture that hundreds of millions of Jews and Christians alike would read for millennia. Her timescale was far too small for that.

I am not blaming her. I am saying that there are many instances in Scripture where the timescale on which God works out his purposes is vastly greater than what we can imagine.

Perhaps the way you or I hold up under suffering may be instrumental in the conversion of someone who in turn brings up his family in the fear of the Lord, so that his daughter's son becomes the next Whitefield or Spurgeon or Carey or Wilberforce. There comes a time when by re-reading the Scriptures it dawns on us that God frequently utilizes and blesses small acts of faithfulness in the context of deep misery to bring

3. She is probably thinking of her husband and two sons. If a relative marries Ruth, and they have children, they will be counted as the heirs and successors of the family line. Property is passed on the same way.

forth blessing we could not possibly have asked for, but would have been happy to suffer for.

The ultimate "timescale," of course (if I may stretch a term), ends up in the new heaven and the new earth. God is getting his people ready for heaven. I do not pretend that elementary truth "solves" everything. But the vantage from the End (see chap. 8) certainly transforms our assessment of many things.

3. If God is the God of the Bible, then for him there are no surprises, no insuperable problems. Far from breeding fatalism, in the Scriptures that truth breeds confidence and faith. It teaches us to trust. It teaches us to read and reread Hebrews 11.

To an omnipotent God, there cannot be degrees of difficulty; there cannot be an unforeseen setback. Elijah flees to the desert and longs for death because the glorious confrontation with the prophets of Baal on Mount Carmel did not bring about the reformation he expected. He is still running for his life from a vicious queen (1 Kings 19). His expectations were false—a frequent cause of depression. God's were not. God had to teach Elijah that sometimes he operates not through the mighty confrontation and the powerful, dramatic storm, but through a still, small voice that reserves to himself seven thousand who have not yet bowed the knee to idols.

Much mental suffering is tied to our false expectations. We may so link our hopes and joys and future to a new job, to a promotion, to certain kinds of success, to prosperity, that when they fail to materialize we are utterly crushed. But quiet confidence in God alone breeds stability and delight amid "all the changing scenes of life."

4. The modern, frequently unvoiced view of God is that he is in charge of the big things, the major turning points; it is less clear that he is in charge of anything beyond that. Jesus in the Sermon on the Mount argues just the reverse (Matt. 6). Jesus *assumes* his heavenly Father sovereignly watches over each sparrow and each flower, and argues from the lesser to the greater: if God cares for even these things—surely of relatively little account on the eternal and cosmic scales of things!—should we not trust him to provide men and women, made in his own image, with all that we need?

The sad truth is that science has taught many of us to adopt some version of the "God-of-the-gaps theory." In this view, God sets everything in motion and allows it to chug along in line with the laws that he himself sets in place. But every once in a while God intervenes. He actually *does* something. We call that a miracle.

Biblically speaking, of course, this is nonsense. I would never deny that God has created an ordered universe. But the biblical view of God's sovereignty is that even now, at every second, he sustains that universe.

Indeed, he now mediates every scrap of the infinite reaches of his sovereignty through his Son (1 Cor. 15:25), who even now is "sustaining all things by his powerful word" (Heb. 1:3). A miracle is not an instance of God doing something for a change; it is an instance of God doing something out of the ordinary. That God normally operates the universe consistently makes science possible; that he does not always do so ought to keep science humble. Above all, this view of God's sovereignty means that we should draw comfort and faith even by observing the world around us—as Jesus did.

5. Yet God is a personal God who responds. That is one of the great lessons of the psalms; it is one of the grand assumptions of the prayers of Paul. We have already observed a number of instances in which David, oppressed by illness, enemies, defeat, tragedy, guilt, turns to the Lord and begs him not to hide his face. The Lord responds, and the psalm ends in a shout of triumph.

This fact goes beyond mere intellectual argument. Unbelievers will simply not follow me here. Consider Paul: he prays three times that his "thorn in the flesh" (whatever that is) will be taken away. When I was a child, I was told that God normally had three answers: yes, no, and wait. It seems safe enough: God can't lose, no matter what happens. But that is not God's answer to Paul. God's answer was this: "My grace is sufficient for you, for my power is made perfect in weakness" (2 Cor. 12:9).

Eventually Paul does not merely put up with this answer: he exults in it. His heart's cry is that in his own life and ministry he might experience the same power that raised Jesus from the dead (Phil. 3:10). Here he learns the secret of it: God's power is made perfect in Paul's life when Paul himself is weak. "Therefore," says Paul, "I will boast all the more gladly about my weaknesses, so that Christ's power may rest on me" (2 Cor. 12:9). The thorn in the flesh helps keep him humble (12:7). As a matter of principle, Paul understands this to be crucially important: "That is why, for Christ's sake, I delight in weaknesses, in insults, in hardships, in persecutions, in difficulties. For when I am weak, then I am strong" (2 Cor. 12:10). This is the New Testament equivalent to the exultation of a David when God himself comes near in the midst of suffering.

The degree of our peace of mind is tied to our prayer life (Phil. 4:6–7). This is not because prayer is psychologically soothing, but because we address a prayer-answering God, a personal God, a responding God, a sovereign God whom we can trust with the outcomes of life's confusions. And we learn, with time, that if God in this or that instance does not choose to take away the suffering, or utterly remove the evil, *he does send grace and power*. The result is praise; and that, of course, is itself enjoyable, in exactly the same way that lovers enjoy giving each other compliments.

I cannot tell you how many times I have visited some senior saint who is going through serious suffering, perhaps terminal illness, only to come away feeling that it was *I* who benefited from exposure to a believer who was already living in the felt presence of God. When my friend and colleague Colin Hemer lay dying, he made jokes about a lengthy manuscript he had almost completed: "It is a great blessing that someone else will have to compile the indexes," he grinned. In his last thirty-six hours or so, as he drifted in and out of consciousness, he spoke the word for "grace" in the many languages he knew. Among his last coherent utterances was an expression of quiet curiosity as to what God would have for him to do in glory.

What is clear is that it is in extremity that many Christians drink most deeply of the grace of God, revel in his presence, and glory in whatever it is—suffering included—that has brought them this heightened awareness of the majesty of God.

One of the hymns of Augustus Toplady (1740–1778) superbly captures the integrity of biblical balance, and shows how the diverse poles in the very being of God, as he has revealed himself to us, conspire to bring comfort:

> A sovereign protector I have,
> Unseen, yet for ever at hand,
> Unchangeably faithful to save,
> Almighty to rule and command.
> He smiles and my comforts abound;
> His grace as the dew shall descend,
> And walls of salvation surround
> The soul He delights to defend.
>
> Kind Author and ground of my hope,
> Thee, Thee, for my God I avow;
> My glad Ebenezer set up
> And own Thou hast helped me till now.
> I muse on the years that are past
> Wherein my defence Thou hast proved;
> Nor wilt Thou relinquish at last
> A sinner so signally loved.
>
> Inspirer and Hearer of prayer,
> Thou Shepherd and Guardian of Thine,
> My all to Thy covenant care
> I sleeping and waking resign.
> If Thou art my Shield and my Sun,
> The night is no darkness to me;
> And, fast as my moments roll on,
> They bring me but nearer to Thee.

God himself is both our shield and our very great reward (Gen. 15:1).

6. There is a sense in which the entire Bible is fodder for this chapter. From beginning to end, it is concerned to teach us to trust and obey.

This means, then, that the object of much of the biblical revelation is not to make us comprehend exhaustively, but something else. Doubtless God could have told us more than he has; doubtless we will find out more things in the new heaven and the new earth. But we are sufficiently self-centered that extra knowledge about God would simply pander to our desire to be gods ourselves.

In short, God is less interested in answering our questions than in other things: securing our allegiance, establishing our faith, nurturing a desire for holiness. An important part of spiritual maturity is bound up with this obvious truth. God tells us a great deal about himself; but the mysteries that remain are not going to be answered at a merely theoretical and intellectual level. We may probe a little around the edges, using the minds God has given us to glimpse something of his glory. But ultimately the Christian will take refuge from questions about God not in proud, omniscient explanations but in adoring worship.

In an analogous way, we conclude that God tells us a great deal about evil and suffering. But the mysteries that remain are not going to be answered at a merely theoretical and intellectual level. We may probe a little around the edges, using the minds God has given us to think through Scripture, seeking to ensure that the polarities of God's character function in our lives as they are modeled in Scripture. But ultimately Christians will take refuge from their questions about evil not in proud theories that explain evil away, but in combating evil, opposing it, especially evil within themselves but also in the larger world as well. Christians will take refuge from their questions about suffering not in bitterness, self-pity, resentment against God, or trite clichés and religious cant, but in endurance, perseverance, and faith in the God who has suffered, who has fought with evil and triumphed, and whose power and goodness ensure that faith resting in him is never finally disappointed.

Questions for Further Study

1. What is the primary lesson to be learned from this chapter?
2. What inferences about prayer (and about election and evil) does the Bible *not* draw from God's sovereignty?
3. If God were not personal, what differences would it make to the way we should pray?

4. If God were not transcendent and sovereign, what differences would it make to the way we should pray?

5. Repeat questions #3 and #4, replacing "the way we should pray" by, first, "the doctrine of election," and then by "the problem of evil and suffering."

6. What instances can you give of God meeting your suffering, or the suffering of someone you know, not with the elimination of the cause of suffering, but with grace that is (to use Paul's term) "sufficient" for them?

13

Some Pastoral Reflections

Anyone who has suffered devastating grief or dehumanizing pain has at some point been confronted by near relatives of Job's miserable comforters. They come with their clichés and tired, pious mouthings. They engender guilt where they should be administering balm. They utter solemn truths where compassion is needed. They exhibit strength and exhort to courage where they would be more comforting if they simply wept.

In the preface I warned you that this is not necessarily a book that should be read by someone who is going through deep suffering. It might help some people; most certainly it would not help others. It is more in the way of preventative medicine: that is, I have tried to establish some firm structures to help Christians think about evil and suffering in biblical ways *before* hard days descend on them.

Even so, because suffering of one kind or another is always taking place, a chapter of this sort may be helpful. It is at odds with the rest of the book. It is less theoretical, and offers a miscellany of counsel to men and women who are trying to comfort those passing through deep waters. Many of the points are offered in light of the discussion in the previous chapters; and, as in the rest of the book, I am concerned with helping Christians, not unbelievers. When unbelievers grieve, there are opportunities for Christians to help and serve and share the gospel; but in this book I am not specifically addressing that challenge (though of

course many of the same things apply). Here I have the Christian in
view.

1. We must recognize that grief normally passes through predictable stages. For example, when someone is suddenly bereaved, it is not
uncommon to find such stages of grief as the following, drawn from a
useful little book by Granger Westberg:[1] "we are in a state of shock";
"we express emotion"; "we feel depressed and very lonely"; "we may
experience physical symptoms of distress"; "we may become panicky";
"we feel a sense of guilt about the loss"; "we are filled with anger and
resentment"; "we resist returning to our usual activities"; "gradually
hope comes through"; "we struggle to affirm reality."

Clearly there is no immutable law about these stages. How many stages
an individual goes through, and how quickly, depends on many things:
how stable that person is, how devoted to or dependent on the one who
has died, how much support is given, how robust that person's faith is,
how habitual that person's walk with God, and much more beside. The
value of recognizing that stages of grief are common, however, is that
the person who is trying to offer comfort will see the telltale signs and
respond appropriately. The bereaved Christian who suddenly starts lash-
ing out with anger and resentment will not be written off as an apostate.
The Christian who at this moment finds little comfort in the doctrine
of the resurrection, so great is the sense of loss, is not to be berated and
rebuked. It would do many would-be comforters good to sit down and
read the moving and candidly personal book of Nicholas Wolterstorff,
Lament for a Son,[2] written after his twenty-five-year-old son was killed
in a mountain-climbing accident.

2. Some grief takes a long time to heal. I have known families—remarkably mature, Christian families—where the death of a promising child
so devastated the parents that it took several years before the mother
could talk about it without bursting into tears, before the father could
talk about it at all. A young pastor I know lost his wife, the mother of
their two children, and about a year later left the ministry. The church
had proved marvelously supportive for the first two or three months.
By six months, older saints, including the senior pastor, were simply
telling him to get on with life, to pick up the pieces, to stop feeling sorry
for himself.

It is possible that some of these things needed to be said—but only
in a context of giving this young man the repeated opportunity to talk
out his grief, to pray with people, to find some continuing help with

1. Granger E. Westberg, *Good Grief: A Constructive Approach to the Problem of Loss*
(Philadelphia: Fortress, 1971).
2. Nicholas Wolterstorff, *Lament for a Son* (Grand Rapids: Eerdmans, 1987).

the children. Pastoral ministry being what it is, perhaps he should have been gently directed toward temporary resignation even earlier—but only as a way of helping him to regain his moorings, not in a way that compounded his grief with a sense of failure and guilt. After he resigned, it took another two years, and a great deal of talk with a mature Christian leader who could give him some perspective on what he had gone through, before he felt able to resume active ministry. My point is that many forms of grief need time.

3. Frequently in the midst of suffering the most comforting "answers" are simple presence, help, silence, tears. Helping with the gardening or preparing a casserole may be far more spiritual an exercise than the exposition of Romans 8:28. The Scriptures themselves exhort us to "mourn with those who mourn" (Rom. 12:15).

4. Many verbal expressions of encouragement should not be based on the assumption that they must answer an implicit "Why?" Not everyone asks that question. Some who need encouragement need reminding of simple things, not profound and complex answers to the "why" question. A young man became a Christian and almost immediately was diagnosed as having a rapid and incurable cancer. As he watched part of his body wither away and other parts of his body bloat grotesquely, those around him found that the greatest encouragement came to him from reciting John 11:25–26 and parts of 1 Corinthians 15.

5. When verbalized answers to anguished cries of "Why?" are required, what and how much we provide will depend largely on what might be called our spiritual diagnosis, that is, our assessment of the needs and capacity of the individual. Some crying "Why?" are not really asking questions; they are simply seeking comfort. Others are asking questions, but cannot at that moment bear more than the briefest reply. When a Christian I do not know very well asks that sort of question, my response to that question may be, "I cannot give you all the answers to your 'Why?' But you may draw courage from the fact that the one who loves you so much he died for you asked the same question: 'My God, my God, *why* have you forsaken me?'"

At some point, more reflective believers will want something more. Some will be ready to read, others to engage in simple Bible studies—for instance, reflections on some of the psalms, or on the prayers of Paul, or on other passages briefly expounded in this book.

6. In this day when many in the Western world have been seduced by some form of the "power, health, and wealth" gospel, it is important to stress the Christian's location—between the fall and the new heaven and the new earth, enjoying the "down payment" of the Spirit but by no means free of death and decay. There is nothing in Scripture to encourage us to think we should always be free from the vicissitudes that plague a

dying world. Of course, it may be easier to say those things to believers *before* their time of suffering rather than *in* it. But where self-seeking, self-gratifying forms of Western Christianity predominate, it is essential to lay out these truths, loudly and often.

7. For one reason or another, suffering is often associated with guilt feelings. The sharpest diagnosis and care are called for. Sometimes there may be real guilt, that is, moral guilt before God for specific sins. Here, if anywhere, the Christian is able to offer good news. Jesus died to take our guilt. Real guilt in the face of suffering must be handled like real guilt in every situation: we must confess it, renounce the sin, ask God for his forgiveness, attempt restitution where possible, and learn to rest in the forgiving word of Christ.

But often there is false guilt, that is, a vague feeling of guilt for which there is no real breach before God. For the Christian, the long-term answer is to establish, on the basis of God's Word, what we should and should not feel guilty about, and thus expose false guilt as nothing less than the devil's lie.

8. Some forms of suffering require active intervention. A wife being beaten by her husband, for instance, requires a judgment: at what point must you counsel the wife to leave him, even to get a court order to provide her with some sort of protection? The case of a child being sexually abused by a relative demands that we bring in police or other services: the need for haste is often balanced by the need for discretion or reasonable certainty. Those serving in poor areas may tackle some problems with carefully thought-out programs of support, relief, education, self-help structures, redress in legislation, and much more. In countless instances, Christians provide—they *must* provide—more than a counseling service or a shoulder to cry on.

9. It is important to offer hope—not only the hope of the consummation, but hope even on the shorter term.

10. Nevertheless, it is important to help people to live one day at a time. When a horrible and terminal disease is hanging over your head, you do not need grace for the end—yet. You need grace for today—just for today. We all are under sentence of death; all of us need grace for today.

11. Above all, we must help people know God better. Too many answers we give are merely intellectual, merely theoretical, merely propositional. We must so teach and counsel and pray with people that we deepen their experiential knowledge of God. We must so get them into meditative and rigorous reading of the Word of God that they draw vast comfort from its pages. At the deepest level, men and women must learn, with Job, that God is very great, and it is an inexpressible privilege to know him, to be satisfied with him, even when—especially when!—we do not have all the answers. Then men and women will learn to rest in his love, and

will return again and again to the cross, where their vision of that love will be constantly renewed.

When C. S. Lewis finished writing his book *The Problem of Pain* (originally published in 1940 at the outbreak of World War II),[3] he wrote a preface explaining that his aim was to address certain intellectual problems relating to the problem of pain. Then he added this sentence:

> For the far higher task of teaching fortitude and patience I was never fool enough to suppose myself qualified, nor have I anything to offer my readers except my conviction that when pain is to be borne, a little courage helps more than much knowledge, a little human sympathy more than much courage, and the least tincture of the love of God more than all.

12. To this end, we must pray for those who suffer. God himself is the one "who comforts the downcast" (2 Cor. 7:6); he is "the God of all comfort" (2 Cor. 1:3). In the deepest suffering, many find it almost impossible to pray. Should not the rest of us intercede for them?

There have been times when I have seen the face of suffering transformed, permanently transformed, in answer to specific, believing prayer. There is surely something unhealthy and deformed about a vision of Christianity that offers counsel but not intercession—a trap into which I have tumbled on far too many occasions. If God is the God of comfort, he, finally, must provide it—often through human agents, sometimes not, but he must do it. So let us ask, remembering that he delights to give good things to his children, and that very often our lack is a reflection of a pathetic refusal to ask (James 4:2).

Questions for Further Study

1. Have you been through deep suffering or experienced brutal, malignant evil? What helped you the most during that period of your life? *Who* helped you the most?
2. What role does hope play in assuaging suffering?
3. How can we help those who suffer to experience the love of God?
4. For whom do you pray? What do you pray on their behalf? Why? To what extent do the prayers of Scripture control your prayers?

3. C. S. Lewis, *The Problem of Pain* (London: Centenary, 1940).

Appendix

Reflections on AIDS

This brief appendix has been included for several reasons. The most obvious is that it is closely tied to themes in this book and therefore provides something of a test case. Transparently, AIDS calls out for reflection on suffering, illness, the sovereignty of God, death—but also (it might be argued) human responsibility and even human culpability. The number of tragic deaths attributed to AIDS continues to climb, with horrific consequences, individually and globally.

Because the subject is tied not only to the harshest realities of suffering, poverty, and death, but also to massive moral questions, AIDS arguably has greater potential for igniting passions than many other issues. Nowadays the acronym AIDS (acquired immunodeficiency syndrome) no longer has to be explained, neither does the basic biology of the "human immunodeficiency virus" (HIV), including its dangerous capacity to mutate to new forms. People have heard of at least some of the drugs used to combat it (especially AZT). Not everyone remembers, however, that the best of these drugs, although they prolong life considerably, neither prevent the disease nor completely cure the patient. In any case, unlike the appendix in the first edition of this book, in this second edition I need not review the basic medical information now available to almost anyone with a computer and a few minutes to search online. On the other hand, the statistics have changed considerably in the last fifteen years, and some of the discussion on moral issues and treatment options needs updating.

The Current State of Affairs

Obtaining reliable statistics is not easy. Statistics published by, say, *Scientific American*, the World Health Organization, and various scientific monographs are far from being in perfect agreement. To add to the mix, some studies focus on the number of people who are HIV carriers (whether or not the individuals have displayed the clinical symptoms of AIDS), while others focus exclusively on those with AIDS.

Even if we allow a 5 to 10 percent margin of error, however, it seems safe to say that more than 40 million human beings now carry the AIDS virus. More than 3 million die from the disease each year, about three-quarters of them in sub-Saharan Africa. The number of people who test positive for HIV is close to being stabilized in Africa, but this is small comfort: it simply means that the number of people who die from AIDS on that continent each year roughly equals the number of new infections on that continent during the same year. Worldwide, the number of infected persons continues to increase in every region, with a total of about 5 million new infections each year. In some regions, the growth is incremental—whether because the totals are already devastating, as in Africa, or because individual countries in a region have aggressively reduced the number of new infections (notably Brazil, Thailand, and Uganda). The sharpest increases in the last two or three years have been in Eastern Europe and Asia. The epidemic growth of the disease in Eastern Europe and Central Asia is driven at least as much by intravenous drug use as it is by unprotected promiscuous sex. Russia alone has more than 3 million intravenous drug users. In Latin America and the Caribbean, national rates of infection are extremely varied: for example, in Brazil, the national infection rate is just below 1 percent (though in some cities, 60 percent of intravenous drug users carry HIV); in Haiti, the national infection rate is 5.6 percent, the highest outside Africa, where several countries have double-digit rates of infection (Botswana, about 35 percent; Zimbabwe, about 25 percent). The death rate of several countries (e.g., Malawi, Namibia, Swaziland, Zambia) is so high populations have stagnated; in others (Botswana, South Africa, Zimbabwe) populations will soon sharply decrease. Although Botswana leads its region in healthcare and literacy, its life expectancy is expected to halve (from about 65 years to about 33 years) over the next decade, the decline driven almost exclusively by AIDS. One of the world experts on the poverty of sub-Saharan Africa insists that AIDS has increased the poverty in Africa by about 50 percent.[1]

1. Daniel Song'ony, *Social Economic Impact of HIV in Sub-Saharan Africa* (Aldershot: Ashgate, forthcoming); idem, *Poverty, Inequality, and Economic Development in Africa* (Downers Grove: InterVarsity, 2005).

Issues having to do with treatments—what helps and what doesn't, what the costs are, who will or could pay—are hotly debated. There is little doubt that in the years ahead many of the drugs that have already been developed will become "generic," driving the costs down somewhat, but the poorest countries will still not be able to afford them. Moreover, many of the drugs, or drug cocktails, have to be taken on strict regimes, to a strict scheduling. Miss a dose or two and all you are doing is helping the virus to develop resistance to the drugs. The Left sometimes gives the impression that universal provision of condoms is the answer. But quite apart from social rejection of condoms in some cultures, the actual statistics are startling. In Thailand, widespread distribution of condoms, *along with* widespread propaganda aiming to encourage more celibacy and more sexual fidelity, has radically reduced the number of new infections each year. In Africa, the only country that has seen a dramatic reduction of new infections is Uganda, and it has done so primarily by warning against casual sex and urging strict sexual fidelity. For those interested in results, as measured by lives saved, as opposed to mere propaganda in the perennial sexual revolution, that hard reality *ought* to influence how at least *some* of the billions provided by Western countries should be spent. The issues are notoriously complex, but condoms alone are *not* going to solve this worldwide threat. As for vaccines, the promise, so far, has always been just over the next horizon.

In America, at one time the disease traveled almost exclusively through either the homosexual community or the community of intravenous drug users. That is no longer the case. A rising percentage of HIV carriers and of AIDS patients are heterosexuals.

At least in America, the reasons why the disease circulated more rapidly in the homosexual population than in the heterosexual population were probably twofold. First, the chances of communicating the disease from one person to another in only *one* sexual encounter are considerably higher among homosexuals than among heterosexuals. The reasons are uncertain, but the most probable is that, since the membranes in the anal passage were never designed for the trauma of sex, the possibility of bleeding is much higher than in vaginal sex. The mingling of blood and semen, both high carriers of HIV, is a potent combination.

Second, studies demonstrate that casual sex—sexual intercourse with multiple anonymous partners—is far more common among homosexuals than among heterosexuals. In one major study, for instance, it was calculated that 2 percent of homosexuals have intercourse with 1,000 or more partners during the course of their "careers" (which for the purpose of the study set the cutoffs at the ages of 18 and 60); 12 percent have intercourse with between 500 and 999 partners; 40 percent with 100 to

499 partners.[2] What is incontrovertible is that the virus is not passed on by casual contact, such as touching, kissing, or even by mosquito bites (the virus does not appear to survive more than a few seconds in a mosquito). It is passed on by casual sex, intravenous drug use, or by an infected mother who is carrying a baby in her womb.

Is AIDS God's Judgment?

There are very strong opposing voices to answer the question, Is AIDS God's judgment? I shall try to respond by enunciating a number of complementary points.

1. If by "God's judgment" we imply that each person infected with AIDS has contracted the disease because of a particular sin, the answer must surely be a resounding negative. To say the least, that would be unbearably harsh on infants born with the disease, or on hemophiliacs who have caught the virus from a lifesaving transfusion taken in good faith, or on faithful spouses who have been infected by an unfaithful spouse. They may be born with a sinful nature, but they have not participated in the sexual promiscuity or intravenous drug use that is the infection's immediate cause in the overwhelming majority of the victims.

2. On the other hand, there is a sense in which all suffering is related to the fall and the curse that disorders the entire universe (see chap. 3). If there were no sin, there would be no AIDS. In that sense, doubtless this affliction is part of God's judgment. But can we say more than that?

3. Consider the analogy of war. In the Old Testament, war is frequently presented as God's judgment on his people. But that does not mean that everyone who suffers in war is guilty of the same idolatry and corruption that brought the nation down. Babies die in wars, too; the righteous may be raped or shot or blown up or starved. But just as these obvious facts do not prevent the Old Testament writers from seeing God's hand of judgment in war, so there is nothing in similar facts regarding AIDS sufferers to prevent us from detecting God's hand of judgment in this scourge.

2. This is one of many such studies, which display a range of figures depending on a variety of constraints. These figures are typical. For useful summaries of such studies and full bibliographical information, see Thomas E. Schmidt, *Straight and Narrow? Compassion and Clarity in the Homosexuality Debate* (Downers Grove: InterVarsity, 1995), 105–8; Stanton L. Jones and Mark A. Yarhouse, *Homosexuality: The Use of Scientific Research in the Church's Moral Debate* (Downers Grove: InterVarsity, 2000), 109–10; and Peter Sprigg and Timothy Dailey, eds., *Setting It Straight: What the Research Shows about Homosexuality* (Washington, DC: Family Research Council, 2004).

4. Even so, we have still not faced the central issue. The plain fact of the matter is that if there were no sexual promiscuity and no intravenous drug use, there would be no AIDS; and those who are most sexually promiscuous are at greatest risk. It is exceedingly difficult—not to say morally and biblically irresponsible—not to see a connection.

For although everyone talks of AIDS and the underlying infection as an "epidemic" or a "pandemic," it is not an epidemic in any historic sense at all. In the plague, for instance, people did not know how the disease was communicated. Eventually the policy was quarantine. But that is simply not the case here. We know the channels of communication of the virus; we know them exactly.

That is why when we are told, both by government sources and by various well-meaning bodies, that "we are all at risk" or the like, we are being told a lie. That is simply not true, in the way all were at risk during the bubonic plague or assorted smallpox or cholera scares. If you are celibate or monogamous (and your sexual partner is monogamous), and you are not intravenously injecting drugs with someone else's needle, your chances of picking up the disease are virtually zero. If you are a hemophiliac, you are at slightly higher risk, but not much (which could not be said of hemophiliacs before 1985). The only way you are likely to contract the HIV virus is if you are involved in a car crash on your way home from work, and the blood of an infected person mingles with yours—or something equally traumatic. If medical personnel take elementary precautions (such as sterile gloves), their chances of contracting the disease, outside the known channels, also approach zero.

These elementary facts must not be uttered with a gloating sneer. But the public is not going to be fooled by half-truths and whole lies, and on the long haul it will prove harder to build a case for compassion, for the dispersal of billions of tax dollars and the like if people feel they have been hoodwinked. The fact of the matter is that the overwhelming majority of those who suffer from the disease have engaged in biblically forbidden promiscuity or self-destroying drug use; and the small percentage of additional people who have suffered from the disease would never have contracted it had it not been for the larger groups. Thus, unlike the plague, the explicit connection between biblically forbidden behavior and contraction of the disease makes it far harder *not* to see the severe hand of God in AIDS.

5. If I may say so gently, it is also hard not to see this disease as a rebuke to the arrogance of the medical profession. I say this hesitantly, for I know many fine physicians and nurses, and more than once my own life has been dependent on their care. Nevertheless, the opening article in one early issue of *Scientific American* devoted to AIDS begins

with a commonplace in the literature: "As recently as a decade ago it was widely believed that infectious disease was no longer much of a threat in the developed world."[3]

I find it hard not to hear God saying, "Do you really think you can ignore my laws with impunity, and treat the resulting diseases with powerful drugs to escape the consequences? You haven't seen anything yet."

Do not misunderstand me: I am grateful to God for powerful drugs that will cure syphilis. Yes, grateful *to God*; for if he sends the ravages, he also orders the universe and works through what theologians call "common grace" to find solutions and treatments. But many successes breed the arrogance we saw in the king of Assyria (see chap. 11), the arrogance of Babel. It is exceedingly difficult for anyone steeped in Scripture not to see in AIDS a firm rebuke of the arrogance of medical science.

6. What then of Romans 1:27? Many conservatives cite this as the "proof text" that exposes AIDS as judgment from God. Paul writes: "In the same way the men also abandoned natural relations with women and were inflamed with lust for one another. Men committed shameful acts with other men, and received in themselves the due penalty for their error." AIDS, it is argued, is one facet of the "due penalty."

A glance at the competent commentaries will exclude this view. The Greek text makes it quite clear that homosexuality itself is seen as the "due penalty" of the "error" of inflamed lust.

7. There is even a sense in which AIDS may be a severe mercy. If God is more interested in our holiness than in our health, in the righteousness of a nation than in its tolerance of promiscuity, this terrible affliction may be one of many forces demanding that thoughtful people ask, "What on earth are we doing to ourselves?" In most of the world, and accompanied by highly diverse social factors, casual sex is not only tolerated but tacitly promoted. Almost never in the media is fornication pictured as a tragedy or a great social evil, still less as an offense against God. Casual sex is amusing, normal, an expression of people finding themselves or their true love, over against the stern legalism of religious rightists who are desperate to prevent people from having fun. We absorb this stance from our youth; it takes extraordinary resolve to stand against it, and when we do we are made to feel ridiculous, old-fashioned, corny—despite the considerable research that indicates there is *more* sexual and personal fulfillment in homes characterized by trust, fidelity, and mutual respect cheerfully offered up to a good and sovereign God who cannot be mocked and who insists that we reap what we sow, than in homes devoted to hedonism.

3. Robert C. Gallo and Luc Montaignier, "AIDS in 1988," *Scientific American* 259/4 (Oct. 1988).

In any case, we are poorly placed to throw stones at those who fall into promiscuity and drug use. Only a little knowledge of the world and of our own hearts reminds us, again and again, as we recall our own temptations and the circumstances and people who have helped us, "There but for the grace of God . . ." And if in some instances those who have been sexually faithful and who are removed from the drug scene nevertheless contract the disease (perhaps from a sexually unfaithful partner, or from an infected mother), I suspect that Jesus would not say to us, "Well, that proves the disease has nothing to do with the judgment of God," but rather, "But unless you repent, you too will all perish" (Luke 13:5).

Compassion and Indignation

If we assume, then, that AIDS and HIV infection are part of God's judgment (though within the categories and restraints outlined above), does this mean Christians have the right to walk away, not wanting, as it were to interfere with the judgment of God? Or should we restrict our help to the relatively few who contract the disease without any personal involvement in either intravenous drug abuse or promiscuous behavior?

Absolutely not! War, if you recall, is also seen as a judgment from God in the Bible. But that does not mean Christians walk away and ignore the homeless, the starving, the wounded, and the displaced that war inevitably churns up. So here: those who are afflicted with AIDS will need help, and the normal healthcare systems are going to prove inadequate. Here is a monumental opportunity to help.

Churches in areas with high incidence of AIDS have opened counseling centers and provided homes for patients with advanced AIDS—places to die with some dignity, after everyone else has turned them out. Human touch, clean beds, warm rooms, food, friendship—these are going to be in short supply as large numbers of infected people begin to display clinical symptoms. And above all there will be opportunities, along with such service, to share the good news of forgiveness by faith in Jesus Christ, who died to save sinners, sinners like me, sinners like AIDS sufferers.

So while Christians utter warnings about God's judgment and articulate the Bible's condemnation of promiscuity and of homosexuality, they must do so with a break in their voice, as guilty sinners telling other guilty sinners where to find relief. And the moral indignation that is a necessary component of any genuine love of holiness must be melded with self-sacrificing love that cares in tangible ways for those who have been caught up in this dreadful disease.

Scripture Index

Subject Index